YOUNG CATHOLICS AT THE NEW MILLENNIUM

The Religion and Morality of Young Adults in Western Countries

THE AUTHORS

Anthony M. Abela is Lecturer in Sociology and Social Policy at the University of Malta. For three years he was Director of the Institute of Social Welfare, having earlier served as *professore aggiunto* in Sociology at the Gregorian University in Rome. He holds degrees in philosophy, theology and sociology from universities in Paris, Rome, Chicago and Oxford. His publications include *Transmitting Values in European Malta* (1991), *Changing Youth Culture in Malta* (1992), *Shifting Family Values: a Western European Perspective* (1994), *Secularised Sexuality in a City-Island* (1998) and *Women and Men in the Maltese Islands* (1999).

Irena Borowik is Associate Professor of Sociology at the Jagiellonian University, Kraków, Poland, and director of NOMOS Press. Her publications include *Charisma in Everyday Life* (in Polish 1990), *The Processes of Institutionalisation and Privatisation of Religion in Post-War Poland* (in Polish 1997), *New Religious Phenomena in Central and Eastern Europe* (1998) and *Church-State Relations in Central and Eastern Europe* (1999).

Teresa Dowling is Lecturer in Sociology at University College, Cork, Ireland. Her areas of specialism in sociology include Ireland, young people, education and religion.

John Fulton is Professor of Sociology at St Mary's College, Strawberry Hill, Twickenham, UK. He holds degrees in sociology and theology from the Universities of Liverpool, London (School of Economics), and Milan. His publications include *The Tragedy of Belief: Division, Politics and Religion in Ireland* (1991), *Religion and Power: Decline and Growth* (1991), *Religion in Contemporary Europe* (1993) and *The Politics of Spirituality* (1995).

Penny Long Marler is Associate Professor of Sociology at the University of Samford, Birmingham, Alabama, USA. She has written a number of books and distinguished articles in the field of sociology of religion in the USA, and has researched both Protestant and Catholic denominations and cultures.

Luigi Tomasi has a PhD in Philosophy from the Catholic University of Milan and in Sociology from the University of Trento (Italy), where he now works. He has been closely associated with the Committee on Social Thought at the University of Chicago and studied under Edward A. Shils, one of the most outstanding social scientists of the twentieth century. Among his published works are *La contestazione religiosa giovanile in Italia 1968–78* (1981), *La condizione giovanile in Europa: Tra società e religione* (1986), *Young People and Religions in Europe: Persistence and Change in Values* (1993), *La cultura dei giovani europei alle soglie del 2000: Religione, valori, politica e consumi* (1998) and *Alternative Religions among European Youth* (1999).

YOUNG CATHOLICS
AT THE
NEW MILLENNIUM

THE RELIGION AND MORALITY
OF YOUNG ADULTS IN
WESTERN COUNTRIES

*John Fulton, Anthony M. Abela,
Irena Borowik, Teresa Dowling,
Penny Long Marler and Luigi Tomasi*

University College Dublin Press
Preas Choláiste Ollscoile Bhaile Átha Cliath

First published 2000 by University College Dublin Press,
Newman House, 86 St Stephen's Green, Dublin 2, Ireland
www.ucdpress.ie

© John Fulton, Anthony M. Abela, Irena Borowik,
Teresa Dowling Penny Long Marler, Luigi Tomasi, 2000
ISBN 1 900621 45 2 (hardback)
1 900621 46 0 (paperback)

Cataloguing in Publication data available from the British Library

Typeset in Ireland in 10/12 Sabon by Elaine Shiels, Bantry, Co. Cork
Printed in Ireland by ColourBooks, Dublin

CONTENTS

PREFACE AND ACKNOWLEDGEMENTS

This book originated in a research group of the International Society for the Sociology of Religion (also known as *Société Internationale de Sociologie des Religions*). The research team has been known as YCARG, Young Catholic Adult Research Group. It was set up at one of the Society's biennial conferences, this particular one at Québec, Canada, in the early summer of 1995. Various sociologists dropped in and out with contributions to the work of the group. They gave a number of papers, including stimulating pieces by Yves Lambert and Marjorie Fitzpatrick. A core group of members then decided to collaborate on a more specific project, from which the present book has emerged, along with at least one other book and a significant number of articles. On two occasions the authors of the national chapters presented their work in progress in thematic sessions of the ISSR's meetings in Toulouse, France (1997) and in Leuven, Belgium (1999). They further discussed each other's work in other informal meetings and through e-mail.

The work has involved bringing together three different kinds of topics: youth, 'Generation X' and other 18–35 age-group studies, like the work of the DEMOS organisation in London; research on late and post-modernity; and research on the changing nature of religion, particularly contemporary Christianity and Catholicism. A project such as ours has also required a wide range of expertise, as well as contacts with the subjects of study. All of us have had an enduring interest in young people and religion, and it has been this more than anything else that has helped us focus. But we have all worked and published in one or more of the other areas as well, and this has provided additional knowledge we have been able to share. We hope that the present publication will encourage others to explore similar topics and not yield too readily to theories on the lack of purpose of contemporary young people or the bankruptcy of postmodern society.

Both religion and morality are in phase of redefinition in our western countries. Morality is certainly not in terminal decline, though some forms of institutionalised religion might be. Also youth is becoming something of an anomalous category, as the early phases of adulthood can range well beyond the age of 24. Youth is often defined as 'incomplete adulthood' and youths are supposed to become genuine adults when they complete the transition by leaving the parental nest, setting up their own home, and finding job stability in the labour market. But job stability has collapsed for the majority in many of our western countries and sexual mores have changed partly as a consequence. Thus the social flexibility of the category 'youth' perhaps becomes unsuitable: it would involve people in a late or postmodern environment who live with a partner, are in or out of work, have a child, or still fail to find employment stability in contemporary society. Irrespective of whether one might categorise people with partners aged 30 or more as 'youth', we decided to study people with some claim to adulthood, but who may or may not have achieved the 'fullness' complete adulthood might bring. We have concentrated on the age group 18–30 because they appear such a central category in contemporary society both as harbingers of what the future might look like and as the group most likely to shape western society over the first quarter of the twenty-first century. We have been primarily interested in what might happen to morality and religion over this period of time, in what ways they might change, disappear or grow. As one of our main research interests was Catholicism, besides the culture of young people, we decided to focus on Roman Catholics, including those affected by Catholicism even if they have abandoned the practice. Specialising on them also meant we could explore more deeply lives and experiences within the constraints of the resources we had at our disposal.

*   *   *

We want to thank those who helped us do the research and write this book, especially the young adults who accepted our invitation to tell their life stories to us personally or to researchers working under our supervision. They gave up their time generously for what were often long and demanding interviews, some lasting longer than four hours. Without their co-operation neither research nor book would have been completed. Reading the accounts has been a humbling as well as an enervating experience, and we hope our young helpers and other young adults will find themselves interested in this volume and in finding themselves there in more ways than one.

There are also individual friends and helpers to thank.

TONY ABELA wishes to thank all those students in sociology from the University of Malta and its Gozo Centre, who interviewed a wide cross-section of young adults under his supervision, from which a quota sample was selected for this study.

TERESA DOWLING wishes to thank the following: Marjorie Fitzpatrick for completing the Dublin interviews; all those who contributed to the study in the Munster area, friends, students, colleagues, the many church and community workers who helped in so many ways including making contact with young people for this study; University College Cork for six months' sabbatical leave which facilitated the completion and processing of the interviews; John Fulton and his colleagues at St Mary's College, Strawberry Hill for their hospitality and friendship; John, Michele and Rachel who, as always, provided love, support and encouragement.

JOHN FULTON wishes to thank Fr Mike Walsh who, despite poor health, helped him considerably with the task of finding 'gatekeepers' to the world of young people. For the same reason, he also thanks Mary Merritt, Caroline King, Tony McCaffry, Julie Clague and a number of clergy contacts in the dioceses of Westminster, Nottingham, Brentford, Southwark, and Arundel and Brighton. Colleagues within the Sociology Programme at St. Mary's College were particularly understanding in helping him with his in-house responsibilities over the period of research: Lemah Bonnick, David Evans, Nic Groombridge, Julie Humphries, Jane Longmore, Mort Mascarenhas, and Beryl Mason. Finally he thanks Anne, Christopher, Rachel, Rebecca and Margaret, for providing that support only loved ones can.

Finally, there is a thank-you from all of us to Ruth Mellor for her work on the cover and to Barbara Mennell of University College Dublin Press, for all her help in the preparation of the book. She was understanding throughout the period and gave us the right advice at the times when it was needed.

FIGURES AND TABLES

1

YOUNG ADULTS, CONTEMPORARY SOCIETY AND CATHOLICISM

John Fulton

The book examines the religious identity of those who have been influenced by Roman Catholicism. It does so against the background of the conditions experienced by most young people in contemporary western society. It is a cross-national, in-depth study of young adults who have been brought up in both a Roman Catholic milieu and today's late-modern world. It looks at how these people, from the 18–30 age bracket, relate religion to their lives, and whether they dialogue with their faith or abandon it as an irrelevance of the past. It is both a theoretical and a realistic account of the lives and values of this group, and how these vary across a range of Western countries.

Our modern societies are secularised: the social institutions of church and aristocracy that dominated the medieval world have been displaced by the even more dominating forces of capitalism and the modern state. Among these states, Great Britain and the US represent Catholics living in cultures shaped by secular Protestant pluralism; Italy and Malta represent the former monopoly Catholic countries of Southern Europe; and Ireland and Poland represent the Eastern and Western fringes of Catholic mono-poly that resulted from popular Catholic alliances with national movements. Our tale is not a tale of statistics: while it lacks in reading the boredom and concentration such a statistical account requires, our story also lacks the numerical accuracy such a study could have provided. It is instead an in-depth account of how young adults come to realise their personal identity in matters of religion and morality, how they develop their personal relationships and what they value in life.

The book concentrates on the specific conditions of young adults, firstly, because of the liminal yet strategic place they have come to occupy in contemporary western societies. They are the future workforce and are already the second most significant consumer sector of our home economies. Skilled as they are to take control over the domestic and international market economy, they represent the likely future of our societies and will be at the forefront in the market and political struggles of the twenty-first century. Yet the majority of them have still not accomplished 'full adulthood': they have either not left their home of origin, or secured a full-time job commensurate with their skills, or taken up a new home of their own (Coles 1995, Furlong and Cartmel 1997). They are also important because they have clearly developed, or been socialised into significantly different moral and cultural experiences than their parents had before them. To cite examples in the area of sexuality, more young adults than ever before cohabit, and put off marriage to a much later date than any western generation since the Second World War. They also have a considerably greater choice of lifestyles than their parents ever had, and may keep the cultures they have acquired even into their old age (Inglehart 1988, Wilkinson and Mulgan 1996).

The purpose of the book is to examine the effect of these changes on the outlook of a specific religious group among them, via in-depth research on a number of their life histories. We shall argue that the present phase of modernity affects young Catholic adults, rendering life both more insecure and more attractive, and changing their experience of religion and morality. Contemporary modernity is both a secularising and a new religious force. Both media and academia often charge that the West has entered a postmodern, post-Christian or post-religious society, and that this change has increased the rate of decline of religious belief and belonging, and damaged personal and social morality, with particular effects on the young adult generation (sometimes referred to in the literature as *Generation X*). We intend to argue, on the basis of our evidence, that while it is true that morality and religion have no longer the public profile and hegemonic power they used to have, they have not disappeared but have changed their location in society. As church-controlled religion has declined, a shift has occurred in personal consciousness in the form of the growth of semi-autonomous morality and religiosity. This shift affects the young adults of today, who are the first major generation to encounter this change in all its fullness. We now come to consider the modern social and cultural developments that are responsible for these changes.

LATE MODERNITY AND YOUNG ADULTS

What young adults are experiencing today crystallises the chief characteristics of contemporary western societies. Fundamental changes in morality and religion are occurring within the age group in particular, and it is likely that the decisions they make at this time are as important to their life as a whole as the decisions made during the period of schooled youth, if not more. If 12–15 used to be considered by the religious specialists of the 1950s and 1960s as a crucial age for decisions on religion and moral purpose, it might well be that the later age group has an equal importance today. The 18–30 age group current in 1998 were all born from the late sixties onwards. They live in a radically changed society from that of their parents. They are part of the first generation to know a society where 'uncertainty', 'risk', 'choice', 'freedom', 'autonomy' 'dependency' and 'lifelong learning' are all prevalent buzz words. The conditions these words express reflect a common set of social realities in western societies. Similar developments are also taking place in a number of Eastern European countries, like the Czech Republic, Hungary and Poland (Tomasi 1998, 1999). However, the peoples of these countries are experiencing far greater hardship, as economic restructuring has adopted a furious pace since the collapse of Communism. Over the past 35 years, the series of dramatic economic and cultural changes in the West have been of such magnitude that a new stage of modernity has been inaugurated, variously called postmodernity, late modernity or high modernity. Often the terms refer more directly to cultural and socio-moral change. But they are always rooted in economic change, and interact across the economic-cultural boundary.

The economic restructuring of the 1970s in the US and of the 1980s in Western Europe has resulted in a dramatic transformation of labour markets. In a bid to retain their dominant role in the world economy, western businesses and their governments developed new technologies to replace labour and drive down unit costs in the industrial sector. This strategy led to a massive decline in industrial employment and to a dramatic growth in the home service sector. Coupled with, and partly developing from this change, was the drive in world communications and trade, which took a mammoth leap forward with the instant communication techniques provided by developments in semi-conductors and computer technology.

The immediate personal consequences were dramatic. Whole labour markets were removed overnight, and unemployment soared first in the UK and later in mainland European countries. In the US rapid geographical mobility of the working population obviated the worst of unemployment. This was in response to the dramatic rise in imports from southeast Asia and the ensuing need to restore economic advantage over Japan, and before the growing Asian economies had reached their 'tiger' proportions. The traditional primary and secondary sectors of mining and manufacturing underwent massive labour contraction. The supply of long term 'jobs for life' in these sectors collapsed, and high-skilled tradesmen had to retrain in order to remain in employment. As the demand for full-time permanent jobs vastly exceeded their supply, wages were driven down not only in the manufacturing sector but also in the rapidly expanding service or tertiary sector.

The lower down the employment market you went, the more jobs became short time and low paid and the more living conditions became insecure. Where men turned down jobs because they considered pay and conditions too poor, women moved in. Early school-leavers, who had always experienced greater instability than most in obtaining permanent work, found there were simply no jobs for them at all. Even part-time work other than making sandwiches and filling up supermarket shelves required skills and corresponding qualifications. Thus full-time education began to get longer and longer, and the retraining and further education of all ages became *de rigueur*. The management of job security by existing companies depended on maintaining product advantage or developing product alternatives, usually by takeover and downsizing rather than through research and development. New companies with new products and management structures tended either to soar to prominence or quickly to go to the wall. Some of the knock-on effects to the professions have been limited, especially where opposition to deregulation has taken place: for example solicitors and lawyers in the UK, academics in Germany and France. In most countries, however, public sector wages and salaries have been held in check while private sector management salaries have dramatically improved, though whole swathes of middle management have often been sacrificed.

These economic changes have partnered cultural and moral changes. We have mentioned the dramatic growth in the service sector. Part of this growth has been in the leisure industries of home entertainment, sport, and health clubs. So dominant is the 'service' culture that even supermarkets, car showrooms, fast food outlets, real estate agents, and even universities have had to promote themselves as 'serving the consumer and consumer choice' and to develop corresponding internal cultures. The consumer has thus become the ultimate individualist, who has taste, choice, and above all 'is worth it'. A consumer culture has come to promote the autonomy of the individual whose choice is paramount and almost totally unrestricted, except when checked by the integrity of other similarly autonomous individuals. It is at this point that the world of production, distribution and consumption elides with the image of the moral, autonomous self, free to choose and enjoy, and free to relate to others as long as the relationship fulfils mutual needs.

The extent to which the populations of our countries buy into this marketed imagery is difficult to measure. However, one thing does appear to be a horizon of choice, possibly also one which has a dramatic consequence if it becomes a widely shared value: namely, the stance that the individual can or 'should' decide that the self become an arbiter of personal moral choice. The individual can decide what is right and what is wrong, and no one person, institution or tradition can advise. This possibility of moral being was available in past societies only to the ultimately powerful or the independent of means. Today, authors are suggesting that it has become a wider possibility, though how wide we shall shortly need to determine.

Late or Postmodernity?

At the level of social inquiry, two types of interpretation of the current state of values, beliefs and morality in general have come to predominate, namely the late (or high) modern interpretation and the postmodern interpretation. Both versions stress that technical rationality has a major function in those central institutions of our societies that we call the state and the economy. Technical rationality means a concentration on working out the stages of the means, rather than the ends, of human endeavour and action. Those who believe that we have now entered a postmodern phase go on to argue that this process of rationalisation has pushed out goals of a higher sort not only from business, the professions, and the running of the state, but also that it has spread to such an extent throughout the public sphere that there are no longer any ultimate values in the shared realm of culture and public life. This dominance of technical rationality in the public sphere so weakens the sphere of personal existence that no one can really believe in an ultimate purpose any more. There are no *grands récits*, religions or alternative secular worldviews, with the result that people are driven towards more intermediate forms of fulfilment. Postmodern theorists believe that the Enlightenment project, especially its belief in science and human reason as purveyors of knowledge and human happiness, has collapsed. Human reason has failed and can never deliver its promise of the good society, a world of equality, peace and positive progress. The assumption for most postmodern thinkers is that the underpinnings of religion collapsed already through the work of the Enlightenment itself. Religion has already had its day and what we are witnessing in the present phase of western history is the steady decomposition of its remains.

For Lyotard (1984) and his postmodern followers, the result is that most individuals live on the surface of things and have nothing to fall back on. Consumerism and self need replace any abiding values of the spirit. It is a WYSIWYG culture: 'What You See Is What You Get' and nothing else. So uncommitted do people become that the (western) universe becomes populated typically by cultural strollers (*flâneurs*) taking in people only on the surface; 'vagabonds' or those who do not belong; permanent tourists, ever moving on to a new experience; and players, whose life and social relationships are a game of no profound consequence, one from which they can withdraw if they are in danger of getting hurt, or which they can 'try again later' (see Bauman 1996). In such a way, not only is postmodernity a world without a vision, but also without any moral absolutes or guidance systems for human action and relationships. We have thus entered not only a post-Christian or post-religious society, but also almost a post-moral society, with little sense of a genuinely social consciousness. These characteristics are manifest, it is argued, in the new generation of young adults, who appear materialistic and immoral, displaying low social consciousness but a high preoccupation with the self and self-image. The conclusion is that the individuals who have emerged in today's society are almost totally individualised, unable to share profoundly in any common human project.

Other authors share Maffesoli's (1995) contention that postmodern existence is not totally individualised, lonely or shorn of emotional life. On the contrary, our period is showing itself to be a time where collective emotions are often expressed, as people move from one set of group experiences to another. The world is full of encounters and experiences of the sacred and enchantment, as people enjoy spectator sport and rock festivals, and share style, hobbies, concerts, new religious movements, New Age experiences and cyber chats. In such a world, it is possible for religion still to have expression, but with little memory of a great past. Today's religion is fleeting glimpses of the sacred, which can be enjoyed while they last, but cannot really structure a rule for life.

The alternative to these out-and-out postmodern perspectives on contemporary culture is the late or high modern view. While accepting the flawed nature of Enlightenment fundamentalism – namely the belief in the *inevitability* of the success of reason to solve humanity's problems and to bring humanity to an understanding of both self, society and nature – most late modernists see the moral imperative of the Enlightenment as still fully operational: to seek unendingly to improve the human condition and the environment in which we live, despite any and all disasters. They still believe that not only is such a vision valid, but that it is in part at least genuinely realisable. A great deal of human destiny lies in humanity's own hands. People of good will, applying their intelligence and other human talents, can achieve considerable successes, even though they will never succeed in a total resolution of the project. Late modernists are still very critical of contemporary society, condemning public spending on armaments and the abuse of the environment, while also pointing out modernity's achieved virtues: democracy, improved health, longer life and greater quality of life, to mention a few.

Who are these late modernists? In the most generic sense and at the popular level, all those who continue unremittingly to seek to improve the human condition. They probably include most people, even many post-modernists. At the theoretical level, and among the sociological community, the name of Giddens (1990, 1991) stands out, but the sentiments are present in all those who accept that the conditions of contemporary modernity allow us all to engage in a critique of society as it is, to sign up to emancipatory projects and to pursue them with vigour until we succeed, whether the goal be banishing discrimination, curtailing spending on armaments, reducing pollution, or preventing or ending wars.

Beck (1992), while being postmodern in his use of the term, tends to stress the process of modernity as, on the one hand, one of emerging equality between the sexes, and, on the other, one of failure by the major institutions of society to support the human individual in its search for meaning. In both these respects, he shares Giddens's general view on the moral emptiness of both state and market economy, and the consequently massive importance of the world of personal relationships, especially intimacy based on sexual expression. In fact, he sees sexually committed love as both in a state of chaos and yet capable of its own emergent *grand récit* (Beck and Beck-Gernsheim 1995). To a certain extent Beck echoes Maffesoli's stress on the emotional and the expressive as filling the void left by a technical rational society, but baulks at Giddens's late modern theme of a continuation of the Enlightenment project (though see Beck, Giddens and Lash 1994).

In the late 1980s and early 1990s, theorists of late modernity were saying that the principal institutions of contemporary society, those of state and the economy, including businesses, do not have a dynamic ethical concern at the centre of their projects. Neither do they have a focus on the superior value of human life in all its personal instances. To an extent, in the swing of the late nineties to centre and left-of-centre politics, most western states have taken on at least the rhetoric of human rights, sustainable development and arms reduction. Also among the rhetoric have been concerns for the state of the family, for people suffering abuse, the deterioration of the environment, and questions over pesticide use and genetically modified foods. But the extent to which governments are prepared to deliver on these agendas, and the extent to which modern politics is capable of doing so, remain questionable. Such a policy would clearly demand both long-term commitment and change in the allocation of national resources. The action they take or fail to take might affect the judgement of who is more right in the late modernity versus postmodernity debate. And there is a peculiarly democratic twist to either course of action: the type of modernity we shall have could depend on people voting for a government saving the people money in the short term but with long-term and dire consequences. Voting for a government with a conscience might mean paying more now but with positive outcomes in the future. However, we shall not be able to blame individual governments or its electors entirely for the present predicament. We have now moved into a phase in which the power of the individual state over the economy is in decline, as globalised economic forces from transnational corporations to the global market delimit its sphere of action. Only globalised political decision making can get us out of the mess into which pollution, exploitation and population imbalance have got us in the first place.

Even if governments were tardy on delivering their promises, would this mean that the postmodernists are right about the collapse of overarching norms and values, and especially in the core areas of personal life? Has individualisation gone so far as to destroy the prospects of any mass ideal-shaping movement, including religion? In seeking answers to such questions, we must first of all accept the changes in society that are actually in progress. In contemporary western countries significantly more people experience greater freedoms in terms of lifestyle and moral choice than previous generations. This is particularly true for those without family obligations, such as young adults. There is an ever-wider acceptance of sexual relationships outside, and before and after, marriage (Inglehart 1988, Wilkinson and Mulgan 1996), though the extent of this change varies from country to country. There is increasing social acceptance of homosexuality, lesbianism, a wide range of ethnic and particularistic cultures, and different basic orientations in terms of overarching values. There are numbers of young people who are preoccupied with their self-image, who are materialist in their values and aims. Yuppies still exist, although they may have already had their day. There are also groups of young people who embrace 'post-materialist' values such as personal fulfilment, peace and outdoor living. There are also young people who can be stirred to support a wide range of good causes full time, sometimes for a sustained period of years. There is some retention of class solidarity among traditional working classes. But the extent of organised solidarity on class lines varies significantly in western countries, with the UK and Ireland probably the worst casualties in trade union terms over the past two decades, and Poland coming out the strongest.

In personal life terms, people still want to find stable sexual relationships and will try a second or third time if the previous one breaks down. Even concern with one's own body can be a move to considerations of spiritual well-being and self-improvement rather than abandonment to short-term materialist goals. In this respect, 'late' rather than 'post' modernity seems the better diagnosis. It is not that morality has disappeared, though it has disappeared as a stable universalised social order and appears increasingly limited to the field of human interaction and discourse. In this field, morality is not crystal clear or objective, but rather general principles remain embedded in the collective memory, while working them out in reality presents alternatives and problems. Morality becomes articulated in encounter, and may result in individuals proposing or determining different values for their personal acts. Morality is acknowledged in a different and less explicit way than in tradition-based societies. Luckmann describes the route of moral communication today as indirect or oblique:

> In [traditional] societies with a generally obligatory moral code and in which interaction based on highly anonymous social roles was less pervasive, moral consensus could be assumed until evidence to the contrary appeared. In modern societies, one could say with some exaggeration, the situation is reversed. Moral consensus can be assumed only after evidence for that assumption becomes available. Among persons who are not reasonably certain about each other's moral attitudes and views, social interaction in general and most specifically, explicit moralizing becomes a risky intersubjective undertaking. Similarity of views on morally relevant issues in social interaction needs to be cautiously negotiated in specific communicative processes between the parties to a social encounter. Even then, the scope of consensus over different areas of social life will be as open to question as is its stability in time (Luckmann 1995: 24).

To some extent, research already corroborates Luckmann's assertion. Inglehart (1988), Wilkinson and Mulgan (1996), and a tranche of youth studies examining youth cultures, such as Furlong and Cartmel (1997), and Tomasi (1995a), all suggest growing pluralism in young people's outlook on life, and a greater focus on the individual and his or her experience as the locus for moral judgement. In a sense, this present volume firms up aspects of this development, while being more precise about the nature of religious change in young people. But it is worth mapping out this growth in experience-centred ethics briefly. It developed among young people in the 1960s and 1970s in countries with pluralist milieus, starting with the US and then, in Western Europe, the UK, the Nordic countries, West Germany and Holland. Then it spread to France and the Latin countries. The current 18–30 generation in all these countries appears to be the first in large numbers to experience this shift towards a do-it-yourself ethics in this field of interaction. The shift is likely to be sustained by successive young adult generations and to become the dominant mode.

But does this mode of constructing moral interaction stretch beyond the interpersonal sphere at all? Most shared values that were based on 'class tradition' are no longer important in our societies. Traditional church-based identities have also weakened, as we shall see. It is questionable, however, whether this shift extends to all *other* aspects of religious and social identity. Is the moral shift so deep in consciousness as to destroy all forms of loyalty and overarching interpretation of one's life and purpose? Though the question is broad enough to embrace humanism, ethnicity and religion, in both narrow and broad senses, all these areas are linked by a common denominator. They represent forms of grand narratives that are supposed to be defunct, or in decline.

The basis for morality has become more dependent on the subject's experience in the encounters of everyday life. This shift in the basis of morality does not mean that the social base is entirely lost. People can still get support for their moral decision making from stable institutions such as the church, but they are more likely to seek it from counsellors, friends, helplines and other media services. They may even find self-support through subscribing to ideologies of human concern. In this volume, we intend to examine the extent to which groups of young adults affected by a specific religious identity respond also morally to the condition of modernity. How do religiously affected young adults see morality? Is it killed off, converted to a preference, or still encountered within a social framework of significant meaning? Is the relationship between modernity and religion a zero-sum conflict, where one gains at the expense of another, or is the experience of young people of modernity, religion and morality actually a very different reality? Let us put the question differently, in terms more relevant to the debate on post or late modernity we have just examined: do young people affected by some form of religious tradition, in this case Roman Catholicism, sustain their beliefs and moral values by insulating themselves from the modern world, or do they face the shift in culture by negotiating morality within the context of or in relation to their religious field? Or do they abandon the religious field altogether, and in doing so replace it either with a more humanist-type referent, or do they resort to *bricolage*, or even to the pose of the *flâneur*?

These are some of the questions we put to ourselves, and which we seek to explore through the analyses of the life histories of young adult Catholics in six different modernised countries. But to understand the effect of social change on religion, and particularly on Roman Catholicism, we must first explore what that Roman Catholicism was in the minds and hearts of its adherents in the generations that preceded those of the present. In fact Roman Catholics have not been simply subject to changes in the secular world of economy and labour markets. Rapid changes have also been taking place in the structure and content of institutional Catholicism itself. Indeed, just as the culture of secularity was changing, so were the cultures of the religious – and the religious perception of the secular along with it.

YESTERDAY'S CATHOLICISM

How then has the situation of religion changed in the West? What was it like before this new stage of modernisation occurred? It would be a long tale to tell, even if there were time to tell it. But a sketch of the situation prior to the 1960s helps understand the depth of the changes as far as Roman Catholicism is concerned. Details for each country are provided where necessary in each of the national chapters (chapters 2–7). Also, some long-term major changes need to be reviewed to grasp the importance of the events of the 1960s, which we shall deal with now. These major changes are spread over the centuries of the modern era itself: firstly, the religious developments of early modern society, particularly the Reformation (sixteenth century); secondly the religious consequences of the political, cultural and scientific developments of the seventeenth and eighteenth centuries; and thirdly the process of rapid industrialisation beginning in England and the Low Countries in the eighteenth century, and developed by Protestant Europe and the US in the nineteenth century. Accompanying these are the changes specifically within Roman Catholicism, which we shall also outline.

Early Modern Developments

The Reformation led to the loss of most of Northern Europe from the hegemony of Rome. As a consequence of its teachings and its empowerment of bourgeois and state power, the Reformation also gave impetus to the following religious changes. First, the principle of individual salvation by faith alone and Luther's doctrine of the calling led to the closure of monasteries. The religious life was played down as a preferred life-path because one could no longer by this means accumulate merit in heaven and thus more easily save one's soul. One was instead called to glorify God in this de-sacralised world, now no longer populated by good and bad spirits. The world thus became the religious field of human endeavour in whatever trade or profession one was called to serve, whether as farmer, teacher, minister, lawyer, tradesman or ruler. And one was also called to fulfil one's family duties as spouse and parent in the same way. Not only, then, was celibacy not seen as a higher way, but a this-worldly ethic replaced the other-worldly ethic of the Middle Ages.

The most direct social consequence of the Reform was a dramatic increase in the rate of institutional differentiation, which took on greater impetus in Protestant lands than Catholic ones. The church as a clerical body increasingly lost its powers in the fields of land ownership, law, social and health welfare, and later in education and control of culture. This development, also known as institutional secularisation, led to the decline of the church's economic, political, cultural and social power first in Protestant countries and later in Catholic ones, where the change took place usually under the banners of anti-clericalism and liberalism. The process was taken further by the scientific and Enlightenment movements, which produced both the modern sciences and democratic politics, based first on the rights of man, and later of woman as well, to the detriment not only of aristocratic domination but that of the churches both Protestant and Catholic.

This differentiation was accompanied by the growth of rationalisation, that is the monitoring and implementation of technical rationality: the careful calculation of means by splitting up stages of material and mental processes in the pursuit of goals whether material and mental or procedural (technology, bureaucracy). Thus science and humanistic ideals aided not only the development of industrialisation and market forces, but also the modern state, as it developed in tandem with capitalism as both the latter's enabler and as the locus for the development of bureaucracy, law, public order, education and welfare. The emergence of the modern state also promoted the emergence of religion's most secular challengers in the field of belief, communism and nationalism, the latter also in its nineteenth-century variant of imperialism and its twentieth-century options of Fascism and National Socialism.

These institutional and class-forming processes were accompanied by a degree of secularisation of the personal life. Though it was not immediately perceived at the Reformation, making the individual directly responsible to God, with increasingly less mediation by the church, put in train the development of the private sphere. It was here that people not only had to become responsible directly to God for their faith, but eventually, in a situation where local village face-to-face relationships would be replaced by the anonymity typical of contemporary urban life, they would become responsible for their own personal morality also: they would become free from the constraints of control by local parish members or their landed gentry and lords. As objectively regulated morality declined, so grew having to take personal responsibility for one's actions. As the process culminated in the phase of late modern or postmodern society, religious believing and belonging became more a matter of personal conscience and decision, with the central institutions of state and market economy totally focused on technical rationality in pursuit of ever increasing wealth – when they were not in pursuit of national protection or enhancement by war. One could modify these state-determined goals to more humanistic and life-quality ones, but one could no longer change them to *religious* goals, given the structures on which modern western society had now been built.

Inside the Roman Catholic Church

With the Reformation irreversible, the Roman Catholic Church found itself no longer the centre of the universe or even of Christendom, which had all but disappeared. This great schism had left the church mainly in power in Mediterranean and central European lands, including Poland. Minority Catholic populations still existed among Protestant ones from the Low Countries across a band of kingdoms and dukedoms to Switzerland. However, Protestants were not tolerated within Catholic lands, while Catholics were in varying degrees in Protestant lands. In this way *monopoly Catholicism* emerged, and persisted well on into the twentieth century (Martin 1978). Its style was to arrange a pact with the monarch and maintain control of the religious culture of the country in return for supporting the secular power. Such a strategy more or less held for the seventeenth and eighteenth centuries, until the watershed of the French Revolution. Even so, it persisted beyond into the twentieth century losing ground slowly to anti-clerical forces in Mediterranean countries, but staying strong in Ireland and Poland, where national confrontations were still to be worked out between Catholic Nationalists and Protestant Unionists in Ireland, and Catholics and Communists in Poland.

Monopoly Catholicism was a form of politics. It meant making the Roman Catholic Church guardian of civil society and its morality, making the ethos of the nation Catholic and excluding other religions from within its boundaries. The ideal citizen was a loyal member of the church from the cradle to the grave. The position and teaching of the church were enshrined in state laws, and the church chaperoned culture, morality and values, with its view of right and wrong. Until the turn of the century, the progress of democratic politics and formation of nation states was possible in Catholic monopoly countries only under the guise of anti-clericalism. To push equality and republicanism, it was necessary to oppose the church, whose stake in the established order of things led the clergy to oppose the very change that would undermine its alliance with the Catholic monarchies of Europe. In the case of Italy, with unification in 1871, Pope Pius IX banned Catholic participation in the politics of the new state, a ban that lasted two decades. Again, when in the 1920s Mussolini and the anti-democratic Fascist Party promised the Pope control of schools and a separate state in the Vatican in return for political support, Pius XI ditched the newly formed Catholic Party for a new alliance with Mussolini. The signing of the *Concordat* of 1929 showed just how ephemeral the Church's conversion to democratic politics had been.

The slowness of the institutional church down the path of modernity was evidenced particularly in three areas of personal life. In matters of thought, the Syllabus of Errors (1864) and the Ultramontane inter-pretation of papal infallibility and primacy (1870) amounted to a block on dialogue with the modern world. In matters of moral conscience, Rome began to focus increasingly on matters of family, sexual morality and Catholic education, where it felt it could still control the individual conscience, given the power of the confessional. In matters of spirituality, Rome also continued to support the development of personal devotionalism among the faithful, seeking to steer them away from matters of theo-logical thought – including the reading of the Bible – and from politics, in an attempt to control that sphere itself through diplomacy and church-state agreements, and to insulate the faithful from the evils of the modern secular world. Early on the papacy recognised its lack of success with the ban on politics, and was forced to develop social teaching particularly in respect of secularity and the state, and to create an active lay apostolate engaged with social and educational problems. However, it sought firmly to place this apostolate under priestly control, with great success until well after the war of 1939–45.

How Pre-Vatican II Spirituality Worked

We have mentioned the essentially devotional character of nineteenth-century popular Catholicism, one which was largely shared by priests and people alike and which persisted into the twentieth century until the 1960s. It was characterised by the cult of the saints, particularly Mary, and the cult of the humanity of Christ, particularly the real presence of Christ in the Eucharistic host. The devotions that were most popular were the Rosary, novenas (nine days of prayer and practices of self-denial) to Mary, other saints or aspects of Christ's sufferings (his Sacred Heart, his five wounds), processions, pilgrimages to shrines, the celebration of miracles and appearances of the Virgin.

While devotions were the focus for the growth and preservation of one's 'state of grace' and closeness to God, the *sin cycle* was a ritualised experience of falling from grace and salvation and then recovering it. It was the principal instrument of social-religious control, maintaining the faithful 'on their feet' in the battle against personal sin and the fight for salvation. It had three essential stages, all highly individualistic in orientation, and which were taught in Sunday schools and day schools to the children from the age of seven, at least from the latter part of the last century. It consisted of the procedure to undertake on the occasion of committing serious or 'mortal' sin. Given the state of moral theology since the scholasticism of the late middle ages, mortal sin was something which could occur all too frequently, given also prevailing views on sexual morality and church attendance. 'Impurity', which ranged from enter-taining sexual thoughts and masturbation to dancing as a 'proximate occasion of sin', and then to petting and sexual intercourse outside marriage, was the cause of most mortal sins among youth, young adults and the male middle-aged, probably with missing Mass on Sundays coming second. Any of these were considered 'grievous', with hell the result if one died before either 'making an act of perfect contrition' – sorrow for one's sin because of one's love for God and a resolve never to do so again – or going to 'confession', the popular name for 'the sacrament of penance', now called 'the sacrament of reconciliation'.

One could never be sure of one's love for God, and could not receive Communion without going to Confession: to do otherwise was considered a 'sacrilege' in church law. So the fervent believer, and probably any lukewarm believer who did not want to take risks, went to Confession. This act of 'returning to grace' was then completed by receiving Holy Communion (the Eucharistic host) usually at Sunday Mass. Confession and Communion were often a weekly, monthly or annual experience, according to how close one was to one's religious practices and how strongly one believed in the moral ordinances of the Church. Because even mental deviation from the norm of 'purity' was labelled mortal sin, the 'death' of the soul was always imminent. The shorter the period between sinning and confession, the more chance one had of going to heaven; the longer the gap, the more likely one was of going to hell, particularly if death was untimely. Consequently, many or most committed people spent a fair amount of their time falling into sin and rising again, and considered themselves inferior to the state of the clergy and members of religious orders who, it was considered, lived the best kind of religious life, with a likely eternal reward.

The spirituality of the sin cycle both mirrored and gave expression to the church's own internal power structure. The powerlessness of the laity in front of sin was reinforced not only by the power of the clergy as gatekeepers of the grace-giving sacraments, but also by the authority conferred on the clergy in matters of church organisation as well as doctrine and morality. It is important to point out that the cycle of sin itself depended on the ministry of the priest. The priest's word was taken as final in both the doctrinal and moral field. It was also rare to find a lay person who had more knowledge of church teaching and theological opinion than the priest, and much less one whose understanding of theology went further than the official teaching of the church.

Devotionalism aided this technically self-centred faith of saving one's soul. There was therefore also a strong element of ritualism, reinforced by the particular sense of the sacred which surrounded worship in the church: a language one did not understand (Latin), objects one could not touch (the chalice, the bread), and people who were to a certain extent unknown and on a pedestal (priests), who not only were the ones inducted into the inner mysteries of the sacred but had considerable control over access to the divine itself. Few laity could consider themselves 'doing all right'. But if they were single and virginal, or widowed and old, and could spend plenty of time praying in church and going very often to the sacraments, they had a better chance than most not only of going to heaven, but of progressing along the path to holiness and avoiding purgatory.

The 'sin cycle' was of particular social importance in countries where Catholics were minorities: the US, Canada and other English-speaking countries. It produced a form of ethnic faith, one where the believers were kept as separate as possible from the wider society and the surrounding culture by the avoidance of marrying out and by frequenting Catholic schools, clubs, sodalities and other church associations. The culture they assimilated was significantly divergent from and antithetical to contemporary Protestant cultures. Such an ethnic faith which kept the secular world at bay could thus mimic the faith as experienced in monopoly Catholic countries, especially in their rural sectors and among those who took the part of the church against the anti-clerical forces of socialism, communism and, in the cities, the perils of urban living, where less policing of individual mores was possible.

In summary, the measures of religious Catholic life were two forms of ritual. Laity and clergy alike shared devotionalism. But the sacramental cycle of sin, repentance and grace was mainly the ritual of the laity, and was replaced or supplemented by the path of holiness for the few religious 'experts', usually the 'secular' clergy and men and women in 'religious life' – nuns, brothers and those priests who belonged to religious orders. This does not mean that all Roman Catholics would have conformed to such a regime and culture. It is likely that compromises were made, and that the further away from core Catholic status one was, the more probable would it have been that one was philosophical and perhaps even a little cynical about such a ritual lifestyle, particularly if one felt the Church did not understand 'the way life really was' out there 'in the world'. For example, it is likely that many adults omitted references to sexual conduct in the confessional, or glossed over them, not necessarily out of shame but perhaps out of distance from the priestly worldview. Even so, the most susceptible to teaching were and remain the young. Many young Catholics of the period may have found the passage through puberty into adulthood quite difficult, especially if they had been informed of the full strictness of church teaching, which focused in a non-contextual manner on sexual thoughts and acts. Also, a 'spiritual sickness' known as 'scruples' was common among those who had experienced some deep conversion to Jesus Christ. Those who suffered from it found it difficult to excise all that was judged sinful in their lives, finding new sins where they had never found them in the past, because of their increased sensitivity to the 'holiness' goal to which they had become converted.

The extent of such phenomena among young Catholics of the time is very difficult to gauge, given the lack of empirical research on the topic in any country. Even so, we can say with some degree of certainty that the most common features of popular Catholic religious sentiment contained emotions of sinfulness and helplessness, and that a number of young adults shared these sentiments. These feelings were partnered by a sense of, and subordination to, the priest who even when he was not a particularly good priest could be relied on, through his fulfilment of the sacramental ministry, to bring God's forgiveness and grace to the constantly errant but penitent Catholic. Provided one did not commit the greatest sins of all, namely becoming a Protestant or losing the faith, there was still hope. God was, after all, merciful. In any case such apostasy usually happened to intellectuals rather than the common faithful, and probably served them right for being intellectuals.

In minority Catholic countries the system did not work very well, as there was continuous and heavy loss of church members to the wider society. For example, in Britain, had the Irish migrants all stayed loyal to Catholicism and their children too, there could well be 15 million Catholics in Britain today as opposed to less than four. In the US, numbers of Catholics are set to increase only because of the massive contemporary influx of Hispanic Americans, which is likely to increase in the foreseeable future. In the West, the 'non-Catholic' world, even in its Anglican and Protestant manifestations, tended to be seen by Catholics and their clergy as an alien and sinful one, a risk to their immortal souls. Also the majority of lay Catholics were working class and the children of Irish and European migrants. The dual pressure of inward-looking spirituality and lack of economic power helped to make Catholics slow to civic involvement. They were mainly politically passive, except for the small minority involved in trade-union activities and working-class politics. There was no Christian Democracy, except for the Catholic Party in Holland, and very little in the way of Catholic Action.

The Overthrow of Pre-Vatican II Spirituality

The Second Vatican Council (1962–5) attempted to engage with the modern world and modify the direction that its predecessor, Vatican I, had taken almost a hundred years earlier in 1870. Vatican II revised Vatican I's statement on the primacy of the Pope by affirming the equal importance of the college of bishops in the oversight of the church. It also developed new approaches to other faiths and churches by introducing ecumenism into Roman Catholicism. Until that time, priests and laity on the margins of the hierarchy had conducted discussions with humanism and Marxism on issues such as democracy and human rights. The same people had been involved in talks with the Protestant and Orthodox, or Eastern, churches. All of these ecumenical activities were now officially internalised into church thinking and practice, and ecumenical officers were appointed to both the Vatican and local conferences of bishops. The Council also produced a set of documents that involved new approaches to politics, poverty and sexuality, and approved the use of the insights of the social sciences for the development of church thinking. Third World issues and the injustices of capitalism came under closer scrutiny than ever before.

In the field of personal religion, the new Council sought to displace devotional religion and the sin cycle with a new spirituality that would embrace whatever aspects of modernity chimed with gospel values. The central rituals of Christian Catholicism were given a new life. By liturgical reform, the individualistic approach to the Mass was replaced by a communitarian one. The rite of the Eucharist was fully partnered by the reading of Scripture. Both biblical and sacramental rites were to be held in the local language of the assembly, replacing Latin. The Reformers had done the same 400 years earlier. The role of the confessional was downgraded, and steps were made to try to change the mentality of the 'sin cycle' of the previous age, by refocusing Catholic spirituality on the development of personal conscience and a social ethic of responsibility towards others. The communitarian trend was thus intentionally partnered by a liturgical, and hopefully preached, pedagogy that proclaimed a greater sense of mission or duty towards the world outside. Christian life was to be lived in a world where Christ could be found among its problems. Roman Catholics were encouraged to engage with society, become active in politics, take on the responsibilities of citizenship, pray and act with Christians of other churches, concern themselves with poverty at home and in the wider world, become 'partners in service' with the clergy.

Of course, the Second Vatican Council, and particularly those bishops and priests who promoted it, had only really drawn up a plan of renewal and modernisation, or *aggiornamento*, as it was called. Getting rid of the old was to prove far easier than replacing it with the new. In fact, not everything was rosy in the Catholic garden. For example, at local level, priests and bishops often disposed of the old ritual practices and reordered the layout of the church without explanation and appropriate preparation of their churchgoing and non-churchgoing parishioners. At central level, the Council plan involved a pious hope that the Vatican itself would be reformed: that the Roman Curia and, to an extent, the papacy would be reformed also, with their powers curtailed and distributed to local and national conferences of bishops, in partnership with their priests and laity. This reform never materialized. A conservative backlash muted the power of the bishops, and dashed hopes of further general councils, as the Vatican bureaucracy slowly exerted its capacity to whittle away the Council's dreams.

There was also a crisis among the clergy, as the new positive approach to sexuality brought thousands of priests and members of religious orders to reconsider their vows. The numbers of religious halved over a period of twenty years, and recruitment to the priesthood, especially in the West, declined dramatically. Part of the crisis was triggered by Pope Paul VI's decision in 1968 to maintain the ban on contraception within the church, despite three-quarters of the commission he had set up voting in favour of its removal – proof if any that the Pope's deeply religious hopes of reform could turn to dust whenever it came to decision-making time.

The emergence of John-Paul II, a deeply religious conservative and yet otherwise humanistic pope, has since led to log-jam in the Roman Catholic Church, and to the emergence of a worldwide conservative episcopate hand-picked by the pontiff. However, a traditionalist revival could succeed only if it produced a strong and numerous clerical *cadre* to propagate its message. But the current shortage of priests throughout the West has now reached crisis proportions, assisted by the conservative agenda to continue the bar on married clergy. Some might include the bar on women priests as a further obstacle, even if certain Catholic – particularly African and Indian – cultures might not be in favour of such a change.

The same period has been marked in western countries by the decline of Catholic Church membership and religious practice. The immediate post-war period had seen a growth, but all that finished in the sixties, as it did for all Christian churches in the West. Decline was most marked in Europe (Ester et al. 1993), with the US affected less, partly because of the

Latino resurgence (Diaz-Stevens and Stevens-Arroyo 1998). Because Protestant churches have been similarly affected, the decline of Catholic religious practice cannot necessarily be related to the failure or success of the Second Vatican Council. The collapse of the sin cycle and of devotionalism may have been in the offing irrespective of the Council, although we are unlikely to be able to prove it either way. Without the Council, the strength of Catholicism might have continued, but probably only by seeking to construct further defences for a fortress church, something which seems unlikely to have succeeded (see Fulton 1997).

It is equally plausible to lay the responsibility for decline at the door of late or postmodernity (see Hervieu-Léger 1993a). In fact, if we look to specialist writers on youth and young adults in various European countries, the appeal is generally to the structural and cultural factors of life in a late or postmodern direction: in France, Michelat (1991) and Lambert and Michelat et al. (1992); in Italy, Garelli (1996) and Pace (1998); in Malta, Abela (1998); in Spain, Elzo et al. (1994); in Poland, Grzymala-Moszczynska (1991) and in Switzerland, Campiche et al. (1992). Only McNamara (1992) in the US attempts to incorporate reflections on the events of and after Vatican II into explanations of the change in young people's Catholicism. We, the authors of this book, have tended to do the same in some of our previous writings. But it remains a possibility that both the collapse of the old as well as the failure to prosecute the new strategy envisaged in some of the Council documents have led to the decline being as great as it is. This argument is necessarily complex; however, it is the one towards which the debate on the subject is now leaning.

THE RESEARCH

Restating the Research Problem

There can be little doubt that dramatic changes have been occurring in the status of religion and morality particularly among young adults in contemporary western societies as a result of late modernity. It is likely there has been a massive change in the basis of beliefs and values, rendering assent no longer automatic, and even precarious and capable of being swamped by the pluriformity, consumerism and instrumental rationality of contemporary life. This book concentrates on how young adult Catholics shape their lives within six countries experiencing varying degrees of late modernity. At the same time, it takes into account the religious and moral messages young Catholics receive from their specifically Catholic environments and how these young people respond to both late modernity and religion together. The samples in each country include those closest to the institutional church, those who are affiliated and who practise their faith in varying measures, and those who no longer practise or are disconnected from Catholic culture. We have looked at their experience of family, school, college and workplace; at their lifestyles, friendships and sexuality; at their social concerns, political values and outlook on the world in which they live; and of course at their religious consciousness, faith and practice. We present key findings from our research from within the context of our young people's individual life histories.

The questions for which we seek answers from the life histories thus collected are as follows. In what ways does late modernity impact upon the religious and moral consciousness and outlook of those young people who have experienced at least some form of Catholic socialisation? Has it already eroded many aspects of religious and moral consciousness among them, and to what extent? Are even those Catholics who remain in contact with the church simply 'dabbling' in religion but without any serious commitment to it? Have their lives become aimless and ridden with materialism? Is what we have in the West a Catholicism in terminal decay, and if so is modern culture to be blamed? What about the changes which the Catholic Church sought to promote 'from the top' in its Vatican Council of the 1960s? Has this impacted, and has it done so only negatively, as Catholic traditionalists maintain? Or have some religious changes succeeded and provided a response to late modern living? Or again, is the young adult scene more complex, and is it impossible to unravel the different effects of modern culture and church reform?

Of course a modest research programme, such as the one whose findings we explore, is not able to say the final word on the matter. Indeed, the reader will spot how easy it is for members of the team to vary in their conceptualisations of the reality thus uncovered. Despite this, a considerable degree of similarity exists in our findings, whatever the emphasis on the explanatory value of different paradigms of understanding. Not only will this 'unity in diversity' come through as the chapters tell their own individual tales, but the final chapter pulls together a number of similarities and differences in the national life histories, and plots a course of interpretation which, although ultimately raising questions about the church of the future and the survival of Roman Catholicism in the West, re-evaluates the effects of both contemporary modernity and contemporary Roman Catholicism on today's young adults.

The Method of Data Collection

The research team worked out a method of collecting evidence that would be the same for each country in both the technique used and the content of the inquiry itself. We were not interested in mere opinions but rather in what the individual's own life values and mindsets were. We wished to probe into the meaning young adults attached to their religious and spiritual encounters, to uncover their priorities in life, and what they really felt about their life situation. Rather than use the survey method, we decided to make use of the life-history method. A semi-structured questionnaire served as a guide in the development of the personal in-depth interviews. We believe we were largely successful in obtaining quality material, capable of yielding information on life experiences, faith commitments and moral outlooks. These materials are consequently also being used for the publication of books and learned articles in our own different countries.

The life-history method, long used by psychologists for medical and clinical purposes, has become popular among contemporary historians, social anthropologists and sociologists, because of its ability to yield quality information (e.g. Josselson and Lieblich 1995). The use of tape recorders, transcription machines and computer packages for qualitative research makes possible a closer scrutiny of the religious and moral perceptions of respondents more thoroughly than before. The respondent is more likely to talk about what he/she understands by the problem rather than fit the self into the answer frames provided by a formal interviewer's written schedule.

The method is especially appropriate for sociologists when they focus on 'the ways in which a particular person constructs and makes sense of his or her life at a given moment'. It becomes 'a vocabulary of motive [Mills 1940] . . . a set of linguistic devices drawn from the existing wider culture which can be used both to re-interpret the past, to fashion the present and to anticipate the future' (Plummer 1983: 105). For example, Bertaux and Thompson (1997) have focused on three-generational data of family experiences and values, and thus introduce broader aspects of subjective meaning into social mobility inquiry than heretofore. For those who form the subject of our study, a part of those experiences and values is religion. At the same time, religious and moral symbols differ from many other symbolic forms in culture, in their ability to excite 'deep seated moods and motivations' (Geertz 1973) in the conscious and unconscious mind of people, and to invite persons to assent and respond to them. Where such symbols are carried within memory, their external appearance incites feelings and sensitises the subject to issues of religious and moral action. The significance of such symbols is more easily articulated by a life-history interview than by a survey. Discourse on one's own life is more likely to reveal what matters to the subject than questions, from an outsider, which may not be of personal concern. A series of closed questions might result in statements based on superficial and vaguely held opinions rather than on long lasting and deep motivations.

The study is based on such life histories collected in six different countries by the team of six sociologists, each of us native to the host culture. The countries are England, Ireland, Italy, Malta, Poland and the US. Of course the life-history account, unless specifically focused on particular experiences of life, could be an unending tale of life's events and a person's opinions on anything from fashion to the worst of traumas. The focused life interview avoids such a scenario by getting the interviewees to concentrate on specific aspects of their life experience and where, if at all, religious and moral issues enter into it.

The sample we used had certain inbuilt limitations. As part of an international project where some research partners were low on financial resources, we had to balance quantity with precision. We opted for a sample of life histories of 18–30 year olds, based on quotas. A quota sample is formed first by working out the criteria by which one is going to recruit respondents and, secondly, by deciding on the number of respondents for each defined grouping. We aimed at a minimum of 45 life histories for each national sample, and we divided this number up into nine separate quotas in the following way.

The two criteria used for the quota sample were (i) *sex and marital status*, and (ii) the *degree of religious commitment* of respondents. The first criteria isolated three categories of respondent: (*a*) single male, (*b*) single female, and (*c*) married or partnered of either sex. The second criteria distinguished between (*a*) core Catholics, (*b*) intermediate Catholics, and (*c*) former Catholics. In order to allow for cultural differences between countries in determining how 'Catholic commitment' would be split up, we assumed a measure of social distance that could operate in different cultures. We divided up Catholics into three groups, according to what, within the culture, would normally be considered a *strong* or *core* Catholic, a middle of the road (*intermediate*) Catholic, and a *former* Catholic. In actual fact, *former* Catholics always tended to be those who had either dissociated themselves from Catholic identity altogether or who had almost completely abandoned religious practice, with little or no intention of improving it. *Core Catholics* were usually those who practised on a regular basis, but who also 'might do something more', such as being actively involved in the life of the Church community in some way. This left the *intermediate* category, which included both those who were not far short of regular weekly church attendance and those who went only a handful of times a year. When in doubt, partners adopted tripartite divisions nearest the sociological practice for their own country.

As can be seen in figure 1.1, the various combinations of criteria produce a three-by-three grid, with nine boxes. This means that we had to recruit a minimum of five respondents to fit each of the nine identity profiles, thus giving us a minimum 45 life histories in each country. Of course, it was not always possible to know in advance into which categories life histories would fit. So over-recruitment to some classes was always going to be likely, and it was also possible to end up short for any single category but only to find out too late, given the tight schedule we were forced to impose on ourselves. Some of the researchers assigned graduate students to collect a large number of life histories from which they selected a more limited number to fit the categories. Partners were left free to include a measure of social class in dividing up the sample, depending on whether access to particular class groups was easy or difficult. Details for each country sample can be found in the relevant chapter.

Figure 1.1. Categories of Respondents 18–30 years old (minimum numbers)

(45 Young Adults 18–30)	15 Core Catholics	15 Intermediate Catholics	15 Former Catholics
15 Single Male	(5) core single males *active, and regular attenders	(5) intermediate single males from frequent to little attendance, inactive	(5) 'former' single males go 1–2 times a year or never attend; may have dissociated
15 Single Female	(5) core single females *active, and regular attenders	(5) intermediate single females from frequent to little attendance, inactive	(5) 'former' single females go 1–2 times a year or never attend, may have dissociated
15 Couples or Individuals (male or female) with partners or spouses	(5) at least one core per couple *active, and regular attenders	(5) at least one intermediate per couple from frequent to little attendance, inactive	(5) at least one 'former' per couple: go 1–2 times a year or never attend, may have dissociated

* 'Active' means performing a role in church-related activities.

In the course of the interviews, each research partner made use of the same life-history schedule. This was to ensure that all respondents would cover the principal aspects of religion and morality within the life-history trajectory. For each stage in life, respondents were requested to speak about the relevant social institutions, events, rituals, relationships, values and beliefs they experienced, how they thought about these at the time, and how they thought of them at the time of interview. The broad lines of the interview are laid out in figure 1.2, and extract the more narrowly religious and moral themes from the general flow of the life histories. The purpose is to show, in Victor Turner's famous phrase, how these young people 'blaze a trail' through their life histories, just as the tribal subjects of Turner's research construct meanings for their existence as individuals and communities through the rituals and mores of social life, though in very different settings and with very different problems from those of our late modern Catholics (Turner 1967). Our young people have encountered religious rituals, images, discourses, persons and places. Some have even spent quality time in meditation and retreats, and undergone moral and religious crises. They have also formed moral opinions on the state of the world they live in and on the church of which they form or did form a part, as well as on the moral questions of the day, some of which have been underlined by the Roman Catholic leadership. Their life histories, then, form the centre of the following analysis of our young adult Catholics in our late modern societies at the turn of the millennium.

Figure 1.2: 'Blazing a Trail through the Forest of Life': Plotting the religious and moral aspects of young adult lives

Social Institution and Sphere of Attention	Rituals, Beliefs, Relationships, Events	Subject's Religious and Moral Assessment
Family	prayer, activities, visitors, relationships, including authority/friendship	Happy at home? Positive moral ethos? Positive religious ethos?
Parish/ Church	attendance, quality of cult, kind of ministers relationships with members	Place of boredom? Beneficial participation morally and religiously? A community of faith?
School(s), Primary (5–12)	quality & kind of religious education and worship, Communion/Confession teachers-pupils, caring ethos	Happy at school? Beneficial participation morally and religiously?
School(s), Secondary, and life generally (12–18)	quality & kind of religious education & worship, Confirmation, retreats, pilgrimages, events, teachers-pupils, caring ethos	Happy at school? Beneficial participation morally and religiously? Crises and personal change?
Self-assessment:	*Quality and content of own religion to 12?* *Quality and content of own religion/morality 12–16?* *Quality and content of own religion/morality 16–18?*	
University/ College	subject of study; friendships, lifestyle; religious faith, practice and moral life	Happy at College? Crises and personal change?
Career/ Workplace	work, relationships, religious and moral aspects	Happy at work? Effect on/of one's religion?
Friendships Today	friends, friends' religious and moral outlook	Lonely, or support group? Good and firm friends?
Lifestyle Today	how weekend is spent, interests outside work (sport, keep fit, music etc.), intimate friends, views on forms of sexual intimacy, activities for others	
Belief-Experience Today	belief in God, religious experience, religiosity, view of self in terms of religion	
Belief-Practice Today	experience and meaning of religious practices, relevance of Church community	
Social Morality Today	religious tolerance, ecological question, equality issues: gender, homosexuality, life issues: abortion, euthanasia, death penalty	
Secular Politics Today	interest in politics, what is wrong with country, welfare, poverty, health care, education, third world	
Religious Politics Today	views on Pope, clergy what needs to be changed in the Church	

2

YOUNG CATHOLICS IN MALTA: SIMILAR ORIGINS, MULTIPLE DESTINATIONS

Anthony M. Abela

On the basis of the behaviour of their present generation of young adults, the Maltese, as elsewhere in the Catholic world, make contradictory forecasts about the future for religion. Pessimists forecast the erosion of Christian values whereas optimists foresee the beginning of an unprecedented new age of spirituality. Church leaders never cease to appeal for the protection of the Christian heritage. They warn the faithful to resist the influence of foreign cultures and avoid the risk of drifting away (*The Times*, 22 September, 1998). However, local theologians find this conservative approach to an ageing, temple-like culture out of step with living Catholic lifestyles and talk of a felt need for spiritual discernment and revolutionary and liberating action (Camilleri 1999: 14). At the same time, the Church's own research institute observes 'a surge in quality' at the end of the millennium (Tonna 1999).

Comparative studies give evidence of both transformations and continuities in Catholic culture particularly among young Catholics. Surveys show how young Maltese adults mix and match relatively high levels of Church attendance with secularised lifestyles. They subscribe to divergent life-orientations such as the religious, the traditional, the individualised and the materialist. Generally, they cherish self-determination and attach less importance to the teachings of the Church. In the new social context, however, quite a few young adults make good use of hitherto unforeseen opportunities to shape new religious meanings and lifestyles as they move from one stage to another in their life cycle. This apparent ambivalence and inconsistency calls for a better understanding of their situation, one that might be helped by viewing their situation as a form of religious and moral journey. Consequently, this chapter traces the religious origins and destinations of young Catholic adults in European Malta.

HISTORICAL OVERVIEW

On the map of European religion, Malta together with Poland and the Republic of Ireland is often seen as an exception to the Latin, Catholic and total monopoly religion (Martin 1978). Its location and ecological conditions are basic constants that shape the historical tradition of the country. During successive foreign occupations lasting until independence from British colonial rule in 1964, Malta developed a nationalism that was rooted in its language, cultural heritage and religion. At a time when the British developed the island as a fortress colony economically separate from Europe, culture and religion bound Malta to the selfsame continent. Malta has since become a republic (1979) and benefits from trade agreements with the European Union, to which it applied for full membership in 1990. Its economy is based on industry, tourism and services. In the new context, social and economic developments are being shaped by and in turn have an impact on politics, culture and religion. In many respects, Malta is at the crossroads of civilisations, a meeting place of traditions.

Malta and its sister island Gozo are situated at the centre of the Mediterranean, 93 kilometres south of Sicily and 290 kilometres north of the African coast. It has an area of 316 square kilometres and a population of 370,000 inhabitants. In 1998, there were 41,600 young adults aged between 20 and 29 years, constituting 11 per cent of the total population. In 1996, one and a quarter million passengers travelled to Malta, of which one million, almost three times the islands' population, were tourists (Central Office of Statistics 1998). During the same year, Malta had a GNP of US$ 8,225 per capita, and low rates of unemployment (3.5 per cent) and inflation (3.9 per cent). On the UN Human Development Index, Malta (.88) ranks 34th place compared to Poland (.874), Italy (.912), Ireland (.915), UK (.916) and USA (.95) respectively in the 51st, 20th, 19th, 18th and 2nd positions (*Malta Human Development Report* 1996).

In Malta, Boissevain (1965), Ganado (1974), and Vassallo (1979) have explained social change in terms of modernisation and secularisation, and Abela (1991–98) by individualisation and value shifts. The process of secularisation goes back to the events of the two World Wars, a succession of political-religious conflicts and the island's contacts with Europe. In the aftermath, the citadel of tradition began to give way, and a portion of the people cut themselves off from the Church (Ganado 1974: 145).

With the onset of independence, industrialisation, and the diffusion of religious reform initiated by the Second Vatican Council (1962–65), the Church had to adjust to a new social role. Social life came under the influence of new aspirations and urban living. Economic and political developments introduced elaborate lifestyles, a quest for luxury and physical comfort. The Church experienced a weakening in its hold over the minds of the people, although it still set the tone for all debate on significant political issues (Vassallo 1979). In the 1980s, there developed a number of new religious movements and a multiplicity of youth, family or mixed groups began to organise the spiritual support of their members and undertake voluntary work in Malta and abroad (Kungress tal-Lajci 1987). Such groups encourage a new style of belonging, with participation on an equal footing for men, women, priests, religious and laity.

The reproduction of tradition still goes on in many spheres of Maltese life. The Catholic Church acts as one of the main stabilising forces. It articulates the value system, provides the role model for behaviour and monitors its performance through the clergy and hierarchy. The code of honour and shame and the idea of the sacredness of women support and intensify the stabilising influences of the Church, the family and ecology, and operate to minimise the effects of modernisation (Mizzi 1982: 237).

Whereas, prior to independence, tradition was powerful enough to redress secularising tendencies, in post-independent Malta, industrialisation, the housing boom, tourism and the media introduced from abroad a new philosophy of life. Maltese society began to adopt foreign customs and religion was dealt a harsh blow (Ganado 1974: 1). Over the past thirty years, young adult attendance for Sunday Mass dropped from 73 per cent in 1967 to 56 per cent in 1980 and 50 per cent in 1995 (Tonna 1998: 20, Abela 1991: 72). Decline in religious participation appears related to a weakening of moral constraint and to change in values.

Change in Values

In the first wave of European Values Studies (EVS) in 1981 and 1984, Malta was found to be the proudest, most religious yet intolerant country, as well as one of the most hard working with the highest levels of family life satisfaction in Europe, closer in attitudes to Northern Europe than to neighbouring Catholic countries. Maltese young people, unlike their peers abroad were found to be very traditional with no strong aspirations for radical social change. Generally, young people were happy, had good social relations, were more open and tolerant than their elders but were passive at work and in society. Their values were shaped more by their family, the environment and the media than through personal reflection on contemporary issues.

More recently, results from a further EVS in 1991 and a national youth survey in 1995 give evidence on how the strict traditional morality of the Church in Malta is gradually giving way to a more open approach to sexuality and its ensuing secularisation. However, the maintenance of strong religiosity in the face of an observed disagreement on sexual attitudes between generations and between the sexes, points to a disjunction between ideal values and actual behaviour.

Young people show greater tolerance than their elders on homosexuality, pre-marital and extra-marital sex, contraceptives, sex with minors, single parenthood, divorce and abortion. But this tolerance is still accompanied by a general disapproval of sexual abuse and prostitution. Young people do not do away with the moral overtones of sexual deviation, though it is possible that the observed change in young people's values on sexuality might lead to a gradual shift in gender relations, marriage and family life in the near future. The magnitude of such a transformation can best be understood through in-depth qualitative studies (Abela 1998).

The Study of Life Histories

Studying the life histories of young adults in Malta and Gozo can contribute to an understanding of Catholic culture in the global society of the new millennium. During the academic year 1997–98, students of sociology from the University of Malta and the Gozo Centre obtained life histories of young adults (18–30 years old). The interviews were conducted as laid out in chapter 1. Participants were assured of confidentiality and anonymity. For this purpose, all names and identifying characteristics have been changed in what follows. From a total of 130 life histories from the islands of Malta and Gozo, a quota sample of 45 was selected for analysis. These follow the three by three classification set out in figure 1.1, p. 24.

Respondents come from a diversity of social backgrounds. Most originate from intact families but not a few show hitherto hidden problems within their families. Quite a few have suffered the loss of a close family member, others have become dependent on drugs and alcohol. Not a few are pleasure seekers. Some find nothing wrong with pre-marital sex, and a few others speak openly about having been abused by a member of their family, church or school. Independent of social origin, young Catholic adults mix and match values, shaping a diversity of lifestyles.

On the one hand, young Maltese adults are rooted in a homogeneous Catholic culture and experience a variety of cultures and life situations on the other. They are exposed to western and European lifestyles through the media and their contacts with the outside world. Various exchanges with tourists, foreign residents, returned migrants and overseas students make possible two-way interaction, the forging of friendships, and both intimate and casual relationships. Quite a few travel widely for long spells of study, work or leisure, and a few others either have relatives living abroad or have themselves lived for many years overseas.

RELIGIOUS UPBRINGING

Most people in Malta are brought up in a religious and protective environment. From an early age they are socialised into the values of the Catholic Church. Regular religious activities include attendance for daily mass, saying grace before meals and prayers before going to bed, reciting the rosary with the family, receiving Holy Communion and going to Confession at least once a week. Between the age of six and eleven, children go to catechism classes run by the Society for Christian Doctrine, also known as M.U.S.E.U.M., or at the parish centre, in preparation for their First Holy Communion and Confirmation. Many serve as altar boys, and a few other boys and girls join the parish choir or play a musical instrument in their church or village band club. Quite a few become members of one of the many church groups or associations and participate in regular activities, such as prayer meetings, Lenten sermons, spiritual exercises, retreats, processions, occasional outings and social events.

Family

Foremost amongst the qualities children are encouraged to learn at home are the values of religion (Abela 1991, 1994). A religious upbringing is an essential component of the traditional family. For most people, the family is the first school in religious values and beliefs. Through their example, parents instil in children a need to observe Catholic customs. For instance, Anna, now a married woman, traces her Catholic identity to the regular religious practices in the family of origin, the strict discipline of her parents, the general environment at home and her early socialisation:

> I come from a closely knit family of four. . . . My parents were both very religious. They really had an influence on my religious beliefs today. We never missed Sunday Mass, we used to say the rosary in the car on the way home . . . and we went to many processions. . . . My sister and I used to be in a prayer group . . . we went on many retreats. I remember watching a video on the Madonna and praying that she would come down . . . I always took Communion very seriously and looked forward to all the sacraments. Unlike many other kids, I was never scared of confession. Both my parents were very strict as I grew older.

Respondents link a Catholic upbringing with good example from parents, saying prayers in the family and voluntary obedience. In such an environment, parents exercise discipline to ascertain assiduous studies and restraint in going out. Lorella, a 19 year old from Gozo, has this to say about her upbringing:

> My brother and myself observe rules almost automatically. There were instances when father or mother had to take a stand, especially as regards studying and lately in connection with staying out late. I do not remember anybody at home teaching me about God or religion but we say the rosary before going to bed. . . . I used to attend catechism lessons in my early years and my parents have always set a good example by going to church almost everyday especially in the evenings.

Peter, a seminarian, who as the son of returned migrants lived his early years abroad, recalls the different roles his parents played and how these related to a simple, happy and formative childhood. Living the early years in a foreign country does not seem to influence the inner workings of the Maltese family, the upbringing of children in particular:

> It was a rather simple upbringing . . . there was formation of character and sound respect for religion. Childhood was quite happy and peaceful. The religious background was and still is staunchly Roman Catholic. Father went out to work; mother stayed at home caring for the family . . . a very happy environment, no tensions nor any of the anxiety we hear of today in so many homes.

Victor, single and 21 years old, member of the Society for Christian Doctrine also mentions the different roles of parents, which are along traditional lines: fathers tend to be stricter than mothers and children are afraid to break the rules. Only small offences are tolerated. When Victor was growing up his parents exercised discipline primarily to raise their children with a sense of values and respect for others, and only indirectly to instil an ethics of achievement:

> Any deviation or undesired behaviour, if discovered by the parents, meant big trouble. . . . I was ready to risk not obeying my mother, but when my father would tell me to do something, I would certainly do it. I was afraid of my father. I would never argue. . . . The relationship with my parents was quite good, except when I went against any of the values my mother taught me. Still, my relationship with my mother would get better quicker than with my father.
>
> They only wanted enough money for us to live a decent life, to get the basic needs. We were never forced to study in order to earn a lot of money. My parents wanted us to study in order to get the job we wanted, and to be able to live happily without lacking any necessities . . . I was taught not to discriminate between people from different social classes . . . and to respect animal life.

Philip, however, a 22-year-old university student, recalls his religious upbringing in no uncritical terms:

From my very first days I had a Catholic upbringing. Throughout my childhood, my parents taught us a sound moral code that was supposed to be always respected in the direst of situations. At home, religion was extremely important. Rosary was said on particular occasions even though I found it senseless. Mass was given special importance even though at that age I did not find it important. As a child I used to go to the nuns to get a religious education but I remember little of it. What I remember is that these classes did not allow one to live one's faith and to cultivate a living faith.

A religious upbringing is not altogether straightforward. Sometimes it is accompanied by parental constraints, ambivalent messages and mixed feelings. On the one hand, religion aims to foster unity, love and trust between the members of the family but, on the other, religious practice is not left to personal choice. This can turn religion into a habit to be enforced by promises of rewards and threats of punishments. It is no wonder that religion triggers negative feelings. Sue, who comes from a family of six recounts:

Our parents brought us up united, we could see how our parents loved each other, and they always gave us a good example. . . . Religion was the only thing they 'forced' on us. Sometimes this made us hate going to mass and there were times when we ran away and went to the playing fields instead. The religion they taught us was not very real, it consisted mainly of mass and rosary before going to bed. Sometimes, it used to be very beautiful and we used to mean what we said, but other times when we did not feel like it, it was just a waste of time. At that age I did not really know what religion was. . . . There were instances when they used to tell me: 'Because Jesus loves you', but most times it would be: 'if you do this Jesus will love you, or else he will burn your tongue'.

Winnie expresses similar feelings:

Mother insisted on morning and night prayers and daily rosary. Every day used to start with mass. Only serious unavoidable circumstances were reason enough to break the rule. I dare say, attending mass everyday was more of a habit than something looked eagerly forward to.

Most children were brought up in a total religious environment. Their games were inspired by religious symbolism and ritual. In their play, children used to imitate the religious feasts. Sabina recounts how she used to 'play church' with her friends:

For the feast of Santa Maria we organised our own procession and dressed up a doll as Our Lady. We would collect wild flowers, borrow candles and walk solemnly in procession along the little street. Mother used to bake a few little cakes for the occasion and we would end our procession with a little party.

The life of religious people is very much regulated by the calendar and activities of the Church. To this day quite a few young people wake up early in the morning to attend mass before going to work or school. Some spend their free time assisting priests to take the Eucharist to the sick at home, reading extracts from the Bible, or singing and playing the guitar during mass.

Voluntary Organisations

Generally, core Catholics are active members of voluntary organisations. These range from the traditional *ghaqdiet* or church-run associations, like Catholic Action, Legion of Mary or M.U.S.E.U.M., to the less structured parish or national support groups and movements which have mushroomed since the Second Vatican Council: the Movement for Charismatic Renewal and its offshoot Christian Fellowship, the Neo-Cathecumenate, and a multiplicity of informal small communities or prayer groups at the parish, inter-parish or national level.

Members of M.U.S.E.U.M. lead a celibate life. They choose to offer their celibacy to God. Being single they are able to dedicate all their time to the Catholic education of others. Victor, for example, spends about three and a half hours a day at the Society's centre, preparing lessons, teaching and organising activities for children and adolescents. Voluntary work, however, is not devoid of its ambiguities and mixed motivations. Paul has this to say about his membership of a religious organisation:

> It is a way of escaping from all my problems and stress . . . my religious club is like a second home. That is where I spend most of my spare time, where my friends are and where I socialise. I do everything with the other members, I even go abroad with them.

Michael, now twenty years old, joined the Legion of Mary after Confirmation. As a member of this group he used to visit and play with sick children in hospital:

> It was not social work that directed me to join this group but my wish to practise my religion . . . to help others in need . . . I was encouraged to share my faith with others and grow in faith. . . . When I was young I just took things for granted, until I began to attend secondary school at which time I had taken the decision to become a priest.

During his sixth form years, however, Michael started to date girls and ruled out the idea of the priesthood.

As they grow older, quite a few teenagers leave behind membership in traditional associations or *ghaqdiet* and join one of the many support groups at a parish or national level. In these groups they talk about all kinds of problems, especially their relations with the other sex. They live a consumerist culture and are not afraid to challenge the laws of the Church. A participant observes:

Some of my friends have had pre-marital sexual relationships but have now come to share the value that sex should be left for the person you are going to spend the rest of your life with, and some are also embarrassed to talk about these experiences. . . . All have a common passion for nice clothes and seek advice from each another on that matter. Although our group is Christian, we base our meetings more on faith than Church laws. . . . Our opinions sometimes clash with the teachings of the Pope and parish priest.

The activities of these groups include: picnics; visits to the sick and old, particularly during Christmas and Easter time; barbecues and days at the beach in summer; weekends in Gozo on retreats and holidays. They also organise national concerts and participate with songs, music and dance.

Quite a few are introduced to new Church groups or movements by their parents. Angela, 19 years old, recalls how she was exposed to Charismatic Renewal from a very young age. She was quite fervent from the beginning, experienced the closeness of God and the occurrence of what she calls 'miracles' in the family: 'my parents have been attending a Charismatic group for the last 16 years . . . it took me some time to realise that not all children are brought up in the same way'.

New movements do not have widespread support. In fact some associate them with sects or denominations. Sabina observes:

People in those infernal groups . . . Charismatics and the like. A lot of clapping and singing and then they're quite happy to pick on someone's reputation and pull it to pieces over a cup of coffee. I don't agree with that sort of stuff. I think they should mind their own business. . . . The Church warns us about the Jehovah Witnesses . . . but these groups are often almost as bad.

People like Sabina prefer to have a private relationship with God. They are unwilling to form part of a cultural religion old or new.

Church Leaders

Although the majority of young people never join a religious group or movement, they all come under the influence of the active members of the Church. In addition to the primary socialisation that takes place in the family, Catholics assimilate the predominant religious culture at school and parish centres, and through their participation in the sacraments, religious feasts and other seasonal activities of the Church. In all these activities they come into contact with priests, nuns, catechists and other active members of the Church.

Young adults give contrasting evaluations of their relationships with priests, nuns and other Church leaders. Certain respondents respect the authority of religious leaders but others think they are concerned only with power. Jo, for example, is convinced that priests are chosen by God, just as doctors, lawyers or other professionals. She feels that priests have an important role and that the Church has a mission to teach social justice. Sue, however, thinks that young people are moving away from the Church because they do not accept anyone telling them 'do this, do not do that'.

Quite a few have friendly relations with priests and nuns. Some seek their advice and find their help useful. For example, whilst growing up, Doris found comfort from a priest because 'it was more of a discussion rather than a confession'. She felt that she could speak freely about her problems. He gave her spiritual guidance and she followed his advice blindly. She says: 'for the first time there was a male benevolent presence in my life. The priest who used to come [to School] usually made mass very interesting. During homily he would convey an important message on morality.'

On one occasion, a priest helped Michael to clarify faith issues that were being challenged by one of his girlfriends. In like manner, Alice who had to decide about the future of her relationship with a Muslim acquaintance, became friends with her confessor when he advised her to do what she felt was right, independently of what her mother thought about the matter. David also appreciates the freedom in the quest for truth and the non-directive approach he came across: 'I first began questioning my beliefs around the age of ten when a priest told us that it was good to doubt things. . . . We believe more strongly when we find answers ourselves.'

Others, however, recall negative experiences. Quite a few avoid priests, religious women and men. Monika has this to say: 'I have a grudge against priests and nuns. After going to a Church school for four years, having an aunt who is a nun and family problems with religion, I see more than just a holy side to them.'

Not a few are afraid to go to confession. Victor, for instance, thinks this is because as a child he was always confessing the same things, and for fear that the priest would make public what he confessed. Another respondent cannot forget a priest shouting at him when he confessed the same sin of masturbation. On this matter, Winnie thinks:

> I could not abide by the priest's exhortation . . . to refrain from these solitary acts. It never really persuaded me to stop altogether. It made me feel some-what guilty, but I could never come to accept the priest's idea *that* that was a sin. I wondered how this could be a sin, since I was harming nobody. I even think so today.

Winnie goes on to say, 'I wish some priests devoted more time to their vocation. the Church would not be so much beset with crises of paedophile priests, secularism, abuse of power. . . .' A chorus of respondents think that the Church has an obsession with sexuality. Nathalie recalls 'priests and teachers always taught me that sex is wrong, and sex before marriage is a sin'. Sharon is determined not to reveal anything about her sexual activity, least of all to a priest. She remembers:

> The last time I went to confession, when I was about 16 years old, the priest wanted to know every little detail about my sexual behaviour with my boyfriend. I am extremely happy with my life and have no regrets whatsoever as to what I do.

On issues of priests, gender and sexuality, Philip voices the position of many young Catholics when he says:

> Firstly, the Church is being discriminatory in choosing only males for the priesthood. Secondly, certain priests can never understand the family and its problems because they are not married. Celibacy can breed selfishness since priests can get accustomed to think only about themselves.

It is not uncommon for certain priests and nuns to take things for granted and a few also to abuse their authority. Similar occurrences have a lasting effect on individuals, who at a tender age are afraid to come out into the open. Fiona, for example, recalls how hurt she felt when a nun at her school made public her family problems: 'you are nothing but an ill-mannered girl. In actual fact you are to be pitied. It is not your fault you were brought up badly, your parents are separated after all.' Fiona comments that after that 'for many years I avoided talking about my parents'.

Nadine feels that at the Church school many nuns led a sheltered life. Their secluded and strict rules turned girls away from religion:

> Nuns are scared of reality. No one could relate to their lives . . . no one wants to be like them. If only one nun was open-minded, maybe a lot of pupils would be different now. They were so one-track minded . . . scared of everything . . . pushed the pupils away from religion. Instead of making religion something from the heart to believe in, it is something you have to do . . . to obey.

Nikita, a returned migrant discovered the reason why her father was alienated from the Church. He once confided how when still a child he was sexually abused by a priest. She thinks this is not unrelated to her father's authoritarian behaviour, his bad temper and violence towards all the family:

> I never saw my father religious. When once I asked him why he does not involve God in his life he told me a very touching and horrifying story. As a child he was an altar boy and very much involved in the Church. One day, a priest who was very fond of him, asked him over to his place to show him some pictures of Saints. My dad was only eight years old. After about half an hour the priest tried to rape him. So he ran for his life . . . he ran away not only from the priest, but from God too. I now understand why he never liked priests and the Church, but I still cannot understand what God had to do with the priest.

At that time there was nowhere for Nikita's father to seek refuge or advice. To this very day, it is not uncommon for untrained administrators of Church institutions to lack those skills for the protection of victims of abuse. Joe Cini, for example, now a 26-year-old single male, serving a prison term for drug-related offences, recalls a priest's indifference towards victims of sexual abuse: 'at the Church institute, the priest knew very well about the sexual abuse taking place, but never did anything about it'. More recently, following similar initiatives overseas, the local Church has set up a commission to investigate reported cases of sexual abuse in pastoral activity (1999).

Abuse in the Family

The incidence of abuse and the protection of perpetrators, however, is not exclusively a matter of Church institutions. Foremost, it is experienced in the private and most intimate spheres of the family. In fact, various forms of abuse take place between partners and siblings, and on children by parents or other relatives in the family. Over the past few years there has been an increasing awareness of the incidence of both domestic violence and child abuse. Many people in Malta are of the opinion that it is not uncommon for children and married partners, women in particular, to suffer emotional (40 per cent), physical (35 per cent) and sexual abuse (28 per cent) in the family (Abela 1996: 71). Such a situation is accompanied by greater demands for shelter facilities and specialised social services. Accordingly, the number of victims who find refuge at 'Merhba Bik', a Church institution for battered women and children, has increased from a low of 36 women and 20 children in 1987 to a high of 140 women and 109 children in 1997. In 1997, the domestic violence unit of the Social Welfare Development Programme was offering help to 307 women. In 1998, the Child Protection Unit of the same agency received a monthly average of 28 child abuse reports, mostly of a physical or sexual nature (*The Times*, 19 January 1999). To address the situation, a White Paper has proposed amendments to the Maltese legislation for the better protection of victims of domestic violence (Parliamentary Secretary for Women's Rights 1998). The Ministry of Social Policy is committed to improving the available services.

The occurrence of child abuse and domestic violence is also evident from the study of life histories. Moira, for instance, who lived for many years with her family overseas, recounts how a lifelong experience of bullying by her older brother, and his being protected by their father, has had a negative effect on her relationships with men:

I have a very aggressive brother who is a fanatic body builder. When he loses his temper he beats me. . . . [Now] I tend to look down on men. I hate any man with a temper. I have become a very strong person and learned to live with the abuse I have been through for 21 years.

Anna, now a married woman, lost her father when young. She recalls her experience of being sexually abused by a friend of the family. For many years she kept the secret to herself, not knowing who was to blame. Only lately has she come to realise the effects this one-time abuse has had on her sexual behaviour and relationships:

When I was about nine a friend of the family abused me . . . I was so shocked that I remained silent and he probably thought that I liked it. I didn't tell anyone for many years because it only happened that one time and he was under the influence of drugs. I also had thought for a long time that it was my fault. I was too young to understand. I later realised how it had affected me. I didn't care about many of the guys that I slept with from 16 to 28, and a lot of the time I didn't even enjoy it. I used to feel guilty because of my religious beliefs. I knew that it was wrong but I did it anyway.

Doris, now a 23-year-old woman, recalls her prolonged experience of sexual abuse, when as a child she was living with her separated mother at the house of her grandparents:

Finding nobody home, my grandfather took the liberty to seat me down in the dining room and asked me to take off my clothes. . . . He paid me one pound when the whole ordeal was over. This secret that we shared went on for three years until I turned thirteen . . . it gradually escalated . . . I never told any member of my family.

Doris feels ashamed to look back:

Although I was aware of my grandfather's wrongdoing, I didn't mind in the least because the more I did the better I got paid. The whole ordeal came to an end when I came across an article that opened my eyes to what was really going on. I threatened to tell on him if he abused me any more. His reaction shocked and scared me. He claimed that I was evil for having seduced her own grandfather. . . . Before I knew it he whisked me off to a far away chapel and pushed me into the confessional booth. He told me it was my only means of salvation. I never uttered a word to the priest about my experience.

Doris went on to say that her grandfather has never spoke a word to her since that episode. He cunningly kept up appearances in front of the rest of the family, and they were never to be alone again. She can never forget what happened.

In another account, Maureen recalls how her father, who had a job overseas, used to beat her mother when he was on 'home' visits. On one occasion he was also extremely violent with Maureen herself. Maureen could not understand why her mother did not denounce him:

When I was 16, father once prolonged his stay in Malta from two to six months. These months were like living in hell. He was even more violent. On one occasion he caught me with my 'fiancée' in bed. He hit me so badly that I had to be admitted to hospital suffering from suffocation problems. My father accompanied me to hospital. When the doctors examined me and asked questions about my condition he kept looking into my eyes. I couldn't tell the truth because I was afraid that when we returned home he would kill me. Up to this time, I used to think highly of my mother, but once she kept silent about my being abused I began to hate her. My aim was to get married and leave home.

It is often argued that present social conditions and power structures in Malta do not favour the denunciation of perpetrators. Victims are unable to break loose from abusive relations for lack of feasible alternatives. Allegedly, in a homogeneous society, priests and other persons in authority succeed in persuading victims to stay in abusive relationships in order to safeguard the unity of the family. Also, the risk of greater hardships and economic poverty deters women from leaving the family. However, with the advance of secularisation and women's emancipation from male authority, young adults in Malta are more willing to take risks in order to put an end to oppressive relationships. In the new social conditions, women have greater opportunities for higher education and a job. Economic independence, freedom of movement, greater mobility and overseas travel all provide new openings for young adults.

TRAVEL MATTERS

Over the past few years, Malta's geographical location and the unprecedented means of communications have made possible frequent and relatively cheap travel to and from Malta. Most of the life histories under consideration have to do with travelling for short visits or long-term living overseas. Participants in the study or their close family members have travelled or lived for some time in another country as a tourist, migrant worker, resident or volunteer missionary. Others have spent much time with foreign visitors to the islands.

It is not uncommon for young people to seek freedom from family constraints and in some cases also from abusive relations. Moving out from the family home, either through marriage, overseas travel, to live with one's partner or to pursue higher education can give a sense of independence and autonomy. While similar enterprises are not devoid of the risks of late modernity, they are often accompanied by spiritual journeys, the experience of maturity and the beginning of a new phase in life. Mark, for example, recalls his first experience of liberty when he travelled on his own to see some friends in Germany:

That trip was the first big step . . . after it, my parents could not say no. . . . Over the last two years I have become more conscious of EU issues and Europe as a whole. I have since travelled a lot and met many new people from other countries. I am interested to meet new people, see new places and what is going on in the world. My friends think that I am not going to end up in Malta and that I will marry a foreign woman and live abroad.

Doris, who was living with her separated mother in Malta, wanted to move in pull and push circumstances:

> At the end of my first year at sixth form, I became restless to the point where I decided to try living with my father, back in England. There were many reasons for my desire to leave the island. For starters, I wasn't getting on well with my mother . . . all my friends were travelling in pursuit of a better education and I longed to be reunited with my father. . . . Mother got used to the idea and deep down felt it was for the better that I move out for a while.

Others travel between the two islands for better opportunities. Most Gozitans who work or study in Malta travel by boat every day. A few others share a flat in Malta and cross over to Gozo for the weekend. Dora, for example, travels between Malta and Gozo every day. During her daily journey she finds time to listen to the music and to think about her future:

> When I am travelling to and from work I have a lot of time to listen to the music. I have time to think about projects for the future. I would like to advance in my career, to marry and have children. I love children, and having one or two of my own would fulfil my life.

Unlike Dora, Miriam and Lorella have found it hard to travel from Gozo every day. After two months Miriam resigned from a course she was studying, because she could not stand the tiresome travelling on land and sea. Instead Lorella has moved to a flat in Malta:

> Given my tight timetable, I need more free time. Leisure has become one of the most important values in my life. I have developed a serious liaison with a boyfriend of my age, which I hope will last. It is too early to say if this will affect my scale of values.

Young Gozitans who live in Malta suddenly experience an independence from their families. This translates into a forced emancipation from the home, less conformity with parental rules and an invariable decline in religious commitment. Some adopt new lifestyles but others do not give in to permissive behaviour. For example, Winnie did not follow the example of her friend. When confronted with a choice she did not engage in pre-marital sex, nor did she consent to have an affair with a married man. Although she abandoned certain religious practices she retained her values in a new situation:

When I started work I could no longer hear Mass or recite the rosary every day. I got used to this after a while. My belief in God and in the teachings of His Church has not dwindled . . . what really happened is that my religious practices declined. . . . One of my flat mates went to live with a boyfriend in another apartment. . . . We never said a word to anybody about the escapade . . . in retrospect, I think that my religious beliefs played an important part in not becoming 'loose'. . . . If I had not been firm, I may have found myself seriously involved with a married man who showered attentions towards me.

Non-resident holidaymakers are often surprised by the extent of permissiveness in Malta, its cover-up and the lack of sexual education for religious reasons. For example, Moira, a daughter of Maltese emigrants who spend their summer holidays on the island, recalls how she lost her virginity:

A boyfriend tricked me into having sex. He did not even realise what he did was wrong. It did affect the way I look at life for sure . . . I know that sex before marriage is against my religion but then I saw Malta as the most religious place around and if people were having sex there, then it can't be so bad. . . . I was drifting away from my religion. . . . Just because Malta is a small island it doesn't mean that it is not in touch with AIDS. The sad thing is that because Malta is so religious they don't teach sex education at school and authorities would rather close an eye than deal with the reality.

Some time later, Moira settled in Malta and joined a youth religious movement:

It was the best thing that I ever did as far as religion goes. I became really close to God. I learned to accept God as a friend and let him take control . . . we were high on life and our new-found love for God. I felt that I became a better person . . . my change scared some people and made others like my parents very happy. I didn't change all my bad habits but I did change some of them.

Challenged by situations of risk and uncertainty, other young Catholics in Malta also experience such a deepening in faith. They find comfort and support in new religious movements. Similar events trigger a journey of spiritual growth.

Getting married and travelling overseas is also a time for change, sometimes of religious reconciliation and maturity. Sabina recounts that since her marriage she no longer sees life as cut and dried. She has come to be much more flexible and appreciative of diversity, different opinions and opposing views. She is fascinated by different cultures and religions. She has rediscovered a personalised faith in God, even if she remains critical of Church morality and traditional religious upbringing:

As I travel overseas with my husband I feel the world shrinking and feel more a citizen of the world . . . my viewpoint has changed. . . . Now I tend to see things as an interesting challenge rather than a threat. . . . I suddenly rediscovered God . . . I made a truce. . . . He took my father but gave me a great husband. I still feel that life is a journey towards an end with God . . . I don't agree with everything the Church says . . . I am also bringing up my children differently. Instead of forcing religion down their throat, I try to explain things and discuss religion, even though they are still young. I hope that I can avoid making the mistakes my parents made with me, and also offer my children all that was positive in my own childhood.

In sum, Sabina and many other young adults who rediscover the essentials of their Christian faith share the belief expressed by Fiona: 'life is a journey and not a destination and all of us should open our hands and welcome the surprises which this life has in store for us'. For some people religious faith remains dormant only to be activated by an unexpected event in their life. Others, however, either because of social conditions or personal choice or both, leave behind their religious faith.

SECULARISED CATHOLICS

Core Catholics generally prolong their religious practices into adult life. Intermediate and former Catholics, however, often undergo a secularisation process. In most cases they grow out of compulsory Church attendance and a strict observance of Catholic morality. Quite a few become cultural or conventional Catholics, a few others grow out of religion completely. Nadine, for example, who considers herself an average Catholic, recalls how she eventually left behind the influence of her religious upbringing:

Until Holy Communion at age seven I was extremely religious, with God and prayers. I used to tell everyone that I wanted to become a nun . . . it all started to die out when it was time for my Confirmation. . . . When I was about thirteen my mother told me it was up to me, as she had done her job. . . . She did not want to hassle or push me, now it should be my own choice. I stopped going, and so did my parents. . . . I do not believe that you have to go to mass and 'sleep' [on the pews] to prove that you are good.

Nadine does not find it important to go to Church regularly, except during Christmas and Easter. Similarly to other young Catholics worldwide, Nadine finds going to Mass a boring routine. Nadine observes how most of her friends were brought up in a Catholic environment. As such 'they can be described as typical Maltese Catholics whose religious beliefs are limited to going to Mass on Sundays but do not really think about God once they are out of the Church'. There are others, however, who are religious without going to Church. Lorella observes: 'no one in my group is a fervent churchgoer, yet they lead a good life, well within the teachings of the Catholic Church and the ten commandments. . . . The Church should liven up the Mass. Sometimes priests put people off.'

Then there are those who distinguish clearly between religion and the ministers of the Church. Exposure to other religions and cultures gives people a critical perspective whereby they come to distinguish between faith, morality and the ministers of religion. Diane, who emigrated to another country after marriage, observes:

> The different religions that I experienced overseas made me question the Catholic Church that I knew from my young days in Malta. . . . Some of the Catholic clergy are not competent enough to make ethical judgements. I consider them as ordinary human beings.

In other instances, young adults are alienated from the Church because they are unable to live by the Church's moral teaching on sexuality. Vicky, a former Catholic, who migrated to Malta when her widowed mother married a Maltese, prefers to be called a 'Christian'. Her departure from the Church is not unrelated to her lifestyle, substance abuse and a guilt feeling for having had an abortion overseas: 'I could not face having a child. I did the wrong thing. I was a coward. I do hate myself for it, but know in my heart that if I ever am in the same situation again, I will probably do the same. . . . Because of this I can't face going to Church.'

Others abandon their faith because they cannot reconcile social inequalities with a just God. For instance, James, who considers himself a libertarian communist, lost his faith when he was 18 years old because:

> I could not understand how God could be omnipotent and still allow disasters and suffering. . . . Spirituality can be found in people and not in institutions. The Church creates a lot of guilt. It wastes time fighting insignificant holy wars like sex before marriage. Instead it should address real problems like poverty in the Third World. It is useless to fight for change within the Church.

Quite a few, however, claim to have lost faith in God completely. Maureen, for example, who separated from her abusive partner, claims that she is neither a practising Catholic nor a spiritual person. She thinks that God does not exist and holds liberal views on morality. She believes that people are happy only out of luck or destiny:

> I am in favour of promiscuous sex and divorce. I favour those political parties that are open-minded and promote divorce. I can't risk starting another relationship and have children . . . I am in favour of using condoms because it prevents getting pregnant.

Monika, who lost her father in her early teenage years, left home because she could not bear the situation. She abandoned all her religious values and beliefs and stopped attending Sunday Mass. She experimented with sex, drink and heavy drugs. She is now cohabiting with a foreigner, has given birth to a child and regained some hope, after going through a dark tunnel with no hope of returning back. My life was in a whole mess and I wanted to escape . . . my newborn baby changed my life completely. Unlike my partner, I never thought of having an abortion. My main concern is to give a good upbringing to my daughter. I have lost all contact with my family, but I am very happy. I do not want my daughter to experience the same hardship I suffered.

Here happiness is found in giving life, with no mention of God and the Church. In fact, unchurched Catholics find alternatives to traditional religious practices in new rituals having to do with caring for others or a fulfilling career, leisure pursuits, fashion, music, 'social smoking', overseas travel or new age religions. David, for example, has been away from the Church for more than six years. He is heavily involved in the Goth Scene, smokes marijuana and practises a Japanese religion:

I used to dress up in gel-spiky hair, leather trousers and jacket. It was fashionable to paint one's face white and put on loads of drastic make-up. I tried all sorts of drugs. . . . Over the past three years I participate on a regular basis in a Light Ceremony.... This includes the removal of negative energies from within your body and mind and enables you to be at peace with others. . . . I find it inspiring and relaxing to have a 'joint' whilst painting or listening to the music.

CATHOLIC IDENTITIES

By way of conclusion, respondents were asked to elaborate on their Catholic identity. Most gave conventional and orthodox definitions but quite a few others came out with personalised and reflexive answers. At the traditional end stand the old style conventional Catholics who think in terms of obeying the ten commandments, hearing mass, receiving Holy Communion, doing what is considered right and avoiding what is wrong. At the post-traditional end, we find adults who are critical of the Catholic Church and shape their own individualised Catholic identity in the changed social context of late modernity.

Here a typology of new Catholic identities is constructed on the basis of the life histories for Malta. Such a typology, however, should not be taken as exhaustive. The types are only models and approximations of real identities. Single individuals might not be able to identify themselves completely with any one type. In fact, individual Catholics might identify with more than one type. There might well be other types that are not represented in this study. Moreover, each type has potential for further differentiation within it, which might not have appeared in the present study.

A first type of modern Catholic identity is focused on *religious tolerance* towards other religions and ways of life. It is not uncommon for the present generation of young Catholics to think that Catholicism entails the acceptance of other religions. In fact, certain respondents were found not to be concerned with the distinctive nature of their religion. They believe that all individuals have the right to believe and adhere to their own religion without imposing their religious views and opinions. This group is characterised by those who find nothing special in belonging to the Catholic Church. One tolerant Catholic said: 'I have the Catholic religion to go by, but it could be any other religion. . . . Other religions may lead to a happy life and Heaven, but I am happy to have been brought up as a Catholic. . . . God will remain a priority in my life.'

A second type of Catholic identity is the *new* or transformed *traditional*. These are able to mix and match traditional Church teachings with a personalised and communitarian experience of religion. Members of new religious movements, the Charismatics for instance, find it important to believe in the Holy Trinity. Still, they think of God as a friend, an intimate person, and not someone 'way up there'. Most of all it means to 'do unto others as you would have them do unto you'. Neo-traditionalists think that a Catholic should respect nature and all creatures. Monika, for example, feels that it is up to the individuals concerned and not a matter of dogma as to how to fulfil their duties. Similarly, Norman finds it important to maintain a relationship with God, to serve his will, as well as to develop good relationships with others, doing away with jealousy, anger and pride.

A third type of new Catholic identity integrates religious *faith with social justice*. These young adults find it essential to include a social, perhaps political, dimension to their spirituality. Vincent, for example, links his quest for spiritual union with God with a need for a greater commitment to social action. He feels

> Being a Catholic gives me the chance to be closer to God. . . . I am very happy yet I would like to serve God and humankind better . . . to fight more for my clients and for the things I believe in. Another important thing I would like to do is to speak publicly [about it].

In fact, quite a few young adults give importance to the integration of their Catholic convictions with a greater commitment in public life. The revived quest for a greater intimacy with God has more the quality of a socially oriented spirituality than a conventional religion. This strand of Catholicism has the quality of post-traditional social Catholicism.

A fourth type of identity consists of *small community* Catholics. Quite a few belong to a Church group or community without, however, feeling at home in the Church. They give importance to spirituality that is shared with others in the community. They are indifferent to the teachings of the

Church. Joseph, for example, is an active member in his 'community' but is distant from the institutional Church:

> I still attend the community but I am rather passive towards my religion. There are various Church teachings that I don't agree with, like [those on] sex and contraception, the death penalty, the way it treats homosexuals. I believe that I can live my spirituality well without having someone dictate it to me. I don't really bother about an afterlife because what is important is the way I live my present life. Helping others, listening to their problems and dedicating time to others who need my companionship are values that I cherish.

Katya also feels detached from the teachings of the Church. She keeps her faith alive by participating in her 'small community' and doing voluntary work overseas. She finds it important to remain attached to the Church as a means of keeping alive a Christian spirituality. However, she would like to see a change in the moral teachings of the Church, making it more relevant to young people:

> I still go to the community because if I stop I would abandon the Church further. Although there are things I disagree with I still feel the need to form part of the Church, or rather Christ. . . . I do not believe that a relationship can progress without a sense of spirituality. In this respect, an experience of mission work overseas helped my boyfriend and me tremendously. . . . I wish that the Church would change its teaching on sexuality and . . . appeal more to youths. At present the outlook is bleak.

A fifth type has the quality of an *individualised* Catholic identity. This group consists of a multiplicity of risk-taking and self-determining individuals who are not concerned to reconcile traditional religion with the demands of late modernity. They shape their Catholic identity in a fragmented social context. They include individualists who take most of their personal decisions by themselves, without much advice. Sabina, for example, differentiates between Christian faith and Catholic morality. She shapes an individualised private religion for herself:

> It's funny how I can believe in the existence of God and yet disobey the rules of the Church. But that's different. The Church interprets the will of God. . . . I interpret it differently. I have the right to lead the kind of life I want as long as I always try to live well and help others do the same. That is the true spirit of Christ. The Church gets bogged down in mundane things that should be left to personal choice. . . . My relationship with God is surely a private thing . . . between God and myself and that's it. It doesn't touch anyone else. . . . I feel that I am still acceptable to Christ.

Those sharing this type of identity are neither willing to conform to a cultural Catholicism nor to accept blindly all the teachings of the Church. They hold that a religious identity is something that has to be resolved by the individual. Unlike the conventional believer, individualised and risk-taking Catholics do not seek the security of the institutional Church. Nadine, for example, thinks:

> Some people find rituals meaningful. . . . Personally, I do not believe that receiving Holy Communion, going to mass or confession puts me closer to God. This is why I do not do it. There is need for someone to lead those who want to be led . . . a shelter for those who feel totally lost. . . . If the Church becomes more open-minded with more realistic views, then it would be good and more a place of unity. The way it is now – for example separated people cannot go to Church – turns people off and does not make me want to belong. They are too prejudiced. I do not think that the Church will become more liberal, but if it does I might change my mind.

Individualised Catholics of late modernity give greater priority to personal intimacy with God than a passive conformity to what in their view are unrealistic views of the Church. At the same time they are tolerant of traditional Catholics. They think that religion meets the needs of people in different ways. Although they live in a fragmented world and a distant Church, they leave the door open for a closer union with a possibly transformed Church of the future.

CONCLUSION

The religious homogeneity of former times is gradually giving way to a multiplicity of Catholic identities. As elsewhere in the world, most young Catholics in Malta start off from a common origin consisting in the main of a strict religious and protective upbringing in the family and the parish community. They are all socialised into the sacraments of initiation at a Church school or parish centre. As they grow older, however, they take separate roads leading to a multiplicity of destinations.

In Malta, core Catholics generally prolong their religious practices into adult life. Intermediate and former Catholics, however, often undergo a secularisation process. In most cases they grow out of compulsory Church attendance and a strict observance of Catholic morality. Quite a few become cultural or conventional Catholics; a few others grow out of religion completely. Some switch to other religions. In the social context of late modernity and the interaction with global society, overseas travel in particular has an important influence on young people's religious journeys. Challenged by situations of risk and uncertainty, some young Catholics experience a deepening in faith. Others find comfort and support in new religious movements. Other forms of exposure to wider cultures can also trigger a journey of spiritual growth.

The emerging Catholic identities have come to displace traditional religiosity, with traditional external morality declining in favour of an individualised spirituality. Young people want to belong to a more open Church that gives importance to spirituality, a sense of belonging to a community, the unity of all believers in Christ, and a Church willing to change with the times. They want a Church that accompanies people on their multiple journeys, thus retaining its social relevance in the new millennium.

3

YOUNG CATHOLIC
ADULTS IN IRELAND

Teresa Dowling

This chapter looks at young Catholics in the Republic of Ireland. It is based on the life histories of a quota sample, the details of which have been provided in chapter 1. We interviewed a total of 55 men and women. Although they were selected in a non-random manner, we believe they are fairly representative of young adults living and working in Ireland today. Among them are young professionals, routine white-collar workers, and people in both skilled and unskilled manual occupations. A small number are unemployed. About one in three are students. Just over two thirds of them are single, and two are lone mothers. The rest are either married (six), widowed (two) or in established relationships. Nine of these respondents have one or more children. We were unable to fill the quota of five for married/partnered *core* Catholics. They seem to be generally few in the population: only two of seven contacted were willing to participate. These were our only refusals. In these circumstances we increased the number of single core Catholics to ensure at least 15 in the core category as a whole.

The men and women we spoke with grew up in a range of different circumstances and socio-cultural environments. They came from Irish cities or their suburbs, from country towns, villages or from farms in the open countryside. Some came from economically privileged families. Others have lived most of their lives in the shadow of unemployment and poverty. Three women came from families of ten and there were two respondents who were only children. The modal size of the family of origin for the sample was four and the mean was 4.2.

While those who contributed to this study differ from each other in many important ways they also share a number of characteristics. They were all baptised into the Catholic Church and were raised in core or intermediate Catholic families. They all attended Catholic schools at both first and second level. In primary school they were instructed in the basics of the faith and each of them was prepared for Confession, Communion and Confirmation as a routine part of their·education. By the time they completed their primary education they all knew they were Catholic even if some already had religious doubts or came from families where there was little regular prayer or practice. In all of this they were probably no different from the vast majority of their peers and indeed their parents and grandparents before them.

IRISH SOCIETY AND CULTURE SINCE 1960

Ireland is a small, relatively underpopulated, island located in the north-west corner of Europe. It is bounded to the east by England, Scotland and Wales, far to the west by the North American continent. About 5.5 million people occupy its 32,500 square miles of land. The Republic of Ireland comprises just over 27,000 square miles of this territory. The 1996 census recorded its population at 3.6 million.

The Republic of Ireland is a Catholic society. Over 90 per cent of its citizens belong to the Church, and the majority of them practise. Until at least 1960 Irish life was influenced more by Catholic social teaching than by any other social or political ideology. The state took a back seat in social and economic affairs and many key areas of social and cultural reproduction, schools, hospitals and other welfare institutions were run by state-aided voluntary groups, generally church dominated or controlled. The Constitution of Ireland (1937), even as amended, is a quintessentially Catholic document. Until 1972 the Catholic Church had special constitutional recognition. Articles on the family, education and the position of women, drew directly on Catholic moral and social teaching and Irish law and church law tended to coincide on many issues. There was a constitutional prohibition on divorce. Contraception and abortion and any literature promoting them were illegal.

For almost forty years little was done to challenge the confessional nature of the Irish State. Inglis argues this was because the Church as a powerful and coercive organisation had established an institutional structure, which successfully socialised generations of Irish men and women effectively controlling opposition or dissent. By the end of the 1960s, various changes had made this monopoly less secure (Inglis 1988).

A Changing Ireland

From about 1960 the Irish State took an active role in economic and social development. State policy encouraged foreign industry to establish in Ireland, and industrial and service jobs began to replace agricultural employment. Cities and towns grew at the expense of the countryside. Government expenditure on and involvement in health, education and welfare increased to meet the needs of a developing society. The modernisation of Irish society was given a new priority.

Social change was also accelerated by the communications revolution, particularly television. The first national station commenced transmission in 1961 and by the end of the decade most homes had a television set. Television provided new knowledge and perspectives on Irish society and on the wider world. It also encouraged and facilitated both questioning and debates. The troubles in Northern Ireland from 1968 onwards, the ideas associated with the civil rights movement and the women's movement all raised questions about the confessional nature of the Irish State. Other media, in particular radio chat shows, furthered the questioning process.

The 1970s saw many changes in Irish society. In 1972 we opted to join the European Economic Community (EEC). In the same year the Irish electorate voted to remove the constitutional provision that gave the Catholic Church a special position in Irish life. In 1973 the Supreme Court ruled that the relevant sections of the Criminal Law Amendment Act 1935, which prevented married couples importing contraceptives for private use, was unconstitutional. In 1979 both houses of the Oireachtas passed a very restrictive bill permitting the sale of contraceptives to married couples (See Whyte 1980). This legislation was amended throughout the 1980s and 1990s and today contraceptives are freely available.

A fear that European law might bring abortion to Ireland resulted in a campaign to provide constitutional protection for the unborn child. The campaign, spearheaded by a group of lay Catholics, concluded in 1983 with a successful referendum to amend the constitution to protect the unborn. However, in 1992 the Supreme Court ruled that the provision permitted a suicidal 14-year-old rape victim to leave the country for an abortion. Despite a further referendum in 1993 the constitutional position on abortion remains unclear. We await further Government action on the issue.

The growing number of broken marriages and the establishment of second unions – some following church annulments – led to the demand for civil divorce. In 1986 a referendum to remove the constitutional prohibition on divorce resulted in a two to one defeat for the proposal. Some commentators have seen this as a triumph for Catholic conservatism though it is likely material considerations played a large part. In 1993 a second referendum to remove the prohibition succeeded by a majority of 0.5 per cent.

When Ireland joined the then European Economic Community in 1973 it was one of its poorest members. Today it is one of the fastest growing economies in the European Union. Nearly half of its young well-educated population is under the age of thirty, with one in four aged between 15 and 29. Unemployment is falling rapidly and economists predict that full employment will soon be achieved for the first time since the foundation of the state in 1922. Emigration, which has been a feature of Irish life since the early nineteenth century, no longer depletes the population. But despite this growing affluence some sectors of the population remain untouched – the poorly educated, the old, and marginalised groups such as travellers.

The changing economic and social circumstances since 1960 suggest to some that the Irish State is becoming less Catholic, that life in Ireland is no longer directed by religious beliefs and values and that the Church is losing its power over the hearts and minds of the Irish people (Kenny 1997). There is a growing number of cohabiting couples, a falling marriage rate and a rapidly rising number of births to unmarried women, from 2.6 per cent of all births in 1969 to over 26 per cent in 1999. Coupled with the number of Irish women seeking abortions in England, such facts suggest the Church has little influence over the sexual morality of this generation. Studies undertaken from the mid 1970s on suggest that young adults, particularly urban men, are less likely to be practising Catholics than other groups in the population. Yet Irish people maintain the high levels of religious practice for which they are noted, albeit at a somewhat lower level than in the past. In 1976 Nic Ghiolla Phádraig reported that over 90 per cent of the Catholic population attended Mass at least once a week. This had fallen to 85 per cent by 1990 (Whelan 1994). By 1998 it had reached an all time low of 60 per cent (*The Irish Times* 2.2.1998). There are few Irish people who seldom or never attend formal religious services though in some urban working class areas less than ten per cent of the population attend weekly Mass.

This is the society in which the young adults we studied grew up. We look at how they were influenced by family, friends, school, church and the wider community as they developed into adult members of Irish society. We look at the choices they have made, the beliefs and values they cherish and the worldviews that direct their lives at the end of the twentieth century.

GROWING UP CATHOLIC IN IRELAND

Family and Community

Most people we spoke with came from two parent families, with fathers in steady employment and stay-at-home mothers. In a very few cases professional women pursued careers while raising their children and some women returned to work when children were established in school. A small number of respondents had been raised in single parent homes, the result of death or marital breakdown.

Family life was generally described as happy and uneventful with no more than the usual rows and squabbles associated with normal family living. The most common exceptions to this were families where there was alcohol abuse, which was the most frequently cited cause of family discord and financial difficulty. In at least three cases it resulted in marital breakdown and separation. In some such families women took up poorly paid unskilled work to support themselves and their children. Children grew up quickly in these circumstances as they took on responsibilities beyond their years to help ease a difficult situation.

Most people had good relationships with their parents even though quite a number of people described their parents as strict, even authoritarian. Fathers were more likely to be singled out as authoritarian than were mothers and core Catholics described their fathers in these terms more often than other respondents. Bridget's father took the line 'you do it or else . . . you are in my house and you live by my rules'. Joe, another core Catholic, claimed his father 'had the last word on everything at home. . . . You could discuss all you wanted, but he was right. You know, it was his house.' Anne, Derek and Conor reported similar experiences.

A small number of middle-class professional parents were more interactive. For example, Orla's parents 'never just said, don't do this. They always discussed everything with us and because there was always respect amongst us. I never really said "Oh, what they're saying is rubbish", you know.' In Garrett's home, 'Discipline . . . was very good . . . it was very fair. A lot of the time I was allowed to make up my own mind. If I decided not to do things my parents would question me and I'd give them the reason why; and they'd say that's your choice.'

Honesty and respect for others were values most parents tried to instil in their children. Hard work was also valued and doing well in school was very important in middle and many working class homes. Sometimes the importance attached to schooling created conflict in adolescence as parents restricted leisure activities particularly in examination years. Several respondents, resentful at the time, now admitted that their parents were right and that a limited social life did them little harm. In poor working-class homes parents worried that children stayed out of trouble and kept clear of the rougher element in the locality. Girls were often more restricted than boys and middle-class children were more likely to be subject to parental supervision than were their working-class peers.

Religion was important in many homes sometimes because parents were very devout, sometimes for reasons of respectability. A number of intermediate and ex-Catholics reported severe parental disapproval and a distinct cooling of relationships when parents discovered they had stopped attending Mass. Some parents tried to force less than willing teenagers and young adults to attend Mass. At least two ex-Catholics still go to Mass to maintain family harmony. In more liberal families young people were permitted to make choices, and while parents may have been upset by their decision not to attend Mass, they respected it and made no effort to impose their will. In one case a very devout mother refused to accede to a local curate's demand that she insist that her teenage children attend Mass as long as they lived in the family home.

In a society in which it is almost natural to be Catholic it is virtually impossible for children to escape the influence of Catholicism. Children from 'staunch' or 'strong' Catholic families were introduced to the faith at an early age. In these families religion was part of the taken for granted world. Parents actively engaged in their children's religious education. They taught them their prayers, took them to Mass and often introduced them to a range of devotional practices and religious organisations as they grew older. Bridget, a core Catholic, remembers being taken to Mass,

> when I was about seven, just before my first Communion. Before that my Mum used to take me into the church and tell me about God and the various things in the church. I felt great being taken to Mass. We used go up to the front and I'd have my book and I'd be able to follow it. Communion was important I remember. My parents would have stressed how important it was. I felt very grown up going to Communion and before I made my first Communion I would have gone up to the altar with my mother to see what it was about.

Deirdre recalls how she and her sister 'were always great company for my mother. She always took us to the novenas . . . and we'd always meet my aunt there.'

Most parents made some effort to encourage children to be at least conventionally religious. Seán now an atheist says:

> My mother liked us to go to Mass and she liked the Christmas and the Easter Mass. My father went to Mass at Christmas. If we didn't go to Mass the mother was unhappy. She was brought up a Catholic and I don't think she ever questioned it . . . so she expected us to be the same I think.

Máire, an agnostic, who grew up on a farm close to a prosperous country town remembers, 'we went to Mass and it would have been unheard of to miss Mass and we all went. It wasn't a big deal. . . . We used to have the stations, the Mass in the house. But that was really only a matter of form, a matter of community rather than a religious thing.' Many intermediate Catholic families like Colm's (24) met the minimum norms: 'they go to Mass, yes, [but] I mean, for promoting extra forms of religion they wouldn't be really [interested]'.

Victor's family was less conventional:

> Neither of my parents were very strong religiously. We never attended Mass as a habit. We always knew there was a religion there. We always knew there was a God there. . . . My mum would have spoken to us about God and about Jesus and when Christmas came around she'd explain what that was all about and things like that. We understood it, definitely we understood it, but it was never something very strong in the house (former Catholic, 30).

Even if parents were somewhat lax, grandparents often kept an eye on the children. Victor and his siblings were encouraged to go to Mass regularly by his grandfather who lived close by. Alan's grandmother regularly checked their religious behaviour particularly as they got older, as did Jack's who resided in the family home. Religion was part of the taken-for-granted world of many communities. Kevin, who grew up in an urban middle-class estate, remembers:

> Rosary was at teatime in my neighbours houses and if I was having tea there, then I'd be saying the rosary twice. I was used to it . . . and you'd be asked into someone's house and they'd be going through prayers and things like this. . . . And we would all go down and say our few decades of the rosary or whatever and go home. It was a social occasion. We had Masses in the estate, open air Masses. . . . And both my parents were from the country so I'd have been to stations once or twice in the country and things like that.

School

By the time most Irish children go to school at age four or five, they are familiar with at least some aspects of Catholicism. This is extended in primary school where religion is compulsory and an integral part of the curriculum (see Drudy and Lynch 1993). Almost everyone remembered primary school as a place where there was a religious influence, even if it was only 'conventionally religious', and many remembered primary school as a religious or very religious place.

By the end of primary school, all our respondents had been instructed in the basic elements of their faith. They had all received the sacraments of Penance, Eucharist and Confirmation and they all knew they were Catholic, even if they already practised irregularly and came from homes in which religion was relatively unimportant. Victor, a former Catholic, who entered his first Catholic school at the age of ten when his family returned from England, graphically describes the impact of this system:

> I only had two years in the primary Christian Brothers' school but you know what the Catholic religion is about when you get to secondary school. And maybe it's just . . . that every day of your life you see a brother, . . . a black habit, a white collar and that all means. The Catholic Church is very easy once you've been given the basic . . . and I think they don't even have to say anything. Just the fact that they're there . . . the memorabilia is on the wall. But all these things are a constant reminder of 'this is what we are about, this is what we mean'. You don't think about it, but all the little impressions become one massive impression and when you come out of that system in a lot of ways those beliefs are instilled in you.

Religious education did not end with primary school. For although religion is not compulsory beyond this level most post-primary schools allocate at least one period a week to religious education and many give it considerably more time than this. None the less, although most people attended religiously owned and run second level schools, these schools were not often seen as religious or dominated by a religious ethos. Emer (26), an intermediate Catholic describes the ethos of her small town convent secondary school as 'run by nuns, but [religion] didn't play a great part in the day-to-day running of the actual school. Academic achievement was of the utmost importance.' Kevin (23) also remembers his secondary school as primarily academic: 'After [first year] I can't remember being taught much religion. We had space for it but it became more of a civics class. There wasn't much with regards anything concrete. . . . Secondary school was very academic, that's how I'd put it.'

Several women also describe convent schools as very class conscious. To quote Emer again:

> [The nuns] valued . . . position quite a bit. . . . I think there was probably an unseen hierarchy almost in that school. There was certainly a preference for people who came from wealthy backgrounds, you know, daughters of professionals and so on. They certainly would have been pets, not necessarily of the lay teachers but certainly of the religious people [the nuns] of the school. Class was important, certainly . . . which seems like a ridiculous thing to say about a religious order, but certainly it was important.

Máire has somewhat similar memories:

> In class terms they had everyone very clearly pigeonholed the minute you walked in the door . . . they created a future that they saw fit for each girl. They didn't rock the boat in any way. The teacher's son or daughter, a lot more was expected of them and they were worked harder and they were

given maybe a bit more individual attention than . . . the labourer's daughter, you know.

Nor are many respondents impressed by the kind of religious education offered in these schools. Seamus (27) who attended a Christian Brothers' school in Dublin has this to say:

> My own impression then was that . . . the religious aspect sort of disinte-grated after second year. There was no particular form to it. Like, we had prescribed books on the curriculum but there was no systematic approach to the teaching of it. I think the whole thing fundamentally just collapsed at that stage.

Deirdre (30) has more positive memories of her convent school but she too was

> disappointed with the classes after Intermediate Certificate [at age 16]. I enjoyed religious classes basically first and second year. Second year, we had a great religion class. . . . It was my first exposure to theology. I thought it was wonderful. I was beginning to understand the liturgy and the structure the Mass took. And I thought this was tremendously interesting. And then after 'Inter Cert' they were more like sociology classes and you know it was good too, but it was all very vague and this was during our religion time.

Colm and Patrick both attended the same community college where Colm (24) claims

> the religion syllabus that we were taught was inadequate, plain and simple. I mean there was stuff being done that should have been done in civics class. . . . You didn't get a comparative religion course where you compare different religions and you didn't get a basic kind of prayer, or shall I say a Catholic religion course either. You know the basics of one's faith (Core Catholic).

The memory of Patrick, 24, is less detailed:

> We had one class a week. We had a chaplain who taught religion. He used to play basketball with us for half of the class. We had books that we went through. But I don't remember much. I think I was already formed as I am by that time. It didn't have much effect on me (Intermediate Catholic).

Some people describe their religion classes as moral education, others as a sort of sex education classes. Others remember general but often undirected discussions on anything they wanted to talk about. Sometimes these were interesting, but a common complaint was that religion classes were frequently badly taught and largely unplanned. In the absence of any obvious curriculum, what was done depended on the teacher and on his or her level of knowledge and interest. As a non-examination subject, most students saw these classes as 'doss' classes, where they had a rest, a chat and a laugh. David sums up, 'in secondary school there was a general apathy about religious classes. They were regarded as a doss subject. Again I suppose it wasn't taught particularly imaginatively . . . many [students] stayed away. There was no enthusiasm there for it.' This lack of enthusiasm for religion classes mirrored a growing lack of interest in religion for large numbers of young people as they moved through adolescence into young adulthood. Cynicism and lack of interest appears to have been the norm and core Catholics often found themselves in a minority in their Catholic schools. But Catholic schools, particularly convent and monastery schools, often provided important religious encounters for students in the form of retreats and special Masses. Several men and women recall these events as important for their personal and religious development.

YOUNG ADULT BELIEFS, PRACTICES AND VALUES

Core Catholics

Core Catholics see themselves as different from their peers. Many of them have always been a little different. As adolescents they were less likely than their peers to engage with the youth culture, experiment with drink or drugs, or have boy/girlfriends prior to leaving school. From an early age many of them were involved in Catholic action groups and other church activities and this contributed significantly to their religious development and occupied much of their free time. Joe joined the Legion of Mary under some pressure from his mother and:

> if I hadn't . . . I'd say religion would have not been important to me at all. I can remember at age 12 and 13 religious things were beginning to bore me a bit. The Legion of Mary kind of checked that and it turned it completely around, like. It has to do with the active apostolate and responsibility. Even as a teenage boy you'd be selling Catholic papers, like. You felt you had a mission. You were bringing the good news, you know, to people's doors and you had a mission, a job to do every week and you came back.

Deirdre joined the Legion while still in primary school and it provided her with a group of like-minded friends. She remembers giving a short talk to a group of Legionaries when she was about 18 and claiming then, as now, that it had been

> the greatest influence in that period of my life and that it had helped me to grow up through the years, that perhaps maybe I would have found [it] either lonely or difficult or strange had I not been involved with the Legion. Growing up was such a pleasure because of my meeting with all the people I met through the Legion. It probably had kept me on a path that was so easy and I felt so lucky.

The Neo-Catecumenate provided the environment in which Anne met with other committed Catholics and, although she has since left the group, her time there helped to develop her faith and increase her commitment.

Sometimes particular events contributed to a strengthening or confirmation of faith. A school retreat gave Derek, Vera and David new religious insights. Derek also became sharply aware of his Catholicism during the referenda of 1983 and 1986:

> I wasn't aware of anything until the '83 and '86 referenda . . . [that] there was a liberal/conservative divide, [that] there were people who were vehemently anti-Catholic, anti-institutionalised religions. I wasn't even aware that my background as a Catholic was a sign against a growing secularism. I wasn't aware that the Church was a body of people, a community that I could be loyal to, that I could stand up for. Or that it was like a barrier that I could stand behind.

The university chaplaincy provided some students from the sample with a Christian community, friendship and opportunities for spiritual development, elements which they found missing in their secondary schools. It was while at university that several respondents developed a new level of commitment, and prayer and Mass became more important in their lives. David (19) speaks of how the meaning of Mass changed for him: 'I always enjoyed Mass. But I started going to the College chapel last year and I became a minister of the word . . . and it kind of developed into near daily Mass. . . . This changed my relationship with the Mass, if you understand. It changed the way I went to Mass.' Vera (21) started going to daily Mass when she joined a folk group at university. When the group broke up for the Easter holidays, 'I found that I missed Mass, so I started to go to Mass every day and I continue to do'. For Derek, too, university provided new opportunities and experiences: 'I remember I used go to a prayer meeting every now and again. It was a Taizé prayer meeting, so it was a lot different to anything I had been to before . . . it's like a lot of chanting and singing. There is a lot more meaning in it and I used to enjoy going in there.'

The core Catholics we interviewed are generally orthodox in their beliefs and practices. They believe in a personal god, in heaven, in the church established by Christ as the way to salvation. They are anxious to know God more and above all to do his will. God is a friend who is always there and who cares. Anna is 18 and still at school. She believes in

> a very personal God, very fatherly. [I] always pictured him as a man who is there and I can talk to him, very personal. It's not someone on a pedestal. It's someone I could have a chat with and have a cup of coffee with, very close, caring, loving, all that. I believe you should involve God in your everyday life. . . . I pray a lot. I have very basic beliefs on what is right and what is wrong.

Colm is 24 and unemployed. He lives with his invalid grandmother for whom he cares, but hopes that some day he may become a priest. He belongs to a number of church groups. His beliefs and practices are quite traditional:

> [I believe in] heaven . . . a just God, definitely, and not one that is in any way fearful, because one should not be fearful . . . belief in the Church and its sacraments . . . maybe not in the Church as, kind of, its system or its personnel but in what it is promoting . . . being good, kind, helpful.

Derek also hopes to enter the priesthood. He tries

> to go to Mass every day. I feel there is a lot of grace there. Living . . . near to a convent of contemplative nuns, I often go in there either for Mass in the morning or for benediction on Sunday or just to do some adoration in front of the Blessed Sacrament . . . and I can always feel an effect on my life. . . . They [the nuns] have a different faith. I would like to think I would have a faith that is built on these [activities]. I would see it as having a simple faith, a really really strong faith.

Many core Catholics attend daily Mass and receive Communion and, like Derek, most identify Mass as important in their lives. Most also confess regularly, though this might be no more than three or four times a year. But Confession was not a major priority. Ailbhe who is very involved in parish work and is a minister of the Eucharist says, 'Confession wouldn't be as important as when I was young. I don't see the import-ance. If you just talk to God he is able to hear you and see what you have done wrong.' Vera (21) also does not find Confession important: 'Providing you are genuinely sorry and God knows what you are doing, it's all right.' However, prayer is important, though it is not always easy to find time in an otherwise busy life. Vera is currently seeking a spiritual director:

> It's a very difficult decision. It's something that I need but . . . sometimes I feel like you are working so hard in the sense for God that you are not actually listening to what he wants. So it's just discipline and I need to know the right way to approach it before I do anything.

Core Catholics are involved in many church activities and Catholic action groups. They are members of the Legion of Mary and the St Vincent de Paul Society. Several participate in one or more prayer groups. They are ministers of the Eucharist, and of the Word. They train choirs and folk groups. Vera works as a full-time volunteer for the dioceses and Derek is a leading activist in an anti-abortion group. Others have cam-paigned on the no abortion platform during the referenda. Sometimes they are so busy prayer may be neglected. Both Joe and Deirdre have this prob-lem and Joe recently cut down on Legion work to develop his prayer life.

A number of core Catholics had religious experiences. The most dramatic was reported by Shane, a 30-year-old married man whose childhood was traumatised by an alcoholic father:

> I was praying as a child, when things were very bad. . . . I got this smell of roses in the room. Now the room . . . would have been very sparse really. I was praying that things would get better and that I would be successful in life and I got this overwhelming smell and I couldn't believe where it came from. I never thought anything till afterwards . . . I realised when somebody said to me that that was a sign – I don't know from whom – that things would turn out [right]. And by golly they did. My prayers were answered. I always remember that event. I was about second year in school [about 14 years old]. I realised something had happened. I felt so privileged.

Other reported experiences were less dramatic but all involved an awareness of God and a feeling of warmth and great inner peace. For three people these experiences were associated with a school retreat, for another a particular Mass, for another it was while on pilgrimage with the Neo-Catecumenate, while one man found God in a Protestant churchyard in New England.

Core Catholics are highly committed to, although not necessarily uncritical of, the institutional church and its teachings. Most are supportive of the Pope and of priests and religious whom they see as doing difficult and often lonely jobs. Vera, Colm and Joe feel the Irish church is excessively clerical and does little to involve the laity in meaningful ways. Vera was critical of it as a male-dominated institution and she resented the exclusion of lay people from salaried positions within the church structure.

On issues of sexual morality the men were far more accepting of church teaching on contraception, abortion, sex outside marriage, and homosexuality than were the women, though Colm was unhappy with the Church's treatment of homosexuals. Alone among the men he felt contraception should be permitted in the Third World. Most of the women condemned abortion, but some were ambivalent on contraception and most rejected the teaching outright. Sex before marriage in the context of an established relationship was acceptable to three of the seven women interviewed though some women claimed they had broken with boyfriends who could not accept traditional church teaching. Women were less likely than men to condemn homosexuality as wrong or a sin than were men and Vera said that homosexuality was 'normal for those made like that'. By comparison with men women seemed less willing to accept 'one set of rules for all'. So, while a number of women accepted that it would be wrong for them to go against the moral teaching of the Church on one or more specific issues, they were less certain that they should condemn others for doing so.

Intermediate Catholics

Although intermediate Catholics were less likely to have been active or committed members of the Church a small number had been involved in choirs or folk groups. Orla, Ruth and Sinéad had all participated in such groups, and Sinéad also served one term on the parish council. As adolescents Sheila, Dónal, Brian and Emer also remained involved in religious activity. Today all except Ruth and Brian are disillusioned with Catholicism in one way or another and have rejected an inflexible and rule-bound church, a church that offers them little by way of transcendence.

Dónal describes himself as

> a lapsed establishment Catholic. A very religious person but it is a very very personal religion. I'd say I'm a practising Catholic . . . very much a practising Catholic but I am not a Catholic who is willing to associate himself with the establishment as it stands at the moment.

Having spent some time away from Ireland he feels little need for organised religion:

> I could go to Mass for 45 minutes . . . or I could sit down on the pier head or go for a walk in a wood nearby or whatever and sort of have a – I felt there was somebody there I could talk to. But it's very much . . . a 'Him and me' thing. I don't feel anybody else needs to be involved. And I find that's more than sufficient for me.

Sinéad (26) still goes to Mass occasionally, 'but not sort of under any pretence of "well here I am obeying your rules". It is more "I'd like to pray" and "there are things I'd like to get off my chest" and things that I'd like to thank God for and things I need more help with. And that is just prayer.' Sheila (30) also goes to Mass, but 'when I want to go. I won't go just for the sake of it. . . . I'll go when I want to go myself. I'll go to pray for somebody or light a candle.' Emer finds Catholicism somewhat unforgiving. She sees her religion as 'very private, something spiritual. It's something between me and God and it's how I lead my life. That is what religion is to me. Now I go to Mass. I like going to Mass, I like being there.'

Brian is a practising Catholic who attends Mass and the sacraments regularly but, 'that doesn't mean keeping all the rules, because nobody does that. Otherwise you'd be perfect. . . . But I agree with a lot of things the Catholic Church says.' He, like most intermediate Catholics, has problems with Catholic teaching on contraception and sex before marriage and is currently in a relationship. He sometimes feels guilty about calling himself a Catholic. There are times

> when I don't agree with the Catholic Church. I know people who want the Catholic Church to change so that it fits in with what they agree with but I don't think that. . . . I think the Catholic Church has its rules. I don't

expect them to change to suit my life. They have their rules and this is what they believe in, you know. I don't expect them to change to become popular, you know.

This slight sense of guilt and a continuing awareness of the rejected rules also bothers Sinéad a little. She admits, 'I'll go to Mass. I'll say my prayers. I won't go up to receive Communion, (a) because I don't go to Confession and (b) I sleep with my boyfriend. I can't have it all my own way.'

Dónal, Sinéad, Orla, Sheila and Emer see themselves as critical or 'thinking' Catholics, as Catholics who live by their conscience, informed by Catholic teaching but not bound rigidly by it. By contrast Ruth, James, Patrick and Cathy give matters much less thought; indeed they might be termed ritualists. All four attend Mass more or less regularly as an obligation, though they do not feel guilty if they miss out the odd Sunday. Patrick is perhaps typical: 'I probably just go to Mass for the sake of it, but . . . I still believe that I have to have some kind of belief.'

Many dream away the time at Mass and think of other more interesting things. Some receive Communion each week but equally they may restrict themselves to the once a year obligation. Few pray apart from this. They all accept Catholicism as something that is part of them but they give it little thought. Along with many other intermediate Catholics they seem to appreciate the social function of religion but show little awareness of transcendence or religious values.

Garrett, Cian, Claire Helen, Martha and Emma retain a Catholic identity although they are relatively indifferent to religion. These are the least active intermediate Catholics. Most lost interest in religion at a relatively young age. They became bored with repetitive and meaningless rituals and today most are alienated from an institution that they see as far removed from their lives and needs. While both men are well educated and from middle-class homes, all the 'indifferent' women are drawn from the most deprived sectors of Irish society. Few ever attend organised religious services apart from weddings, baptisms and funerals, but most claim they pray from time to time. Many like Cian (21) 'wouldn't pray for exams or anything like that, but if something – say someone died or someone was very sick I'd just pray for them. I wouldn't say it was regular, more a reaction.'

Intermediate Catholics generally reject church teaching on sexual morality. Most believe that sex was a normal part of an established relationship but few condone promiscuity. None of these men and women accepts church teaching on contraception. Indeed, many argue that sexually active adults have a responsibility to control their fertility and protect their health by taking appropriate precautions. There is less consensus on abortion. Some condemn it out of hand; but most defend the woman's right to choose and even those who would not choose abortion themselves would not condemn anyone who did. This attitude of 'live and let live' is very common among intermediate and former Catholics and is also reflected in their views of homosexuality. Although some find the practice disgusting or unnatural, individual rights prevail. Generally euthanasia gains acceptance on similar grounds although some fear human rights abuse were it generally permitted. Few approve of capital punishment.

Intermediate Catholics tend to judge moral issues on grounds of human and individual rights. There is no absolute code of behaviour that is right for everyone. Morality is a matter of making choices in a given set of circumstances. The only limiting condition is that decisions should not harm others or violate their rights.

Intermediate Catholics are more critical of the Church than are the more committed core. Many refer to the recent scandals and recount stories of clerical hypocrisy. Some are saddened by these events but the tone tends to be more condemnatory than sorrowful. But most try to be fair and rarely are all priests condemned for the sins of the few. But trust has been breached and it will take time to rebuild confidence in the priestly role. Some convent-educated women remember the nuns who taught them as old fashioned and out of touch with the real world. Their view of the world holds little meaning for young people at the end of the twentieth century. In Orla's view, 'the religious stuff was so dated, it was old fashioned. It was holding us back.' Few would seek advice from a priest or religious for 'they are not streetwise' and their lives are removed from the real world, particularly the world of the poor and the deprived. None of the most deprived of our respondents knows any priests, though community nuns are seen by several poor women as real friends, 'just like ourselves, not like nuns at all'.

Former and Distant Catholics

Of the 15 people in this category only two, Yvonne and Jack, describe themselves as atheist. Yvonne distanced herself from Catholicism at an early age partly, she thinks, because of the anger and confusion she felt at the death of her father when she was ten.

> When my father died the local priest spoke to me and I remember thinking there was no sense in what he was saying. My father's doctor also spoke to me and he made more sense. He tried to address the issue of death from the perspective of a child rather than this grand big scheme that we all had to understand. . . . I remember being angry at the ceremonies and the superficiality of the whole ritual. I remember being angry at the priest the way he treated my mother.

She continued to practise intermittently into her teens but remembers, 'as I got older being angry, angry with authority as vested in the priest, angry with political statements, awful priests from the pulpit. . . . I remember having the sense that really the promises entailed within religion were nonsense.' Today she has broken totally from the Church and is raising her two children without a religion. This is not an easy path in Ireland and she baptised her first child in deference to her parents-in-law.

Jack is a mature student. His atheism dates from about age 16 when he left school and went to work. Living away from home he did not bother to go to Mass and, as he thought about religion:

> it seemed that this is not true, its not grounded in fact, it is superstition, hocus-pocus, and there is no way I can support these theories. . . . Then after a while I began to think about it and I began to see atheism as a religion in itself and as time went on I honed it down more and more, particularly since I came to College and had access to other views. Now I'd be a complete atheist.

Kevin, Seán, Elaine, Ellen and Máire all define themselves as agnostic. Kevin comes from a very devout and traditional family as does Elaine. Like Jack, Kevin could not accept what he describes as

> mumbo jumbo aspects of faith like immaculate conceptions and virgin births and transubstantiation. That last is a big problem. That was earlier. So I dismantled these kind of magical mythical elements and I was left with a kind of Life of Christ thing, as a kind of a humanist thing. And now I've dismantled that as well and I have – no, I'm still left with that to a degree. But if I have religion or a faith in anything it would be in a man called Christ who did or maybe didn't exist, it's actually irrelevant I think, and his code would be OK by me.

Elaine too found belief difficult and religious ritual boring and meaningless. She emigrated at 18 and ceased all religious practice. But her little girl was born in Ireland and she was baptised. She will make her Communion and Confirmation at school like everyone else. Elaine is doing this for the sake of her very devout parents, even though she believes none of it and many of the ceremonies disturb her.

Geraldine, Siofra, Emer, Sarah, Victor, Conor and Richard all say they are non-practising or lapsed Catholics but they are indifferent to religion and have little interest in the Church. Although a theist, Alan claims he cannot call himself a Catholic because

> I disagree with a lot of what the Church teaches. I do believe that if you are to call yourself a Catholic you must do so. While the Church is unwilling to change, we have to change and that means that we have to leave the Church. We can't expect to live our lives by a set of values that are against what the Church preaches and still expect to be called part of the Church.

Yet Alan and his non-Catholic wife have agreed that, should they have children and remain in Ireland, these children will be brought up as Catholics by Alan. This kind of decision is one that many distant Catholics will probably make. Most claim they will marry in church, baptise their children and send them to Catholic schools. In this way they will fit into Irish society easily. Several respondents claim this is what their non-believing siblings are now doing with their children. One core Catholic describes this practice, which he believes is widespread, as 'making children official'.

It is perhaps not surprising that it was among ex-Catholics that we found the greatest criticism of the Church. There was criticism of its power in key areas of Irish life and of its capacity to prevent change. Church control over Irish women and their sexuality was an issue for several women. Although some of the socially concerned recognised that nuns and priests make important contributions to social justice issues, their motivation was questioned. All ex-Catholics welcomed the apparent decline of the Church in Ireland.

VALUES, HOPES AND ASPIRATIONS

While respondents differ from each other in their levels of religious commitment and on many issues of sexual morality, they display considerably more uniformity in their hopes and aspirations and in what they value in their lives. Family and friends are extremely important and a major source of happiness. Where men and women have established their own families they take precedence and children are their main concern. In most cases young adults retain close ties with parents about whom many worry as they get older. Regular contact with siblings is also common, and they all believe that family members will assist each other in times of need. Although many of these young people acknowledge they hold different religious and other views to their parents, they none the less believe that parents and family are the most important formative influences in their lives.

Most of these young people wish to love and be loved, to find someone with whom they can share their lives but, except for core Catholics, this does not necessarily involve marriage. Of course there are many that wish to marry, but some would say not now and some could not yet afford it. A small number of women oppose marriage as an institution of little benefit to women and there are respondents in established relationships that see no need for marriage to confirm the bond.

Few of these young adults are particularly materialistic. Most want a secure future, to own a house 'to give the children a chance'. But material possessions are low on the order of priority for all but a few and only one woman from a particularly deprived background identifies money and possessions as very important in her life. Most just want to be happy and happiness is linked to people and, for some, to enjoyable and fulfilling work. But they are young and aware that life is for living, for having fun and they want this too. As Ellen remarks 'life is before death'.

Looking at Irish society in general there is concern that happiness eludes many people in our society – the poor, the homeless, the marginalised – and there is an awareness of deep divisions and persistent inequalities in a society that is rapidly becoming affluent. A number of respondents, particularly those with strong humanistic values, believe that the more fortunate have a duty to pay back in some way. Some have engaged in voluntary work at home and abroad, but at time of interview only three respondents were actively engaged with justice issues, with Amnesty International and with literacy groups. Environmental issues are a worry to a small number of respondents but their involvement does not go beyond recycling a small amount of household waste. A few women are vegetarians but as a matter of personal preference rather than any strong ideological views on ecology or animal rights.

Our study of young Irish Catholics shows patterns of both continuity and change. Being Catholic remains part of Irish identity, an identity that is constructed and confirmed in family and/or school and in many areas of Irish life. It is an identity retained in varying degrees by most of those whose life histories we collected. This said, there is little evidence of 'the simple faith', the unquestioning acceptance of Catholic teaching as imparted by authoritative figures. Some core Catholics apart, young Irish Catholics seem unwilling to accept that there is but one way to live one's life. Yet there is little evidence to suggest they have abandoned shared values or that life is a kind of do-your-own-thing free for all. The evidence from the interviews suggests young Irish people have many beliefs and values in common. Chief among these is a commitment to human and individual rights, whether expressed in traditional Catholic or in humanistic terms. There is evidence of a growing tolerance associated with this commitment: the right to be different, the right to choose, the right to be yourself and act in according with your own conscience. And there is evidence of social concern for injustices in Irish and other societies. In addition, there is a reaching out to the other in the expressions of caring for family and friends. There is a selflessness in the orientation to children and parents – a recognition, even among those who describe themselves as individualists, that a meaningful life is shared with others.

Although many young Irish people no longer accept church teaching on sexuality, there is little evidence of widespread promiscuity or approval of it. Most young people seek stable relationships bound by love and loyalty, if not marriage. There is a strong sense of commitment and responsibility to children and to ageing parents. There is great loyalty to family and friends without whom many would feel bereft and among whom mutual help is the norm.

Young Irish people may be different from their parents in many ways. They grew up in a different world and face different challenges. Their lives are more complex. They face a whole range of choices every day. But they do not lack commitment. They do not lack beliefs and values. Rather, faced with an uncertain and ever changing world not easily handled with recipe knowledge, they have to make choices from a range of alternatives unknown to earlier generations. It could be argued that they are truly moral.

4

YOUNG ADULT CATHOLICS IN CONTEMPORARY POLAND

Irena Borowik

RELIGION IN POST-WAR POLAND: FROM CONFRONTATION TO PLURALISM?

Poland is almost monolithic in religious terms. Ninety-five per cent of its 38 million population consider themselves Roman Catholic, three per cent belong to religious minorities with the Orthodox Church being the largest (500,000 members), and the remainder are mainly Evangelical and Lutheran. The most successful at recruiting new members in recent decades are Jehovah's Witnesses (currently estimated at 100,000) and, in the last few years, the Pentecostal churches.

The fall of Communism radically changed the legal status of religious communities. A new law in May 1989 facilitated the official registration of religious bodies (Urban 1998). Many religious organisations registered as a result, especially as state borders were also opened up. There are now over 150 recognised churches and sects in Poland (Pasek 1998). Nevertheless the main actor on the religious scene remains the Roman Catholic Church.

The role Catholicism plays in Poland is influenced by two important factors. The historic link between religious and national identity is one. The other is the Church's role in preserving national identity during the times when Poland was partitioned and when it was under Communism. In the last few centuries when Poles did not have their own state, and in the recent past when the state was subordinated to the Soviet Empire, the Church was the only social institution preserving the language, traditions and memories of a glorious past. In effect, Catholicism united almost the whole of society despite any difference in education or social class. The history of the struggle for an independent state turned Polish Catholicism into a kind of civil religion (Morawska 1987; Borowik 1997b), where religious and patriotic symbols were inseparable as definitions of Polish identity, as the stereotype 'Catholic Poland' indicates (Nowicka 1997, Mach 1997, Szajkowski 1983).

After the Second World War, being Catholic meant being anti-Communist. The 'religious and opposition subculture' (Johnston 1992) reached its highest point with the arrival of a Polish Pope in Rome. Catholicism in Poland was dominated by its role as preserver of national identity and locus in the struggle for an independent Poland. Political and religious goals overlapped, as the social teaching of the Church on the dignity of the human person came to express the fight for human rights against Communism. Religious socialisation relied mainly on two institutions, the family and the Church, for religious instruction had been removed from the school curriculum under Stalinism. There were also no religious programmes on the radio and TV, and the Church could not defend its position in public life. Church buildings and altars became a place for anti-Communist protest and sermons became its most common weapon.

How did young people fare in this period, and how has the situation changed since 1989? Surveys on the topic have been conducted in Poland since the end of the Second World War. They show that the level of religiosity and religious practice has been high, especially in comparison to Western Europe. Poles see themselves as believers. The extent of religious belief varied in different periods of time and according to different surveys, depending on the content of the question, from nearly 70 per cent to over 90 per cent. Over 40 per cent of the adult population attended church at least once every two weeks.

Some idea of the strength of belief can be gained by looking at Table 4.1.

Table 4.1. Religious beliefs in Poland

Category: Belief:	Rural 1967 %	Urban 1969 %	Youth 1989 %	All Poles 1990 %
Holy Trinity	93	84	(in God) 71	86
Goodness of Christ	94	82	74	–
Eternal reward/punishment	87	74	68	62
Resurrection of the body	61	54	32	36
Hell exists	–	–	51	41

Sociologists of religion explain the differences in responses in various ways: as nominal Catholics; as those who pick and choose their beliefs and values; as 'Sunday Catholics' (Piwowarski 1996); as a result of the social processes of 'individualisation and de-institutionalisation' (Mariański

1995); or as a result of the growing privatisation of religion (Borowik 1997b). Davie's famous phrase 'believing without belonging' (1994), which she applied to the UK, cannot be applied to Poland as the picture shows sometimes the opposite process, 'belonging without believing', that is going to Church without having faith in its beliefs or moral code. This typical Polish response shows how religious ritual and the church parish can express faith in the nation and its moral values.

When we turn to look at research findings on specific traditional moral values in Poland, however, we soon become aware of the growth of only partial acceptance of, and even opposition to, certain norms promoted by the Church, especially among the younger generations (Borowik 1996). There is no research strictly comparing the younger and older generation, and so there is some risk in making inferences from published research. Even so, a careful review of the literature does show up the following differences between young people and their parents' generation:

1 In general the number of young religious people declines by about 15 per cent compared with adults. More of them are agnostics and atheists, although there are generally only small numbers of atheists throughout the population (six per cent).
2 Children and youth have different religious experiences. A good illustration of this is the present state of religious instruction, which was introduced into schools in 1990. At primary level (age 7–15), over 90 per cent of children take part, while in the secondary school (age 15–19), and particularly in urban areas with over 500,000 inhabitants, the percentage declines to 49 per cent (Koseła 1995: 102).
3 The young contest the norms of Catholic morality to a higher degree than the old. For instance, only six per cent of young people disapprove of contraception compared with 17.7 per cent of adults (Borowik 1996: 93). For a sample of core Catholic youth, the figure is 37.9 per cent (Borowik 1997a: 132).
4 Young people appreciate their individuality more than their parents. They also appreciate the values linked to it, such as making their own decisions, independence, and self-fulfilment. In case of moral conflict fewer than ten per cent refer to the Church's teachings or advice (Mariański 1995: 155). In the open question asking to whom young people would look for advice, fewer than three per cent mention Pope John Paul II (147).

The changes brought about by the fall of communism have had their impact, especially in terms of people's expectations of the institutional Church. There is growing criticism of its involvement in politics, and people consider morality to be more of a private matter than a concern of the Church (Borowik 1997b: 137–45). Trends in Poland now suggest that the numbers of distant and former Catholics are growing. This is why in our research we sought out a significant number of them, to find out more in particular about the processes of disaffiliation.

SAMPLE AND FIELDWORK

The research was conducted in two stages. The first took place in 1996, in a small town south of Kraków, Maków Podhalański. The town was selected for two reasons. The first one is linked to the fact that small towns and villages in Poland are the places where traditional religious belonging is strong, and where the parish has an important integrative role as well as exercising social control on young people and their attitude towards religion. It would be easier here to find if there is a generational change of religiosity, as any lack of traditional values would be more obvious than elsewhere. The answer to this question could only be an indication of change, as we did not interview the parents to see if they conformed to the traditional model. The second reason was the known political attitudes of the town's inhabitants, who proved to be the most right wing in Poland in the presidential elections of 1995. It was here that Lech Wałesa (the candidate of the right) received the highest vote in Poland. It could equally be considered as a sign of the high influence of the Church in the town, as the Roman Catholic Church openly supported Wałesa's candidacy. With the help of the students of the Institute for the Scientific Study of Religion at the Jagiellonian University (Kraków) it was possible to interview over 100 young people, including young adults.

In 1999, the second stage of the research took place in Kraków. The main focus of this stage was to balance the sample in religious terms, i.e. to find agnostics (which was impossible in Maków) and to expand the group of core Catholics, as it was too small after the first stage of research. As a result of both stages of the research, a sample of young adult life histories for those aged 18–30 was selected, and the details appear in Figure 4.2. The sample is not representative especially in relation to education, as we have an over-representation of students. The main reason for this is that distant and former Catholics can be found more readily in this group. In terms of level of education, the most varied group is the self-identified 'religious by tradition' and falls into the category of intermediate Catholics. Among them are a baker, two joiners, two teachers, a sailor, a secretary assistant, and a dressmaker. Core Catholics number among them a nurse, a gardener, a sailor, a laboratory assistant and a number of college and university students.

Figure 4.2. Young adult Polish Catholics and former Catholics

Commitment: Sex and marital status:	Core Catholics	Intermediate Catholics	Former Catholics
Single men	8	12	10
Single women	9	13	9
Partnered men/women	2/3	4/6	3/3
Total (82)	22	35	25

As far as age is concerned, respondents were spread throughout the 18–30 year range. Not surprisingly, most of the married were between 25–30 years old, though two of the married women were 22 years old. One couple lived together, 23-year-old Jan and 22-year-old Katarzyna. Some of the respondents were born in the countryside on farms. However, they now live in Kraków and go home about twice a month. Most of those interviewed in the first stage of research are still living and working in Maków Podhalański, a town of 5,000 inhabitants.

Collecting the life histories took from two to six hours, depending on how much respondents wanted to say. In the main, respondents were interested in talking about their life. Some of them were annoyed if their stories were curtailed. Others did not wish to talk about sex, arguing on grounds of intimacy and privacy. However, for some it was the preferred subject and they wished to give details. Some people described their life in a very ordered way, while others talked in unending sentences, with many repetitions and breaks. Some respondents used slang that defies translation. This is why in some quotations original terms are given in brackets.

FAMILY LIFE, SCHOOL AND FRIENDS

Family Life

Only five of the respondents grew up in single parent families with one or more brothers and sisters and, exceptionally, with grandparents. The largest family had nine members – two parents and seven children – but that was an exception. The emotional way in which respondents described their first memories and time before school suggest that it was a very important time for them and their future life. At this stage the group could be divided into two: the majority who described their early childhood as a very happy and joyful time, and having a strong feeling that their parents cared for them and were interested in their problems, and the minority who did not. The first group felt they had stability, certainty and a very close relationship, both with the closer and broader family and good relations also with neighbours. Exceptionally some experienced traumatic events: one person the death of the father, three of grandparents, and one girl the suicide of her aunt, a fact that traumatised her family. These mainly positive evaluations are not contingent on material status: some families were very well off, having their own house and small business, and some were rather poor. Only in one case, that of Mariola, a single parent and an alcoholic, do present traumas appear linked to past ones of constant lack of money: 'a few days after I get my money, I spend it on wine and vodka. When I have none left, my mother brings me food and cigarettes.' The happy childhood of many is linked to the fact that they were born and grew up during the 'Gierek years' of prosperity. At that time, most Polish children did not lack the necessities of life: though what counted as 'needs' for children were generally limited by a restricted market of goods. As one life history records, 'money was no problem for children, as their parents never gave them any'.

A minority of respondents linked their unhappy childhood to inter-parent problems, arguments being the most frequently cited and alcoholism the least. Another problem here could be the permanent lack of time parents had for their children, perhaps because of the long working hours. The death of a mother was definitely the worst experience for one respondent. He declined to talk about it but repeatedly interjected 'if my mother had not died my life would have been different'. Aged 23, he had been thrown out of university, had no place to stay and spent his life working out 'how to get hold of a bottle of vodka'. We may assume that his mother's death, coupled with his father's lack of physical presence – a long-distance train guard – lay at the core of his predicament.

Nevertheless, the majority of life histories showed a very positive childhood experience. Some of the reasons given for it by respondents were: few responsibilities, fun with friends, few problems, feeling safe and plenty of free time. The success of their childhood was confirmed by the fact that those respondents who loved children already had children, or were thinking of having them; all said they would bring up their children the same way as their parents. The values they most frequently desired in children were honesty and obedience: 'my parents were religious, and my brothers and sisters were good. Mum and Dad expected me to go to church, to be obedient, get good results in school, and look up to my elders.'

Going through the life histories, the impression of the very different roles mothers and fathers had in the lives of respondents is striking. Frequently fathers were described as cold, distant, absent, busy, hard working, quiet, dominant and authoritarian. Mothers, however, were warm, tender, caring, friendly and helpful. Some respondents commented, 'Mum has got used to it'. It appears that parental roles in Poland still divide along traditional lines, with the husband as head of the family and breadwinner and the wife as housekeeper and child-carer. Only occasionally are fathers described as active in bringing up children. Grzegorz sees his father as 'an exceptional, wonderful man', a good example to follow, who 'teaches me how to live' and engages in conversation on 'all the important problems of my life. When I was small we used to go for a walk almost everyday. Now we go for a glass of beer. I know my grandfather did the same.'

Almost all parents paid a lot of attention to the education and achievements of our respondents at schools. In 'unhappy' families, authoritarian fathers punished some of our interviewees for getting poor marks: 'every fail (*pała*) meant a spanking' (Paweł); and Monika:

> Whenever [Mum] went to parents' evening at school, I was frightened. I used to keep quiet about the really bad fails (*dwóje*). When she came back home, I always knew when she was angry and was going to beat me. Though sometimes she didn't . . . she sometimes told me off for three hours. . . . Her telling-off was so painful that a beating would have been preferable. But no, she had to go on repeating the same thing over and over again: 'You should learn, it's the most important thing. Why don't you learn . . . why don't you ask. You have a sister, she will help you, we will help you.

Relations with parents seem to become more complicated with time, especially as the crucial period of adolescence arrives. Our respondents here split into two. One in four did not experience trouble with parents. An examination of the life histories showed them as adolescents not forcing their own point of view and following the rules laid down by their parents. Other life histories describe all sorts of problems at home: the unexpected births of brothers and sisters in three cases, parents controlling every move, and being kept in the house. They describe parental shifts in attitude towards them, especially by fathers, which resulted in parents losing confidence in them and becoming less open with them, with the consequence that parents tried to dominate them and paid more attention to neighbours' opinions than to their children's. The worst experiences here were those of the girls, perhaps confirming the different standards Polish society demands from young men and women.

Friends

As the children grew up, the more important their friends became. They already had, of course, friends and playmates in the playground in early childhood and at primary school. Respondents referred to one or two friends of the same sex spending time with them after lessons. But after moving on from primary school at the age of 15, friends became the most important group in their lives. They compared themselves with them, valued their esteem and shared values and experiences. In the secondary school our sample initiated meaningful relationships with one or two people and stayed in touch with them even when they travelled far from home or experienced changes in their life course, such as marriage, a changing lifestyle and children. The importance of these relationships can be compared with sexual love, although best friend status appeared the more stable.

Those in our sample who were continuing their education in secondary school, college and university talked frequently about freedom, friendship, love, community, tolerance, independence, and self-realisation. They also talked about graduation and having a happy family life, being independent financially and having their own flat – or house, in the case of the older interviewees. Given present financial difficulties in Poland, having one's own flat seemed to be one of the most important practical dreams of young adults. The majority of respondents in education at present live either with parents or in student hostels.

In terms of leisure time, the main feature of almost all of the life stories was that, almost without exception, it was time spent in drinking, and going to discos and parties. A few mentioned using soft drugs – in one case hard drugs, with forcible medical treatment organised by parents. Often being with friends happened only at leisure time; they were the only friendship events for those young men who had entered the labour market or were unemployed. Typical phrases in the life histories here were 'my life turns around drink and parties' and 'my life is dominated by drink'. For students there were additional activities. They talked about trips to the mountains, the cinema and music concerts, reading good books, and chatting. Those who had girl or boyfriends spent time with them. Core Catholics devoted a lot of leisure time to religion and religious activities. We will deal with these later on.

While the emphasis of interests is different according to whether one is a student or is in the labour market, a common attitude is a lack of interest in politics. The majority participated in the last presidential elections, by voting for one of the two candidates, Kwaśniewski and Wałesa. Respondents saw it as their obligation to know about and vote for the candidates. But otherwise, most life histories displayed an open lack of interest or disillusionment with politics: 'politics is immoral'; 'it's very boring, nobody is interested in it'. Marta's opinion is quite typical:

> There is so much rudeness in it and accusing each other, and that's perhaps why I do not like politics . . . everything they do they do only for them-selves. . . . Every one of them is looking only for his own interest . . . looking for back-handers and returning them.

Most of the young adults did not even have a genuine political preference. Only one described himself as conservative and another as an anarchist, and nobody in the sample belonged to any political organisation or group.

Education and Work

There is a significant difference between young Polish adults' attitudes to primary and secondary education. Most saw primary schools (age six to 14), as places they did not like. Teachers were authoritarian and punitive and appeared to hate the job. They 'did it only for the money'. Only a minority found teachers who were likeable and had an impact on their adult life. Interestingly, the negative view did not seem to depend on student achievements, as this same attitude was present equally among those who had difficulty in primary school and those who did not. For our sample, primary schools consisted mainly of marks and tests. Some respondents stressed their experience of school as a place of unequal treatment: how teachers preferred the privileged, richer, and better dressed to the poorer and less well dressed pupils, who were often ignored or criticised by the teachers themselves. Relationships with teachers were described as authoritarian, with children totally dependent and subordinate.

Respondents saw high school (age 15 to 20), in a completely different light. It is a place where friendship appeared as the most important single element, while education, results and teachers come second. It does not mean that second-level education is not important for them. Most saw it as a happy or successful period in their lives, although some saw it as a difficult period, and, exceptionally, a very hard time. High school students have to be almost gifted intellectually to get a university place. In part because of this, some of the respondents, and some of their parents, were not interested in pursuing a high school education. They focused on having a job and money as soon as possible. Some of them had already graduated at age 18 from their three-year course in technical school. Another group, having finished primary school, effectively went into the job market, but often ended up unemployed. For these, 'learning was never easy'. Only in one case did a young man regret not continuing his education. It is worth noticing that those who stopped their education at primary level or after vocational school came in all cases from parents with a similar educational profile, whereas the majority of students at secondary school or university had parents who had been to high school. This is in line with Polish statistics which show that, since 1989 and the collapse of communism, only three per cent of university students have come from the lower social classes.

Both those who left and those who stayed on at school stressed the low importance of religious instruction in school and how small an impact it had on their lives, even though almost all of them attended the classes. Our older respondents still remembered catechism in the churches (religious instruction was introduced into the curriculum as an option in 1990, which that group never had). In their opinion it was much more interesting and inspiring than school lessons where, 'it became as any other lesson but without being as important as maths or Polish'. One respondent remembered the intolerance of one teacher towards those not attending classes in religion. Another strongly criticised the priest who took the class. Respondents referred to attending religious instruction as an obligation and not as a choice. Others provided a motive for their attendance, saying, 'I was going there because everyone did' or 'it was taken for granted', or 'I wanted to have a certificate'. Some respondents stressed that if they did not go they would not know what to do with the time, because religious instruction took place in the middle of the timetable. Another simply saw it as convenient to have it at school rather than church. Three people pointed out that in their school religion was strongly promoted by teachers. In one case it was possible to get a question on the Ten Commandments in the maths class. But in another school, the head teacher had a wholly negative attitude towards religion.

After religion in the family and going to church, religious instruction in schools seems to be the next factor socialising young people into religion. But only four respondents judged religious instruction as having deeply influenced their life, leading in their case to membership of the religious organisation 'Oasis'. The priests who taught them made a profound impression on them. But in the case of other respondents, priests were a big disappointment. For instance, finding out that a priest who taught them had fathered two children alienated two respondents from the Church.

The Effects of Marriage

For our married respondents, values and lifestyle changed significantly with having a family. Most leisure time was spent at home with the children and it was normal entertainment to meet friends in a similar position. However, lack of time and money had become a major problem:

> Normally if you work hard and honestly you should be able to buy things within a certain period of time. . . . Here a worker cannot live on an average wage, not to mention buying a car or a flat. . . . We live with my in-laws and it is not easy. We can't afford to buy or rent a flat (Alina).

Perhaps people with their own families are more able to make comparisons with their past childhood and adolescence than single respondents.

The young married couples thought that the situation in the past was much easier for young adults than today: 'I see that life was easier in the past. My mother says the same. People were less compliant. We had a car and sometimes we even went abroad on holidays. Later on we still had the same car, but there was no money to buy petrol.'

RELIGION AND THE LIFE HISTORIES

Core Catholics: Religion as Personal Experience – 'God moved my heart'

Those significantly committed to their religion came from varying social backgrounds. However, there were some common elements at family level. They more frequently described both parents as very involved in religion compared with other respondents. In one family, there was a nun. In another, the mother was an organist's daughter. Core Catholics had more brothers and sisters than average – as many as six brothers and sisters, with only one having a single sibling. Their situation was well expressed by one of the respondents, who had had catechism classes at church from the age of four and could describe his home as 'dominated by spiritual values; we frequently attended church and mother read the Bible at home. My father used to say that everything we have is a gift of God and we should respect it.' Also family evening prayer seemed to be typical in this group. In addition to regular church attendance, the families of core Catholics brought them into closer contact with priests and parish churches than in the case of the intermediate and former groups. For instance, their mothers used to bring flowers to church to decorate it and also helped with church cleaning.

For some core Catholics, church worship provokes great emotion: 'in a crowded church, when an organist is playing music loudly and all the people are singing, I feel really moved. I feel the presence of God' (Mateusz). Religion and a personal relationship to God seem to be the most important factors shaping their lives. Personal religious experience in particular is a striking element:

> I believe [God] always helps me. I pray frequently and also in difficult moments of my life: exams, taking decisions, going on a long trip. . . . I believe he is listening to me and protects me from evil. If I have done something good I know that God is pleased with me and I feel good.

God serves as a personal model for life. Bartłomiej, 23, expresses it as both his wish and challenge: 'I would like to be at least half as good as God'. Faith serves as a sort of sense, provides energy to live happily and helps in difficult moments. It forms among this group of core Catholics points of ultimate reference not only for life but also for death. Anna, 22 and an unemployed laboratory assistant, says: 'when I was a child, death was one of my fears. Now I know that after death I will be with Christ.' Religious beliefs appear to form frameworks for interpreting reality in all sorts of different areas: family life, friendships, one's own inner life and external political change. One of the respondents sees the new government led by first premier Buzek as formed under the influence of God. These respondents feel strongly that God gives direction and sense, supports their attempt to be better, and helps them not to be afraid of death, because 'after death we will meet Him'. They talk about a deep personal contact with God that would be described as mystical experience in the relevant literature: 'once while praying in chapel a miracle happened . . . my prayer became so free that words flowed from my mouth. . . . I wanted to become a good priest but I understood that it was not my destiny, that it was not God's will' (Piotr).

Mateusz, 18, reports that he feels God's presence sometimes in church, or looking at the miracles of nature, such as landscapes. Beata, 22, reads the Bible every day of her life, 'because God is the biggest thing in my life'. Another respondent compares praying with breathing, and 'if you do not breathe, you know, you simply die'. Mariusz and Marta describe their different religious experiences more extensively. Mariusz's vision took place while praying in the church at night:

> About midnight something really strange happened . . . it was also seen by three or four other people. We all somehow looked up while we were invoking the Holy Spirit. Suddenly I looked and simply saw a bird. I saw a bird that was flying, from one side to another and then higher. And honestly I thought at first it was a trick, and that somebody had set free a canary and that was it. But then I thought straightaway that this explanation was unrealistic, a bird flying at that time of night.

Later on other members of his sodality told Mariusz that such things happen in times of intensive prayer and he started to interpret it as a distinctive experience, important for him as a personal encounter with God. Marta is not attached to any religious movement, and she has a strong individual type of religiosity:

> A good few years ago, I felt I saw God. One day I was cycling. I saw such a beautiful sky. . . . There was a cloud from which rays of sun beamed out. I was seeing something like – you just see God. Because God can be seen through nature, through what he created . . . he can talk to people in this way. That is what it was like for me, I don't know, like a smile of God. . . . And I felt so good at that moment and I remember it just as strongly today.

Personal religious feeling among core Catholics in Poland is also strongly supported by belonging to religious communities and groups. In the life histories people mention their membership of Oasis, the charismatic movement, the Community of Good Friends, the Catholic Youth Society. These groups appear to play an important role in their life, organising their timetable for the week. Their friendships thus develop with members of religious sodalities, as well as building shared values such as love of God, love for others, the search for truth, appreciation of freedom, and belief in redemption. Key values are religiously founded and explained. Truth is the truth of God, freedom comes from God, and life is sensed as guided by divine destiny. The Pope is seen as the highest authority on earth.

From this perspective, the Community of Good Friends is of special interest. Young people founded it independently of Church authority and priests. One of the members of the group describes their activity:

> We spend time together on Sundays in the presbytery at Przegorzały (a district of Kraków). We speak a common language, my friends and I. It is a religious one, but there is no doubt for me that it's a good thing for young people to be able to talk about life in religious terms (Robert, 19).

> We go to visit holy places together. We don't call it a pilgrimage, we simply go there, pray and relax together and then come home. We also help the Church sometimes, as for instance with the Pope's visit, or with a meeting of young Christians (Arnold, 22, student and friend of Robert).

Religion within this group of young adults has a practical influence on their lives, as it takes up most of their leisure time. Every Sunday is devoted to it. After Mass, which they always attend, they have meetings with their religious groups and then further meetings later for animators of Oasis and members of the charismatic movement.

Some core Catholics feel that the 'others' in school are different from themselves. A vocational school student explains:

> They talk about money to buy hi-fi, a trip abroad . . . Their only knowledge of the supernatural is taken maybe from *The X Files* [the television series and film]. They criticise priests. I am different. I don't drink, I don't smoke, I don't use bad language.

All of them respect the moral teaching of the Church. They are against the liberalisation of the law on abortion, do not accept divorce, and are convinced that having pre-marital sex is sinful – although one young man says he is too weak to observe it and another that he knows he will break it. Others are convinced that God will help them not to break Catholic norms. For instance, Robert says: 'I resolve not to have inter-course with a woman until I am married, and I know I will stick to it.' Another core Catholic, 22-year-old Arnold, has had a regular partner for two years: 'at the start, I had a problem with the Church teaching but I don't think I have contradicted it. I think that having pre-marital sex is [usually] a sin, but as long as I make love to only one woman my conscience is pure.' Other young men do not wish to talk about it, perhaps indicating that they find it a problem.

We have said that almost all core Catholics had core Catholic parents. The only one who did not is 24 year-old Dominika, currently a student, who experienced a conversion that became the turning point of her life: 'the most important, the most crucial day in my life was 4 July 1995. My eyes were opened and I saw my life: how I lived, what I was doing, how I related to others, you know, I saw all my malice. God moved my heart. It changed everything.'

Before her conversion she ran away from home, went to France, and lived on drugs and prostitution. After her conversion she came back to her parents and continued with her education. It seems that religious experience changed not only her internal world but also the objective features of her life. Talking about it, she is deeply engaged and many times expresses her conviction that 'God holds everything in his hands'. She also has a sincere regret concerning her former friends who still live as she lived before and some of who 'maybe already buried'.

The Intermediate: 'I'm a Catholic – but let's keep it in perspective'

One of the striking differences between core and intermediate Catholics concerns the role of the church and priests in the life of both groups. In the case of the first the Church figures crucially in the organisation and disposal of their time, and with the second, considerably less so. The latter also tend to criticise the institutional church at least more openly than the former. In the life histories of the intermediate Catholics, criticism is directed at three issues. The first is the political involvement of the church. They express the opinion that the Church is 'too involved in politics', and 'should be more concerned with the morality of the people and help those who are poor'. Jan, 27 and a married man, clearly states:

> The Church should be decisively separated from politics . . . the Church and the Pope should play a significant role in forming morality, but they must not make the decisions: they must not judge the people. Decisions have to be made by people's own free will. The power to judge is God's.

The second issue upsetting our intermediate Catholics is what they see as the materialistic and financial interests of the clergy. Respondents give examples of priests who have good cars and fix high stipends for celebrating baptisms and weddings. A 22-year-old married woman, with one child and several worries about the shortage of money, complains:

> My friends have a rather high opinion of the Pope, and they love him because he is so good. But priests change their cars and complain that the faithful

do not give them enough money. The local parish priest in the village has sent both his children to university and then shouts out to his parishioners that they are sinners. But the worst thing is they meddle in politics.

This last quote brings us to the third form of criticism: the immorality of priests who talk in sermons about sexual relationships being acceptable only in marriage while they themselves do not observe celibacy. This behaviour deeply affected at least one of our respondents:

My faith folded over the priest who had two children. The priest who came to our parish later on talked openly about evils within the church itself. This [openness] broke down my unbelief. But if you come to realise that a priest has a child . . . these are things that really upset people. But I now know one thing – there is a God.

Authoritarian and narrow teaching is also a source of criticism, as one respondent observes: 'I try to live by Christian rules but the Church makes me nervous with more and more commandments'; and another:

The Roman Catholic Church in Poland has become an institution that only frightens people. The priests make me nervous. The Pope might be starting some reforms, but I do not see any changes yet. Because of this, I am like my friends – we reject the church hierarchy.

While our young intermediate Catholics criticise the Church far more than their elders, they otherwise represent the conventional attitudes towards religion of their families and community. This means they identify themselves with Catholicism in spite of their criticisms. The majority of them attend church – less regularly than core Catholics – from once a month to a few times a year. Sometimes their parents force them to go, but even so they do not abandon their links with the church. A typical expression they use is, 'I am a religious person – but without going over the top', or, in more detail, 'I am not religious . . . I don't always go to church, but go sometimes. No, I said it wrong. I am simply average.'

Being 'average' also means they will have a religious wedding in the future, have their children baptised and socialise them in the Catholic worldview. Dorota's explanation is quite typical for this group:

My family was very religious. We went to church every Sunday. My parents prayed together every morning and evening. I was brought up to respect my religion and tradition. My parents have always cajoled me into going to church. I still do now, but just to keep the peace.

If one looks in the life histories at self-descriptions of 'being religious' and 'going to church' one finds they mean the same thing in Poland. This is why some respondents stress they are Catholics and believe, but do not practise. This was the case with a 23-year-old student of German philology:

I stopped going to church more or less in the third year of high school. My parents stopped going even earlier but they always stressed we should go without them. Maybe it was just habit. Then I realised that it is hypocrisy and only for the eyes of others. But when I told my mother about my decision she was angry. I was surprised. I knew I was right this time. . . . It doesn't mean I don't believe in God. I do believe and I pray, but I just don't need a church. Religion is a very personal matter for me.

In this writer's opinion, the student's attitude will probably change as soon as he comes to have his own children. Marta in her narrative expresses both her present rejection of the church and 'coming back' to it later in life: 'Mother is angry with me sometimes . . . I have to have a reason for not going to church. She is upset with me because of my radical views, that I am not going to invite priests to my new flat at Christmas, or that I don't have to have a church wedding.' But later on, as she talks about her future family, she says:

Quite definitely I will take my children to church when they are small, so that they get used to it from the very beginning. But later on, if they don't wish to go to church, I won't force them. If they say that the priests make them nervous, I'll suggest they go to another church, maybe they will find a better one, with a wise priest who teaches them something important in life.

The transcriptions show that the lives of intermediate Catholics are dominated by secular values, even in spite of their church attendance. There is no time to think about religion, its values and preoccupations. Friends and their own key values are about 'having a good time', going to 'nice parties with nice people', and earning money especially for those who are already working or have families. The majority of them favour divorce, if and when necessary. They have more doubts on abortion. But those who hesitate do not use religious arguments like core Catholics. They do not appeal to the sanctity of life and mortal sin. Intermediate Catholics see the issue as a moral problem not linked to religion, where each individual case is solved separately by those involved directly in it. This general subordination of religion is given a life-course spin by one of our respondents:

We don't have time now to think about religion and the supernatural. As soon as we're old and drawing our pension, and our children are grown up, our life will be much quieter. Then we will sit around the table with a cup of tea and think about what is going to happen to us in next world.

Distant and Former Catholics in Poland: 'There is no absolute and objective truth'

The third category of life histories we gathered brings us to those who describe themselves in such terms as 'I am not a religious person', 'maybe I could be called an atheist', and 'I am a secular man. I do not think about religion'. The majority of them were brought up in Catholic families but only one describe his family as deeply committed. Usually their parents went seldom to church – only on the big occasions – and there was no family prayer or any other form of religious life, such as reading religious literature together or talking about religious matters. Respondents still took part in religious instruction at school, although two withdrew in high school.

They divide into two: those who express complete indifference towards religion, and those who seem to lack religious feelings but remain interested in religion, sometimes more than intermediate Catholics, by regretting in some way their loss of faith. Mariusz, 23, a student brought up in a 'very religious' family, lost his faith gradually and without any drama:

> Somehow at the end of primary school [at 15] my objections to religion began to surface. Earlier I was a deeply religious person. The problem was: what was the sense in going to church? Some of the issues seem absurd now, such as 'what if somebody bites your left cheek, do you let him bite the right one too?' . . . There were other questions also. . . . I didn't look for another faith, I tried to create my own system of values.

He does not feel any need for religion. The same occurs in the case of Ryszard, who says, 'I do not need God in my life. What matters most is the people around me and the things that happen here. It is said that God is love: people can love. It is said that God gives life: people can give life, and can take it away.'

In another case, drifting from religion was linked to a dramatic event in the family during the high school years. The respondent's aunt committed suicide: 'it was the day that shattered my views on life, everything . . . it was the day I doubted the whole of Christianity, all its rituals, all that system. . . . That was the day I left the faith, although I respect it because of my mother.'

Beata has 'never believed in God'. In another case, it was probably the distance between the respondent's world and that of her parents that started the drift. Her alcoholic father even went to church when he was drunk, remaining aggressive towards her mother and herself both before and afterwards. As she ironically interprets it, 'maybe he thought that after he prayed, the Lord God would make us forget all the pain he had inflicted on us'. Her mother, a cleaner, knew little if anything about religion: 'once I read the Bible and I told her that Jesus Christ was a Jew. She was so surprised, and she answered that Joseph and Mary were Polish names. . . . Sometimes I go to Church but I don't believe in God. It does not make any sense.'

Sometimes leaving religion behind is not linked to decisive thinking about the problem, as in the case of one respondent who was brought up by parents belonging to the elite of the ruling Communist Party, which means they also never went to church. What is of special interest is that his father tried to convince his son to go to church, despite his own allegiance. Nevertheless, 'my father always slept long on Sundays, and I wanted to do the same'.

The life histories show that our distant and former Catholics have quite varying attitudes towards the Church and its hierarchy. Some are completely indifferent to it, some describe themselves as enemies of the Church 'because it is an institution of oppression, and of intellectual and emotional violence' (Ryszard), and some end up defending the Church in discussions with intermediate Catholics. As was said before, the majority of Poles define themselves as believers. Representative samples show that fewer than 20 per cent of young Poles are unbelievers or find religion irrelevant. Perhaps the reason for the variety of views on the church among this section is revealed to some extent in the strongly indi-vidualistic character of some of these life histories. The most important value in this group is self-realisation, which they understand as finding their own way in life and realising their own potential. This value comes top in different areas of life: three students talk like this in the context of their education, future work and relationship with a present or future partner. A further two respondents, contrary to those with a positive view of life, have more of an alcoholic view. As both their life histories show, their life is poor, there are no important values or events, and the most important item on the agenda is 'sitting around the table over a bottle and talking about whatever'.

Perhaps because the majority of young people identified themselves with religion, our distant and former Catholics often found that either parents or friends and sometimes teachers tried to convince them to return to their faith. A respondent who stopped going to church had a long conversation on the subject with a teacher who tried to force her to see at least a priest-teacher and talk it over with him. The parents of some of our faithless respondents were angry after finding out about their loss of faith, and took some time to accept it. One friend tried to prove God's existence to a respondent and to convert him, but, as he said,

I showed him empirically and analytically some of the inconsistencies in the Bible. There are rules governing the world. If we call them God, then God exists. It could be said that it is a kind of equation or a set of equations, the regularity. . . . There is no absolute and objective truth. . . . I understand faith as resigning from freedom: from freedom and from responsibility.

CONCLUSIONS: RELIGION AS THE CULTURAL HERITAGE OF POLISH IDENTITY

Almost all our Polish respondents consider their present relationship to religion to be the result of both their early religious family socialisation and their own later experiences and decisions. They consider religious education in schools as having little impact. In terms of their general values, the majority, including agnostics and atheists, see their family of origin as the single most influential factor. Almost all respondents describe their families as Catholic. They refer to Sunday Mass attendance as the main indication of this. Some also speak of traditional holidays as religious events for the family, but only a small minority refer to the family practices of evening prayer and being taught prayers.

Going to church on Sundays has the character of an obligation rather than a choice. These young adults tended to find it a boring occasion when they were children and often said they were forced to go. Even where the father never went, the same pressure would be brought to bear. As one respondent says, 'Christian values were present in my home. Parents taught us these values. They made sure we went to church by asking us what the sermon was about and other questions.' For those who still live in villages and small towns, further pressure comes from neighbours. In the words of another respondent, 'people would think that I am a member of a sect if I didn't go'. Marta, born and brought up in a village and at the time a student in Kraków, criticises her village friends:

> Actually it is irritating that they deceive their parents, in the sense that they tell them they are going to church, even fool their neighbours, and when they can't be seen they go to have a beer instead. It is senseless for me. . . . If somebody is 20 years old or more and no longer has to obey parents or go to church, why do they do it? If they don't want to go, then they don't go! They should do it openly, not go somewhere behind the church with a bottle of beer in hand. I simply don't like it.

There are plenty of examples of parents maintaining high social pressure on their children in such matters. Even those who describe themselves as agnostics and atheists are pressed by their own parents and the social climate to baptise their children, teach them religion and ensure they take religious instruction. They fear they will be seen as 'different', which means being 'non-Catholic'. Religion was rarely a matter for discussion at home. There were no religious books or newspapers, and the values to which children were introduced, such as obedience, honesty, and politeness to others, were never given a religious context. As teenagers, respondents were introduced to knowledge of sex by friends, newspapers, books, and sometimes from an older sister or brother. In rare cases where parents spoke of it, it had no religious reference. The only different group here was the 'core Catholic' families.

Mariański (1995: 341) is convinced that, in the cultural and religious field, there is 'a silent revolution' going on in Poland. On the basis of research conducted in 1988 and again in 1994, he affirms the growing discrepancy between the values of the young and their parents. This gap has now reached such an extent that 'young people will no longer go back to the value system of their parents. Change is now outweighing continuity' (Mariański 1995: 341). This is certainly true for our life history sample, where the change was especially visible in the area of politics. Their parents' generation was involved in the Solidarity movement, which had ten million members in 1980, and had an underground political life fighting Communism. But our younger generation rejects any involvement in the 'dirty matters' of politics. That is a striking generational change. But talking already about a generational discrepancy in the field of religion is premature as there is little other research to support or compare with our results. Growing criticism of the church and priests among intermediate Catholics rarely meant leaving behind religion or one's Catholic identity. It is quite possible that even some of the distant and former Catholics will come back to the Church at least formally when they have their own families and children. It could be argued that at the present stage the most significant changes in Poland are not occurring on the religious 'surface', namely in declarations of Catholic identity or regular religious practice. Rather, they are taking place in the relationships between the religious institution and the people, between priests and laity, the politics of the clergy and the expectations of young Catholics. In a way, what we have reported from the life histories is the failure of the institutional church to adjust its politics to a new consciousness of the relationships between morality and religion on the one hand and politics and the state on the other. In a long-term perspective, this conflict could well have an impact on the religion of future generations. Certainly it would be quite naive to expect sudden changes in a mindset which has dominated Polish culture for some time.

5

YOUNG ADULT EXPERIENCE IN ITALY: TOWARDS A RELIGIOUS AND MORAL SUPERMARKET?

Luigi Tomasi

ITALY SINCE 1945

The lives of contemporary young people in Italy have to be seen in the light of developments in Italian society since the Second World War. The years from 1945 to the end of the 1950s were years of transition. Democracy and social difference reappeared, as new political parties and trade unions developed after years of monolithic Fascism. However, a traditionalist Catholicism permeated the culture of young people and the Catholic Church was still 'hegemonic in the lives of Italians' (Brunetta and Longo 1991). Under the all-seeing eye of the Church authorities, regular religious practice was maintained.

Matters changed in the decade that followed. They were the years of the Second Vatican Council (1962–65) and the innovative impulse it generated. But it was also the time when Italians in general began to develop their own interests and lifestyles, giving rise to great changes that have left an indelible impression on the culture of young Italians. People believed that the Council would put an end to the Tridentine style of Catholic worship and behaviour and bring about a change in the spirit and sense of religious faith and belonging. So for young people it was a time of new religious awareness and enthusiasm. But the failure of the Church to carry through the reforms envisaged in some of the inspiring documents of the Council had a negative effect on young people's expectations. As they realised that the changes were going to scratch only the surface of Italian society, they came to regard the Church no longer as 'God's people in history', but merely an institution of power. The result was an anti-establishment religious ethos that led to the explosion of protest in 1968, in which young people sought a role in the institutions that governed them (Tomasi 1981). This proposal was totally opposed to the control of young people's lives by church and school, and provided both a threat and an alternative to the system. It thus provoked a crisis in all the traditional Catholic associations and movements.

These religious developments also have to be seen against the political upheavals of the period and of the years that followed. The five years up to 1973 were ones of industrial unrest, and included the 'Hot Autumn' of 1969, the first energy crisis and a long recession, all of which heightened people's fears and anxieties. In the end, a number of political and business scandals completed the circle of disillusion and distrust, and the traditional communal ideals of the Italian way of life gave way as social and personal interests fragmented. From the 1980s onwards, growing social heterogeneity found expression in the growth of cultural pluralism throughout civil and political society. A substantial divide opened up between Italy's social institutions and its young people, who now embraced 'other' values derived from industrial society and the transformations associated with it. This is the period of various youth movements in the country with their various brands of spirituality.

In the 1990s up to today, with its culture of late modernity, young Italians appear to have accepted religious values and faith in more authentic and genuine ways, but at the cost of the Church's decline and the loss of its influence on the lives of young Italians. In other words, young people are still open to sacred values, but these are often expressed in an individualised manner. Research has shown a substantial growth in what we call a 'generic' religious attitude that does not have a specific church referent: an attitude that no longer relies on the religious institution but opens the door to an indeterminate, but perhaps no less intense, religiosity (Donati and Colozzi 1997). However, this new religiosity has tended to become self-referential: it selects from the repertoire of gestures, symbols and words proposed by the Catholic Church those which best meet the needs of the moment and are best adapted to personal, contingent circumstances.

At the end of the century, the Church's social influence on the lives of young people seems rather limited, although in general terms it still has a certain weight in determining the ethical beliefs of those closest to it. On many important issues, however, not only the more religiously incoherent and secularised young people, but also those who more closely embrace institutional religion, show marked independence of some of the Church's teaching (Cesareo et al. 1995, Garelli 1996, Tomasi 1995). These features are confirmed by the results of the research that we now present.

The fieldwork was conducted in the northern Italian province of Belluno, an area of mixed urban and rural environments. Of the 45 life histories, 25 per cent were then at university, with 15 per cent of them undergraduates and 10 per cent postgraduates. A further 25 per cent were graduates in employment, although their jobs did not match their educational qualifications. The other half of the sample were in possession of upper secondary-school leaving certificates. Of particular interest is the high level of schooling received by our young respondents' mothers. The following presentation of their religion and values concentrates on each quota in turn, providing a detailed description of their experiences through extracts from the transcripts.

FAMILY VALUES AND THE EARLY YEARS OF YOUTH

Young Catholic Adults: Single Males

The life histories show that *core* Catholic single males had excellent relationships with their parents. They were generally middle class and few of their fathers were regular churchgoers:

'My father is a believer but not a practising Catholic.'

'My mother is a believer and attends church. But my father had some bad experiences in the past and has distanced himself.'

The family played a decisive part in the formation of their life values compared with their schooling:

'School has not altered my values.'

'My values have never changed. They are those that I learnt in my family.'

'During my time at school I never experienced religious crises because my faith has always remained intact.'

These interviewees had mixed experience of early schooling, some noticing bias among the nuns that taught them:

'My experience of elementary school was wonderful.'

'The school certainly imparts important values and very often, as in my case, they were close to those I learnt at home.'

'The great defect was that the nuns always favoured some groups over others.'

'My values have not been changed by school. The change came when father died.'

'My experience at school did not alter my values. Indeed, it reinforced them because it confronted me with different and worse realities.'

Antonio's reply is of special significance. An only child who lives in the country, he praises the example of his parents, 'who not only professed the faith but lived it'. He gives a positive description of his childhood: 'I must say that I had a good childhood, I was very happy. I grew up with the right values, warmth and affection. I don't think I could have had anything better.'

With the *intermediate*, or less committed single males, one finds that:

'The values at home were always family and honest work. To these my mother added religion.'

'My relationship with my parents has always been good, though when I was little I was more attached to my mother because Father worked abroad for a while.'

'My parents are believers but they only go to Mass on certain occasions.'

The responses of this intermediate group on early schooling are similar to those of the core male group, yet they emphasise the near total lack of religious education. These young men belong to the medium-to-low social classes and they regard money as important. They do consider themselves Catholic, but think that merely paying lip service to church precepts counts for little. Alberto, who has a flexible relationship with both Church and religion, explained: 'In certain respects I find the Church too restrictive. I don't think my life will be affected whether or not I go to Mass.'

The families of the *former* Catholic single males mainly belong to the middle class. In general, these young men emphasise the religious marginality of their parents: 'my parents believe, but they only go to church on special occasions'. Some of them stressed the permissiveness but also the purpose of their parents' style of family living:

'My parents made the mistake of giving me too much freedom.'

'For my parents the essential values were those of the family together with money and self-fulfilment.'

Relationships with the mother are generally good, while those with the father are more problematic, and possibly connected to the relationship between religious practice and lifestyle. Paolo declares that he went to church not out of faith, but in order to make a good impression on the others:

When I was little, my father was the first to go to Mass. He always took me with him and woe betide me if I didn't go. Outside the church he did as he damn well pleased, but we still had to go to Mass. . . . My father went to Mass, but then he behaved contrary to the church's principles: he only went to Mass to be seen.

Single Females

The *core* single females are all university students and belong to families with a medium-to-low and traditionalist lifestyle. These committed young women say that at home they were taught behaviour 'in keeping with religion' and that they have always been religious: 'when I was little I always went to Mass and to catechism, and I recited the prayers. Everything was very religious.' Great emphasis is placed on their link with their mothers:

> 'Mother educated us all according to the old rules. She has the sincere values of the poor.'

> 'My relationship with my mother was closer and deeper than with my father.'

Values were traditional ones:

> 'My parents' values have always been those of family, honesty, and religion.'

> 'My father was a believer but he only went to church on certain occasions.'

> 'Our values were those of the family, of honest work and of religion. My parents were and are very Catholic and they are regular churchgoers.'

Interestingly, 'at home, our use of language was always rigorously controlled'.

The majority of these women attended state secondary schools, where religion was not a problem: 'the religious aspect did not bother me because it was a normal consequence of what I had at home'. The importance of the family in religious education is strongly emphasised by Barbara:

> Not even at teacher training college was the religious side encouraged. I didn't notice this shortcoming because we followed Christian principles at home, and we lived them on an everyday basis. . . . Belief in God helps me to live better.

Good relations with clergy were typical of the group: 'my good fortune was to have a Franciscan friar as a teacher. I was very happy with him and still have exceptional memories of him.' Some respondents declare that university matured them considerably, but their values are still those they learnt at home.

As regards the *intermediate* or less committed single females, their values are again those of family and honesty. But, in terms of elementary school, they confirm the core Catholic experience of teaching nuns:

> 'Being taught by nuns was not a pleasant experience.'

> 'The nuns were strict and had favourites.'

'I believe that two years being taught by nuns in nursery school, and then five years of elementary school, again with the nuns, have conditioned my life, because it is easy to be brainwashed at that age.'

This group's lower appreciation of religion can perhaps be explained by the behaviour of both parents in each case, who tended to have only a lukewarm attachment. Silvia, Matilde and Marilena had similar experiences of parental religious practice. In Marilena's words, 'there was never any formal religion at home. . . . My parents were both believers but they only went to church on certain occasions.'

The link between past religious observance and making friends is very strong: 'as I grew up, I always went to church, because going to catechism makes you more part of the community, and going to Mass helps you make friends. Today I have distanced myself somewhat.' It may be that their lukewarm practice is also linked to antipathy towards the Church:

'I don't believe very much in the people who make up the Church.'

'You can't preach poverty and be surrounded by luxury. That's a moral contradiction. I think if I don't behave well, if I need help, I believe that God gives it without my having to comply with the Church's rules.'

Certain Masses have significance for them: 'there are Masses that I always try to go to, as on Christmas Eve, when you find an atmosphere that you don't find otherwise'.

The families of origin of our *former* Catholic single females all had two children and were middle class. Friends belonged to the same social class and the same work environment. They shared the same lifestyle and had the same idea of healthy living, 'in which you cycle or walk as much as possible, rather than use the car'.

The parents of these interviewees are not religious except in one case: 'my mother has always been very religious, a practising Catholic, and she still is.' And another: 'I don't know if my parents believe in God. I think they do, but I believe they feel their religion to be private and nothing to do with formal religion.' Carla says:

My parents call themselves atheists although I have received all the sacraments. I was keen to go to Mass, but when I got up on Sunday morning to go to church, they used to say to me, 'what do you want to go to church for? Staying in bed is better'. There was no religion at home and the only religious person was my sister, who has converted to Pentecostalism.

The majority of this former Catholic group say that when they went to Mass as children, they went with their grandmothers.

Their key values were honesty, freedom and respect for others. Some emphasised family membership, which they found extremely important:

'my family's values have always been those of belonging, personal dignity, honesty, and rigid adherence to the rules'. They were families in which money stood in high regard: 'the value which has always predominated in my family is the search for money, especially for my father, who focused the family on this.'

The majority of these interviewees had a happy childhood: 'up to ten years ago I had a good relationship with my parents. There was a lot of physical and verbal communication; mine was a golden childhood.' The relationship with the mother was generally closer: 'I had a stronger relationship with my mother because I physically spent more time with her.'

Usually, the mother was less authoritarian than the father. The group also view nun teachers positively: 'I passed my time in elementary school very well, where education was rigid, strict and oppressive, although I didn't realise it at the time'. This ethos changed over time so that 'I now give much more importance to persons than to things'.

Most of those who have been to boarding school are hostile to priests because of the psychological abuse they believe they suffered: 'I have never been able to see priests as mediators between God and me, because if you live honestly and respectfully [you are fine]. What the Church considers sinful I do not consider to be such.'

Young Couples and Individuals with Partners or Spouses

The *core* Catholic members of this quota, both men and women, come from families with four or five children and emphasise close dialogue at home. Their parents were believers and churchgoers:

> 'We always went to a Mass that didn't clash with other chores.'

> 'I was never forced to go to Mass, and that allowed me to grow up seriously religious.'

> 'My parents were authoritarian, and religion was the norm at home.'

They all stress that values were the simple ones:

> 'Our use of language was acceptable and in keeping with religion.'

> 'My parents' values were always those of family and dignity.'

> 'My parents aim was always to have harmony in the family.'

While most owe their religion to their parents, this is not the case for Emanuela:

> My parents were never authoritarian. It was grandmother who took charge at home . . . and she smothered us with Catholicism. We've always been believers and committed churchgoers. On Sunday we had to confess and go to Mass. Always.

These core Catholic young spouses are aware that education has supported their faith. But they had different experiences of nuns:

'The experience I had at school did not alter my values. Indeed, it reinforced them because it confronted me with different or worse realities.'

'The education that I received from the nuns was excellent in every respect.'

'They greatly supported religion in class, and we always said a prayer at the beginning of lessons. When I went to middle school I noticed the change.'

'The nuns were rather authoritarian, and there was always this distance between pupils. The great defect that I noticed was that they favoured some people over others. The religious side bordered on paranoia. This affected me profoundly, also because they made speeches about rebellion that you can't imagine.'

Their religious values did not change as they moved on into adulthood: 'I altered when I changed from being single to being a wife. My husband supplemented the values I had.'

The life histories of the *intermediate* or less committed Catholic couples show that they did not always get on perfectly well with their parents, although the latter have always lived according to Christian values: 'my parents are very religious and go to Mass very often'. Grandmothers figure again in a religious role: 'my support group was not my parents but my grandmother'.

This quota of intermediate Catholics belong to the cultured middle classes, and some of them attend church every Sunday. However, their parents were not authoritarian: 'my parents never imposed a particular type of behaviour on me'. But they all had slight contact with religion:

'There has never been a strong sense of religion in my family. My parents are both Catholics, but they almost never go to Church.'

'I now realise that we didn't pray and we didn't talk much about religion, but I knew my father cared about it and my mother was very devoted to the Madonna.'

'Going to Mass was a pretext to see friends, but then I began to grow closer to the Church.'

Most of these interviewees attended state primary schools, and here too religion was forcefully present:

'At elementary school I had teachers who cared greatly about prayer.'

'Sometimes there was only religious education that session, and I must say that it was rather boring.'

For Elisabetta, it was otherwise:

There was an hour of religious education at middle school and I always attended with interest. At that time I went to Mass every Sunday and I sang in the choir. In adolescence I changed my habits somewhat. I was and still am a believer but I drifted away from the Church. I never had enough time, and the Sunday commitment was the first to give way. I wasn't sorry not to go to Mass any more, also because I didn't feel distant from God. I'd only chosen a different path.

The general opinion of this group of intermediate married Catholics is that school did not alter their values but reinforced them. They display religious maturity and freedom of choice: 'I think that believing in God is very important, but it should always be a free choice'.

The accounts of *former* Catholic couples show family values still leaving their mark:

'The values that my parents gave us when we were children were those of family and serenity.'

'The values of my family have always been those of work and being a family.'

They also explain the context for this group's lack of religious practice and belief, while also emphasising underlying values: 'the values we received were Christian ones, although my father was not a churchgoer, while my mother was'. Other replies highlight the artificiality of belief:

'We had always been churchgoers, but that's because we were forced to go by my mother, not because we believed in it.'

'There was never a formal type of religion at home, the language was normal, and prayers were never said. We went to Mass because we had to, but when I stopped going nobody said anything.'

Mariafiore emphasises the influence of Church history on her:

We were always churchgoers in my family. We went to Mass on Sunday, we recited the rosary in the month of May, we sang in church. Today my twin sister and I no longer belong to the Church because, with our knowledge of history, we have discovered what the Church has done in the past, and the hypocrisy of modern priests who don't practise what they preach. We've left for these reasons as well.

The bad example set by priests emerges from other replies: 'I hate priests because they don't practise what they preach. I've seen priests doing the nastiest, ugliest, filthiest things.' Frequent reference is made in these cases to an exclusive relationship with God: 'I often and willingly talk to God. I consider Him more a friend than a person to fear.'

One life history describes a bigoted mother, but with a less narrow-minded father: 'he's always been a believer but not a churchgoer. Sometimes he goes to Mass on feast days'. Again the maternal grandmother comes in for praise: 'she was fundamental in my childhood'.

PRESENT RELIGIOUS BELIEFS AND VALUES

Single Males

Core Catholic single males connect their view of sex to religious and interpersonal commitment:

'I think of sex in religious terms.'

'It is difficult to talk about sexual abstinence before marriage, but my belief is that everything should be related to the principle that if two people really love each other deeply then the sexual relationship is the characteristic of that love.'

'I am in favour of sexual abstinence before marriage. I believe that it is the duty of a Christian to obey the rules that the Lord has given us.'

The interviews reveal a contradictory attitude between, on the one hand, a belief in the rightness of the Church's precepts and, on the other, a need to justify personal experiences and those of family members even if they conflict with religious teaching. Take, for example, this passage from Giovanni's life history:

I've never had sex, and I believe that religion has influenced my decision not to. I have never viewed sexual experience as sinful, but as a rule established by the Church for our own good . . . I believe that the divine should be part of marriage. If the Church tells me that I must wait until I'm married, then I'll wait, even though I don't know the reason why. I go to Mass every Sunday, and now even sometimes during the week. The rules of the Church are just . . . I don't condemn homosexuals. I have an uncle who's a homosexual. If a person is happy living with someone of the same sex, I don't find that a problem. . . . I have a crucifix in my room but I've got to change it. I have the impression that the old woman who lives with us has made it impure because she blasphemes while dusting.

Involvement in voluntary work is very common, and so too is attendance at the parish youth club: 'at home, the main value is being of service to others, and I do it willingly because I feel rewarded'. When asked about their friends, these core Catholic young men reply, in words similar to Pino's: 'the majority of my friends call themselves religious. However, not all of them are as observant of the Church's rules as I am.'

Our sample of core Catholic single men also want to bring up their children according to religious principles: 'when I have children, even if my partner is not a churchgoer, I shall take them to Mass and attend to their Christian upbringing until Confirmation. Then they will be old enough to decide for themselves.'

Opinions are also generally positive on Confession, Communion and Mass:

'Confession is a manifestation of one's shortcomings, a release. Mass serves to strengthen one's faith. Communion is very important, like prayer.'

'I go to Mass very willingly. It is a way of being with others and with myself.'

'Communion is important because I feel good if I take it.'

These informants do not usually talk about the Church as an institution, but their judgement is mainly favourable on those church rules others find contentious:

'I feel very deeply about abortion. If a person has been conceived, there is an obligation to give it life.'

'I am against abortion, although if I had to decide whether to keep a malformed child I would have problems, because I wouldn't know what to decide.'

'I cannot accept abortion because you have a child inside you. Although in the case of rape victims I wouldn't know what to say.'

'As regards euthanasia I don't believe that it is right because God has decided when you must die. The same applies to the death penalty.'

They are not attracted to new religious trends, although they are at times superstitious: 'I don't want to read my horoscope because I'm afraid it will condition me'. They do not believe in spiritualism and are tolerant of other religions. Their deepest values are religion – 'God is my greatest support' – self-fulfilment and the family, though civic consciousness also has a place: 'I believe in justice and I obey the civil regulations, although the politicians who represent this country are thieves'.

The *intermediate* or less committed Catholic single males sometimes consider marriage a formality. Their replies highlight considerable freedom in sexual matters:

'Religion has not influenced my sexual behaviour.'

'I'm Catholic but I believe that sex is something natural.'

'I believe that the Church is mistaken to forbid the use of contraceptives.'

'I do not believe in abstinence before marriage but I do believe in faithfulness.'

The confidants of these young people are members of their own peer group, friends who exert a sometimes very strong influence on their values. Few of their friends go to Mass, but many of them are believers: 'I think there is no desire to go to Mass but there is a great deal of respect for the Lord'. In general, these friends are markedly indifferent to the Catholic Church:

'We speak badly of the Church as an institution.'

'We occasionally talk about the Pope but never positively.'

But some in this group of intermediate Catholic men are distrustful of others: 'I don't have friends because I'm not interested in having any, given that I don't trust people'. In any case, although friends are the main confidants of these interviewees, the family is still their main source of support.

Like their female counterparts, they have different opinions on religious practices, but are generally negative on Confession. Their practice is infrequent. While they still believe in God, they are low on religious experience. However, some replies in the area are interesting: 'I've never had a real religious experience, but I have experienced some strange coincidences which made me say God exists.'

Sometimes belief in God is tied to life-experiences, and so too is unbelief. Luigi relates:

> My father went up into the mountains and he was missing for days. I prayed long and hard for him to be found alive. . . . When they told me that he was dead, I felt terrible and I lost my faith for a year or two. The parish priest told me that the Lord always listened to children. Then I added things up and told myself that I'd prayed so much but I'd been betrayed. I didn't believe again for a long time.

These young people express different opinions on the death penalty and that abortion is sometimes justified. They are against euthanasia, but with some margin of doubt: 'I don't think euthanasia is right but if I was in a terminal situation I would ask for it'. They are tolerant of other religions, but consider sects, particularly the violent ones, to be like the crusades of the past – retrograde and pointless. Some do not condone homosexuality: 'I don't like homosexuals because their behaviour is against nature'. They are against racism and express concern for the environment and oppose hunting, which is popular in Italy.

Former Catholic single males have very open attitudes on sexuality:

> 'Sexual promiscuity intrigues me.'

> 'I don't believe in sexual abstinence before marriage.'

> 'I want to point out that I'm comfortable with being homosexual. I'm convinced about it and accept my situation.'

We must remember that this group is from lower-class backgrounds. Their friends' lives 'are mainly dominated by money, although they do not earn very much and are dissatisfied with the work that they do'. What the group value most, though, was freedom. In general they find friendship important, whereas the values of their families of origin are of little significance: 'I don't believe that I have ever taken my family's values seriously'. Their lives appear to be governed more by external factors than by internal ones. As Paolo explains:

I consider myself a non-believer. I'd like to believe but I have no basis to do so. Yes, I'm rather an individualistic person. Material goods and image are essential to me. You're not judged for what you are but for what you appear to be. The first impact you make is an external one.

Prayer is only rarely of importance: 'the only thing worthwhile for me is prayer. Perhaps if I came back to God it would be the first and perhaps only thing I could do'. They are critical of religious practices:

'Mass, Communion and prayer are practices of a system that I don't agree with, and they don't mean anything to me. I hate Confession because by it religion lets you live with all sorts of wickedness.'

'Mass, Communion and Confession are useful and important for those who believe; for me at the moment they have no value.'

Voluntary work is quite common: one is section head of the local blood donors; another is a bone marrow donor. Death holds few fears for them: 'I'm not afraid of dying, but I'm afraid of being ill and suffering'. Euthanasia 'is all right by me if someone asks for it when they are still lucid and not confused'.

Abortion has greatest acceptance among this group:

'I think that abortion is a good thing.'

'I accept abortion at the beginning of pregnancy, after a certain period, no.'

'It's right that there should be abortion, it's right that you should be able to choose. I don't agree when they say that someone who has an abortion has not accepted their responsibility. According to me it's taken up more than anything else because [people] can't give a tranquil life to the newborn child.'

The majority of them oppose the death penalty:

'I'm against the death penalty. I believe that people have the fundamental right to decide on their own life.'

'I believe that life imprisonment is worse than the death penalty.'

'I'm in favour of the death penalty when someone has deliberately killed another person.'

These former Catholics believe in telepathy, but not in astrology. They stress the freedom of their lifestyle: 'until recently my life was more controlled; today I'm rediscovering the roots of my life'. They are tolerant of all religions provided they do not invade one's personal sphere and are open-minded towards sects: 'there are interesting sects but I don't agree with the satanic sects'. Homosexuality does not bother them: 'if homosexuals are happy then I don't have a problem about that'.

Single Females

The *core* single females, unlike the single males, are markedly liberal with regard to sex. Alice and Lisanna have never agreed with the Church's rule that prohibited pre-marital sex. Barbara tells her own tale:

> So that I could be with my boyfriend one summer, I told them at home that I was going to work at a summer camp. Instead I went on holiday with Carlo. When I came back from this escapade I was pregnant. At home the myth of virginity collapsed – it had always been put forward as the safeguard of personal dignity and Christian values. My parents were very disappointed in me.

Family upbringing sometimes determines sexual values: 'the fact is that my parents were committed believers, and my values were therefore clear. I knew that I would only have sex with the person that I was going to marry.'

In general the life stories of these core Catholic single women show them to have been less constrained than their male counterparts by the Church's moral and ethical precepts:

> I realise that I go against the rules of the Church in moral matters, but I must say that there are criticisms to be made of the Church. I am a believer and a churchgoer, but that doesn't mean that I'm a bigot or uncritical.

They place great importance on prayer and church practices, though not without exception:

> 'Prayer for me is the moment when I speak to God.'

> 'I go to church, and I believe that if you have faith then Mass is very important. I don't like Confession. Communion is the fulcrum of the Mass.'

> 'I believe rather less in Confession because I expiate my errors by myself.'

Nor are these women particularly interested in the membership of societies and clubs, although they show great respect for others: 'I would be content if, at the end of my days, I could say that I hadn't done too much harm to the people I'd met'. They also express some scepticism, if not hostility, to new forms of spirituality: 'I remain bound to the ideas of God that I have. The new forms of spirituality indicate a great problem for mankind today – that is, the need not to feel alone, abandoned.'

They are opposed to the death penalty: 'I am not in favour of the death penalty, firstly because it does not work as a deterrent, and secondly because I do not believe that one human being can decide on the life of another.' They are discerning in their opinions on abortion:

> 'I'm not in favour of abortion. But I am in favour of a law that gives women the right to choose.'

> 'Abortion in a certain sense reflects a personal choice, which can be made only in certain situations.'

These young core Catholic women are very tolerant towards others, and also towards other religions. They believe strongly in prayers of intercession, and are opposed to fundamentalism. Much emphasis is placed on freedom of choice, the family, and care for others: 'I believe that what matters most in life is respect for humankind, for diversity, the importance of protecting the weak and the poor, of trying to give everyone a decent standard of living.'

The *intermediate* or less committed single females express reservation rather than condemnation of sexual promiscuity:

'I think that sexual promiscuity leads to sterility in the relationship and is therefore useless.'

'People who indulge in sexual promiscuity are unfulfilled, also because you can have everything physically but little feeling.'

'I feel pity for young people who have the misfortune of being homosexual or lesbian because of the way they are seen by others.'

They also express slightly different life values from core members. While they share the values of freedom and fulfilment, the intermediate Catholic women also include money in their short list. They have believing friends who are like most of them in that 'they don't go to Church very often'.

They almost never talk about the Church, and if they do, they are critical of it, mainly as regards the ecclesiastical hierarchy and its alleged great wealth. Whilst they express little interest in voluntary work, their attitude to worship is different, and also critical:

'I believe Mass can be a moment when you communicate with him in whom you believe.'

'I believe that Mass is a very important collective occasion which keeps your faith alive.'

'Confession annoys me, I don't like it.'

'I don't like Confession at all, in that I believe that you can have a dialogue with God without a go-between.'

Their comments on Communion are positive. They also value prayer: 'prayer is a way to directly communicate my state of mind, a need that I have, a thanksgiving'.

Some in the group are irked by the fact they find themselves fully nurtured in one religion without having had the choice of an alternative. Maria clearly expresses their common desire for a quiet life: 'I usually go out with a group of friends and we never talk about serious matters. It's a way of hanging out together and being relaxed.' They accept euthanasia, but take up different and more differentiated positions on abortion:

'I've always been against abortion. I don't believe that I could ever do it, but I believe that there are certain cases in which it is justified. For example rape victims, or situations in which the child cannot grow up happily, or also in violent circumstances or family conditions.'

'Abortion is all right by me in particular cases: for example, forcing a girl to have a baby against her will is bad.'

'I accept abortion when bringing the pregnancy to term would endanger the mother's health. I also accept it in cases of sexual violence.'

They believe that the death penalty is something terrible, whether the offender is guilty or not:

'Of course, there are persons who commit such atrocious things that the only punishment that they can inflict on them is the death penalty.'

'In some cases I am more in favour of torture than the death penalty.'

'I don't think that the death penalty is right, but mistakes are made in all institutions.'

They generally dislike sects because, they believe, sects deprive individuals of their freedom: 'I don't like fundamentalists and sects, but I don't include them in the same category as the other religions. They are extremes of faith which bring nothing good.'

The *former* Catholic single females accept premarital relations: 'I think that everyone is free to do what they want while respecting the freedom of others'. They acknowledge that the meaning of their religious practices have not changed since their school years, but their participation has mostly ceased. They have given up worship, even at Christmas and Easter. They are highly critical of religious practices: 'I regard Mass, Communion, Confession and prayer as social conventions. I have my son take Communion and go to Confession for social reasons, so that he won't be marginalised.'

These former Catholics have conflicting opinions on astrology and spiritualism. They do not keep icons or religious memorabilia and they are not attracted by new tendencies like pagan revival. Marilisa declares: 'I'm not an atheist but I follow certain principles. I can certainly call myself an ex-Catholic. The best description of me is a pleasure seeker.' the rest clearly value thrift: 'I save quite a lot, but more than anything else I don't waste things'.

These single women tend to have a mixed bag of friends. Some have friends who 'are dominated by love and selfishness'. Others have friends who 'don't consider themselves to be religious, and they don't go to Mass'. Others have friends who 'value money and savings'. No one is interested in voluntary work. Like their male counterparts, they are negative about politics: 'I am increasingly disillusioned with politics. Italy is a country of cheats where merit is not rewarded.'

The majority of them are opposed to abortion:

> 'One of my convictions is that abortion is murder, whether it is performed on the day of conception or three months later.'

> 'I'm against abortion; I think it's something to be left to the consciousness of the individual person.'

Judgements on homosexuality were positive: 'I think that people who come to terms with their homosexuality or lesbianism are to be admired.'

Partners or Spouses

The *core* or committed couples are strongly anchored to their religion and have a close interest in others: 'although I've had moments of difficulty I have never lost my faith.' And again: 'when I finished my studies, I devoted my time to voluntary work'. The values in which their friends believe reflect strong religious conviction and strong family ties. They value prayer highly, while acknowledging their own shortcomings:

> 'Prayer is fundamental for me, both private prayer and prayer in its community and church form.'

> 'I don't think I'm very good at praying because when I finish, I realise that I've only asked for things.'

They also express positive attitudes towards Communion whilst having misgivings about Confession:

> 'I'm rediscovering Communion now.'

> 'Communion is the climax of the Mass, and they are both practices of great importance for a believer.'

> 'Confession is important because it lets me enjoy the highest moment of the Mass which is Communion.'

> 'I don't often go to confess, but when I do I feel really liberated. It's like going to the doctor who cures you.'

These core Catholics also make criticisms, albeit veiled ones, of the clergy: 'I believe that the priests are a bit too powerful and are too attached to money. I prefer the friars, who take the vow of poverty; luxury is not a characteristic of God.' Nonetheless they are greatly appreciative of Mass: 'Mass is a way to be close to God', and 'on Sundays I go to Mass with my daughter, but without being oppressive about it'.

Much criticism is made of abortion, euthanasia and the death penalty:

> 'If I had been the victim of violence and became pregnant years ago, I would have had an abortion. Today I'm not so sure.'

> 'I would never have an abortion but I think it is right for there to be the legal possibility to have one, but it shouldn't be seen as a contraceptive.'

'I don't know if I'd ask for euthanasia. If someone asked me to do it, I wouldn't have the courage but would instead ask for God to take him away as soon as possible.'

'I don't think that we can decide the lives of others. Life imprisonment would be better.'

They have a certain respect for homosexuals: 'you should show respect for them. They should be allowed to live their own lives'. In general these young people accept parity between the sexes but not equality: 'everyone has well defined roles and it's pointless trying to equalise them'. Some criticise esoteric practices and others accept them:

'I don't believe in astrology or in telepathy, or in spiritualism. I strongly believe in prayers of intercession.'

'The most critical phase of my life has led me to believe in, that it is better to seek astral or telepathic powers to give me a sign.'

'Wanting these practices is a form of weakness.'

Instead they express aversion to sects and fundamentalism, because 'they are exaggerations and distortions of faith'. Although they accept other religions, they invariably reject the Jehovah's Witnesses: 'It annoys me when the Jehovah's Witnesses ring at the door to say the same old things and disturb good people.'

In general these core Catholics do not belong to environmental associations, nor are they interested in animal rights, but they do recycle. They have been brought up to believe in justice and honesty, and they have crucifixes at home. Their values remain those of the family of origin:

'The values that my parents gave me are the same as those that I have today, but I have made them my own.'

'I don't believe that I've changed much since I was at school. My values are those that my parents gave me, and I try to pass them on to my children.'

Finally, these married respondents care more about others and are more sociable. They also show greater interest in politics, as evidenced by Maria:

I don't have strong political ideas, but when they held the local elections in my village, I attended the rallies in order to decide who to vote for. Perhaps I'm a bit lazy, but I think that politics should be seen as something distant and inevitable. However, criticising is very easy, but you must have alternative proposals.

For *intermediate* couples the most important values are family, work and friendship. Work is closely connected with the value of thrift, which characterises all the intermediate Catholic couples. Deborah explains this position as a natural consequence of her education:

> My parents brought me up to be thrifty, so that before I buy anything I think about it very carefully. I'm always afraid that hard times will come and that it's better to save. I realise that this is our typical mentality, which has advantages and disadvantages.

Considerable emphasis is placed on values like personal fulfilment, the community, and religion: 'my friends don't go to Mass but they consider themselves believers'. And, 'I don't go to Mass on Sundays. I only go on important occasions.' They also stress, sometimes forcefully, the way their religion has changed with marriage: 'my religion didn't change until I got married. While I was living with my parents I did what they told me.' They have a varying understanding of Mass, Communion and Confession:

> 'Mass is important for me because it is the moment when you're closest to God.'

> 'I don't agree with Confession.'

> 'The priest is a go-between and I prefer to speak for myself.'

> 'I'm against Confession. It's years since I last confessed, and consequently it's years since I last took Communion.'

> 'I confess directly to God without the mediation of the priest, whom I don't trust.'

These interviewees give great importance to health, but they are not interested in the environment. They are opposed to sexual promiscuity, but also to abstinence before marriage. They are sometimes involved in social activities: 'I'm doing a course so that I can help others'. They are mixed in their views of the Church:

> 'I cannot speak badly of the Church as an institution because I've always met good people.'

> 'I cannot forgive the way the Church wastes money.'

> 'The clergy is useful but I don't agree with this greed for money.'

They are partly critical of the death penalty and feel strongly on abortion rights:

> 'I'm not entirely against the death penalty. Given that there are people who have killed, why shouldn't we do the same to them?'

> 'I've never thought deeply about the death penalty. I don't think it is right. Violence cannot be solved by further violence.'

> 'I've always argued that the right to have an abortion should exist.'

> 'I find it difficult to accept abortion but there are situations in which it is necessary.'

These young people have similar attitudes towards euthanasia: 'I respect the right of others to choose as regards both abortion and euthanasia. I'd never want euthanasia for myself, but I respect those who want to relieve their suffering.' The same approach is also evident in opinions on homosexuality: 'I don't understand how you can be homosexual but I respect their decisions'.

There is little belief in astrology. They also consider themselves non-racist and in favour of equality between the sexes with some specifications: 'I believe in the equality of the sexes, but there are things that women should do and others that men should do.' Overall, these young people are self-aware and judge reality with their eyes open.

The *former* Catholic couples are open-minded on sexual matters: 'I don't believe in abstinence before marriage, I find it absurd'. They are not opposed to sexual promiscuity provided that both sides agree.

They are critical of the Church: 'faith can never be called into question, but the rules imposed by the Catholic Church can be'. At times they are highly critical of the clergy: 'I must say that the priest of my village is a very ignorant person'. On other occasions, as in the case of Mariafiore, the clergy are criticised for exploitation: 'people's ignorance has enabled the Church to gain what it has and to control people's minds. If the parish priest said that something had to be done, it was done, and that was it'. They accept Mass but criticise Confession, because 'the Church must keep up with the times'. They are uninterested in voluntary work and Catholic associations. They strongly oppose the death penalty, but have different opinions on euthanasia:

'The death penalty is a difficult issue. It is not up to us to decide whether or not to take a person's life.'

'I'm against the death penalty because no one has the right to take away a life.'

'However much a person was in pain, I wouldn't be able to put an end to his suffering.'

'I believe that if a person asks to die he should be allowed to go peacefully.'

Telepathy again is preferred to astrology and spiritualism: 'I don't believe in astrology although I've had my tarot cards read. I believe in telepathy and I would like to be telepathic or sensitive. But I don't believe in spiritualism although it's a topic that fascinates me.'

These interviewees are very concerned about health. They are against fanaticism and the new sects and cults that have appeared in Italy in recent years.

CONCLUSION

Two contrasting trends emerge from the analysis. On the one hand, there is increasing secularisation to the point of apathy and indifference to God. On the other, there is continued recognition of the presence of God as a point of reference around which to reconstruct personal identity – that identity which some theorists hold is now disintegrating in the ideological void created by modernity.

In Italy today, young adults generally accept religious values, in particular as expressed by the Catholic religion. But then, unlike in the Northern European countries, world religions and denominations other than Catholicism are only residually present in Italy. Despite secularisation, religion still plays a part in the formation of youth identity. This is not to imply that all young adult people embrace it; rather, that for those who choose religion, it becomes a central pivot for the other human aspects of life in the construction of personality.

Two features emerge in particular. First, much more than in the past, religion has become a matter of deliberate personal choice. Second, faith and religion have become functional to personal growth, an important piece in the mosaic of personal life and self-fulfilment.

The religiosity evident in the life histories of our young interviewees is strongly influenced by the cultural climate of egocentrism, narcissism and radical individualism so distinctive of popular youth today. An important dimension is the perception of sin, given its crucial relation with God. Today in Italy, in fact, it would be wrong to say that the sense of sin as guilt has been superseded. It has not disappeared. However, the guilt felt at sexual expression is fading, whatever the context considered, because there is a declining perception that anything sexual is a matter that concerns God. This, therefore, is one of the areas of human behaviour that has become secularised. In fact, 80 per cent of the interviewees declared that religion did not figure in decisions on pre-marital sex, a further sign of shrinkage in the area of religious experience. Greater tolerance was shown towards this issue compared with homosexuality, for example.

As regards the Church, young adult Italians admire it more for its humanitarian work than for its role in the formation of consciousness. Jealous of their freedom to make personal choices, they find it difficult to accept any external pressures of an ethical type. This confirms the existence of that moral subjectivism which, although an expression of the right to take one's own decisions, also signals rejection of objective moral norms imposed from outside.

The critical attitude of young Italians towards the Church does not necessarily express an underlying hostility. Instead, it is often prompted by the desire and hope for improvement. A significant minority of these young people has a positive relationship with the Catholic Church even though they are to some extent critical of it. One notes that churchgoers are increasingly critical of the Church as an institution. This is by now a general trend. The most significant aspect of this criticism concerns Confession, which is rejected by the overwhelming majority of the interviewees. Added to this is the disagreement over sexual and family morality, which is widening the rift between the Church and young people.

It is also worthy of note that when the family of origin is strongly Catholic, then so too is the son or daughter. In any event, half of the interviewees considered that the values given to them by their families of origin were valid and to be preserved. Finally, almost all of them expressed tolerance for marginal beliefs and behaviour.

One may therefore conclude that – although faith was still a factor in the interviewees' production of individual and collective identity – the spirit of modern times has eroded the observance of religious principles, justifying total or partial selection among them. Are we moving towards the age of the religious supermarket where one chooses what one wants from the religious goods on offer?

6

YOUNG CATHOLICS AND CONTEMPORARY AMERICAN SOCIETY

Penny Long Marler

THE MAKING OF A YOUNG AMERICAN CATHOLIC

The story of young American Catholics in contemporary society is a story of three generations: the grandparents, pre-Vatican II Catholics; the parents, Vatican II Catholics; and their children, 'generation X', post-Vatican II Catholics. It is a story of movement from a largely immigrant, urban and working-class Catholic 'ghetto' to the suburban, middle-class American mainstream, of movement from the anti-Catholic platforms of the 'Know-Nothing' party and the Ku Klux Klan to the 1960 presidential inauguration of the wealthy Catholic John F. Kennedy. Finally, it is a story of movement from nineteenth-century piety, prayer books, and parishes that provided an institutional anchor for Catholic laity 'cradle to grave', to late twentieth-century Catholicism: one of peace and justice movements, parish councils and priest shortages (Dolan 1985, Castelli and Gremillion 1987, McNamara 1992, Davidson et al. 1997).

The grandparents of the current young adult cohort witnessed both the peak and zenith of the Catholic ghetto. They still reflect the distinctive, lingering nineteenth-century ethos of devotional Catholicism. Until at least the mid-twentieth century, the Catholic mini-state defined the thought and actions of its inhabitants. Roman Catholicism's actual identity as a subculture insulated it from the internal divisions that characterised American Protestantism. What also worked to preserve it was the fact that most Catholics lived in ethnic, working-class enclaves in urban areas. They had neither the financial nor social resources to take an active part in middle-class America.

After the Second World War, a number of events conspired to push Catholics out of the subculture. The 'G.I. Bill' allowed war veterans to attend Catholic and secular colleges, and upwardly mobile Catholics began to move from city to suburbia. Two prominent Catholics led the 1950s anti-Communist crusade, and in 1960 the first Roman Catholic president was elected on the strictest church-state separation platform to date. Over the two decades following the war, Roman Catholics became an active part of the American mainstream and perhaps better Americans than their Protestant neighbours (Herberg 1960, Greeley 1977, Gallup and Castelli 1987, D'Antonio et al. 1995).

Then everything fell apart. In November 1963, John F. Kennedy was assassinated. America entered the 'conflict' in Vietnam, thousands of young Americans were killed, and a massive peace movement rallied support *against* the war. Social justice movements erupted across the country promoting equal rights for minorities. A youth inspired revolution of 'sex, drugs and rock and roll' initiated unprecedented moral experimentation (Kennedy 1990). 'Question authority' was the watchword of the era that witnessed Watergate and Nixon's attempted cover-up. Concurrent changes in the Church promoted by Vatican Council II reforms did little to discourage such trends, as we have seen in earlier chapters.

The style of Catholicism of the Vatican II generation continued to reflect loyalty to a Catholic heritage. However, a new centre of Roman Catholic identity developed, as the Catholic school replaced the immigrant Catholic neighbourhood. Also, the majority of Catholics now supported birth control, and many American clergy 'soft-pedalled' the contrary papal teaching. The divorce rate among Catholics climbed and official marriage annulments increased from 700 in 1967 to a startling 25,000 in 1978. Between 1968 and 1978 nearly 5,000 priests resigned. The Vatican II generation began to follow the culture and their consciences more than the Church, and these attitudes and actions still persist among them (Greeley 1977 and 1990, Dolan 1985, Schoenherr and Young 1990).

They also persist among their children, the members of today's young adult generation. The dominant theme of the 1980s and 1990s for young Catholic adults has been absence, particularly from church. With increasing levels of divorce, and hyperinflation in the late seventies and early eighties, more women entered the workforce. Children were shuffled from parent to parent and more spent time alone after school, feeding off popular culture in heavy doses via television, the video, music and fashion trends (US Bureau of the Census 1996). Their expenditure was supported by summer jobs, part-time work and the generosity of 'guilty' parents. The idealism of the sixties gave way to the cynicism of the eighties and nineties.

Today, Catholics look more like Protestants in social terms. Increasing numbers are moving to the sprawling suburbs of metropolitan areas, and the number of Catholic schools is declining. As a result, the majority of Roman Catholics are now educated in public schools and universities. More are marrying outside the faith, further straining the transmission of Catholic beliefs and practices. In the absence of the insular Catholic ghetto, the conflicts between liberals and conservatives that plague Protestants now beset Catholics. Tensions exist over the form and scope of lay leadership, women's roles, and other church teachings (Castelli and Gremillion 1987, D'Antonio et al. 1989 and 1995, McNamara 1992).

Also, Post-Vatican II children are also absent from church. They place a higher priority on being Christian than being Catholic. Denominational identity has become a personal choice and faith a matter between 'me and God'. They question church teachings on papal infallibility, abortion and birth control. They are uninformed about Church practice and teaching, lack a vocabulary to interpret their Catholic experiences and believe that whether something is right or wrong depends upon the situation. It is no surprise, then, that recent research reveals a linear decline from the oldest to the youngest cohorts on key indices of Catholic belief and practice: they are less orthodox, want greater democracy in the Church, and attend church less than their parents or grandparents. Two thirds of them are Americans first, and Catholics second (Davis and Smith 1996, Davidson et al. 1997, D'Antonio et al. 1995, Hoge 1981, McNamara 1992).

The Sample

The 45 young American Catholics whose life histories have been documented were all 18 to 30 years of age. Their accounts are consistent with recent research on the post-Vatican II cohort, but are novel in bringing two sets of previous findings together. Davidson et al. (1997) examine 'Catholics without parishes' by cohort through interviews and a national sample survey, and McNamara (1992) examines the attitudes and opinions of seniors at a large, suburban Catholic high school with some attention to the disaffected. The findings of both studies are consistent with our own for the core or 'super core' and 'distant' young Catholics ('distant' is a sub-division of 'former' Catholics, as will be seen below). But a middle or intermediate position is less documented, and that gap is addressed in this chapter, alongside findings for the other groups.

In their national survey, D'Antonio et al. (1995) do not examine results by age cohort, nor employ qualitative methods for interpreting commitment. However, they operationalise three categories of commitment among Catholics, and confirm that moderate and low commitment

Catholics tend to be younger, and the high commitment group older. Our research builds on the D'Antonio findings in three ways: it employs similar criteria for defining commitment, focuses on the post-Vatican II cohort, and is based on the qualitative method of life-history analysis.

Life histories were collected in late 1997 and early 1998 by upper-level undergraduate students in the social sciences and religion at Samford University in Birmingham, Alabama. The sample was selected according to gender, marital status, and commitment categories (see figure 6.1). Criteria for selecting and categorising interviewees by commitment were similar to those established by D'Antonio et al. (1995) for nuclear, modal, and dormant Catholics. 'Nuclear' Catholics said they attended Mass at least once a week, said the Church was one of the most important influences in their lives, and indicated they were unlikely to leave the Church. 'Modal' Catholics said they went to Mass at least monthly, said the Church was important to them among other groups, and were in the middle on a scale measuring the likelihood of leaving the Church.

Figure 6.1. Young Catholic life histories for the US

(Total: 45)	Core (15)	Intermediate (15)	Former (15)
Single male (13)	Matt, Joel, Jim, Ty *Super Core:* Sam	Cal, Randy, Brad, Chris	*Distant:* Mike, Nick, Doug *Dissociated:* Mar
Single female (16)	Katie, Holly, Pam, Victoria *Super Core:* Carol	Cecilia, Mary, Beth, Sherri, Joanne, Ann	*Distant:* Margaret *Dissociated:* Maria, Amy, Julie, Krystal
Couples or individuals with partners or spouses (16)	John, Jane, Nicole *Super Core:* Paul, April	Jack, Brandi, Kevin, Coleen, Gary	*Distant:* Stella, Ryan, Suzie *Dissociated:* Peter, Rebecca, Alexandra

'Dormant' Catholics gave the lowest commitment response on two of three items: Mass attendance, importance of Church, and likelihood of leaving the Church. Consequently, in 1993, 28 per cent of the national sample was classified as nuclear, 56 per cent as modal, and 21 per cent as dormant. Not surprisingly, the 55 plus age group contained the highest percentage of nuclears, and the 18–29 group the highest percentage of modals and dormants. In our sample, 'core' corresponds to nuclear, and 'intermediate' to modal. However, the 'former' category, while corresponding partly to the dormant category of D'Antonio, also includes persons who no longer consider themselves Catholic and either claim no religious affiliation now, are in transition to another religious option, or have switched to another denomination.

The sample is predominantly southern. While Roman Catholics are not historically dominant in the South, the population of Catholics is the fastest growing and the youngest (Gallup and Castelli, 1987). Most importantly, regional analysis of national opinion polls shows that Catholic respondents in the South are closer to the national average on most demographic and opinion items. Southern respondents were only slightly more likely to say they felt 'extremely close to God' than other groups, and slightly more likely to view homosexual relations as 'always wrong' (Davis and Smith 1996).

CORE CATHOLICS: FAITH THAT WORKS FOR ME

Victoria was born and raised in Gainesville, Florida. Her father was an accountant and her mother, she said, 'dropped out of college to raise me'. Her sister was eleven years younger. Her father was 'raised Methodist because it was kind of a household word. If they wanted to go to church, they would and if they didn't, they didn't have to. [When] he got to a certain age he just didn't go to church.' When her parents were first married, Victoria explains, 'my mom would go to church and he would stay at home . . . but it was when I was born: he told us the story that he held me and looked at me, and he saw Jesus. It was like, "wow", and now he's just as much of a Catholic as, you know, my mom.' Her mother's side was Catholic: 'they always went to church [but] we didn't see them on a regular basis. I always worried that my [Methodist] grandparents were going to go to hell because they didn't go to church'. She explains that the early values taught in her home were 'the good, in terms of values and morals, and the conservative – go to church, family comes first, drugs [are] bad, no premarital sex'. Religion was always

> very in-the-family. It wasn't just the Church. We brought it home. We talked about things a lot . . . we'd be sitting in the parking lot waiting for something and I would say, 'so, now, was Jesus, was he really real?' And it was, 'you learn things and as times change, we change as well'. It was a very open-minded religious type of education.

Prayers, particularly informal ones, were encouraged and considered important. First Confession and Communion took place in the second grade:

I remember the processional. I got to be first in line and I had a candle and we sang, 'Are Not Our Hearts Burning', and we walked down the aisle. I don't remember much of the Mass. I remember the fact that I got to be the first one to receive Communion. I don't actually remember receiving it, which is funny. And then I remember the breakfast afterward . . . the big party. But honestly, the memory that I had was walking in with my candle, singing. I think at the time it was a very enriching, new thing.

Victoria went to a private, Baptist pre-school and kindergarten: 'they taught Bible verses. You'd get up there and you'd recite from memory and you'd get a prize, which I totally disagree with. I think understanding them is what's important.' After that, she attended public schools. One 'special teacher' stands out: 'my fourth grade teacher was Jewish and she taught us Chanukah when Christmas time rolled around'.

Victoria's parents were very open about sexual matters, and she felt she could go to them with almost any question. Her father had been sexually active when he was young, and he discussed frankly the pressures that led to premarital sex:

My parents were very truthful in the fact that you're going to want to have it. It's something you are going to have to, you know, put that line and say you can't cross this line. . . . They, however, let me know that if I did decide not to wait they weren't going to banish me from the house and that they would still love me very much and that God wasn't going to send me to hell if that was something I decided.

Victoria drinks only in moderation and believes that sex outside marriage is a 'sin'. Still she and her Catholic friends disagree with many of the 'strong views' of the Catholic Church. She thinks its view 'is just wrong. I don't agree that contraceptives are bad . . . that abortion is bad. . . . The fact that only men can be priests is wrong.' She is concerned about the present Pope's views, but will not be put off by him. She concludes, 'we're there to help it change. You know there is a lot of good in Catholicism . . . we hope to stick with it and make it right.' Her criticisms of the Church appear closely connected to her liberal Democratic political views: 'socially, I'm very much for equality for everyone whether that be blacks, whites, females, males, homosexuals, heterosexuals. . . . I don't think anybody should be held back.'

Most of her college friends are religious, and they share her moral outlook:

All of them think that everybody should be kind to each other because everybody should be peaceful and that violence is bad. How they go about doing that is different . . . some of my friends are very morally conservative . . . others are more hippie-ish. But they all, you know, the underlying similarity is they all [believe] God is their life. And whether it is Catholicism or Methodist or Baptist or Jewish, there is a God and that without God you're not going to get the peace.

Religion is 'very important' but, 'in terms of going to Mass every Sunday, not necessarily as important. . . . Having a relationship, a personal relationship with God – knowing God as your friend, I think, is essential.' Still, Victoria attends Mass regularly, and she and her father play softball on a parish team. She recently switched from her childhood parish because there was 'some political stuff going on at the church'. The religious education directors, a husband and wife team, had developed a monthly inter-generational program called, 'May We Grow'. 'The entire family comes', Victoria says, 'for me it's a phenomenal program'. According to Victoria, the religious education position was cut from two positions to one and 'this couple has five children and they can't live on one salary . . . so they had to go somewhere else'. Because the parish has two music directors, she concludes, 'it was kind of saying what [the priest] thinks, is important. Families aren't as important.'

Victoria says, 'I think of God as being a spirit that is everywhere. . . . I don't think any one religion is better than another in that each person has to find out what is best for them individually.' That is what Victoria desires for herself: 'I want to be the best that I can be. You know, that sounds so cliché but that's my goal, to do what God wants me to do and do my best to make this world a more equal and just place to live.'

*   *   *

Victoria and six other interviewees in the core Catholic sample are from outside the state of Alabama: Victoria and Paul from Florida, and the other five from different surrounding states. The rest were reared in local metropolitan areas. Also like Victoria, the majority were reared by Catholic parents and supported by strong Catholic extended families. All but three have 'cradle' Catholic parents. Joel's father converted to Catholicism from Methodism and Katie's mother, who was a Baptist, converted when she married: 'mom . . . could never be anything but Catholic . . . it would be harder to convert from Catholicism to another religion because you would be losing a lot'. Holly, on the other hand, is a fairly recent convert to Catholicism and her parents are Baptists.

Only Paul, a married 'super core' Catholic, was raised by a single, divorced parent and about half report the presence and active involvement of grandparents. Jim is at the University of Huntsville working on his Master's. He remembers spending 'a lot of time with my mother's parents because they lived really close in town. We'd go to church with them. . . . The whole family comes to their house [even now].' Ethnicity, too, is an important part of the church and family mix for Jim, whose mother is 'Italian . . . she runs the [family] kingdom', and for Katie whose father is a 'very Irish Catholic' providing her with aunts and uncles who are nuns and priests.

Half of these young core Catholics, like Victoria, emphasise the importance of having had a 'religious atmosphere' at home. Carol and Sam, both super core Catholics born and raised locally, say their families 'talked and prayed together' and that 'going to church together was a big thing'. Sam remembers 'walking up with my parents when they went to Communion . . . folding the money to put in the collection plate was another big deal'. When Sam was in high school his father was diagnosed with cancer:

> You're like, wow, this isn't right because you don't think this is going to happen to you and all it's done is made our family a lot closer. [Dad] had only three weeks but he made a whole year. In that year we grew really close as a family, religiously. Just bonded. . . . I asked him if he was afraid and he said, 'no'. . . . He went straight to heaven, I mean, I'm almost sure he did. . . . He was a real saintly man and he was a real good dad, real good husband and real good everything and he went through a lot of pain his last year of life. And you would think one family would be torn up and distraught over all this. [Instead] it was an acceptance.

Jane and Matt explain their families 'always prayed at dinnertime and at bedtime' and had 'family prayers at Advent and Lent'. Ty remembers his family reading the Bible together and Nicole's family 'blessings at meals, and rosary three to four times a week.'

Unlike Victoria, most cores attended Catholic schools for at least some time: one third attended both Catholic elementary and high schools, one third attended Catholic elementary school only, and three attended only Catholic high school. Sam attended public schools only, although he is and was very active in his local parish, serving as an altar boy, and becoming involved in the youth group throughout high school. For those who attended Catholic school only, the experience was more formative than family. Pam, raised in Iowa, college-educated in Georgia and recently moved to Birmingham, says, 'attending a Catholic high school, going to church, praying, the outward signs that you have faith influenced me more during high school. It became important to be a visible Catholic.' John, married and an industrial engineer raised in Missouri, remembers his Catholic school education fondly and emphasises the twin importance of excellent academics and lifelong friends. Paul echoes, 'I wouldn't trade my Catholic education for anything.'

April, who is now teaching at a Catholic school, especially remembers Mass at her high school. She explains, 'we did have great school Masses . . . You did not realise that you were at school when having Mass. The bells were off. The phones were off. Everybody was at Mass.' Religion classes, April says, focused on community service rather than studying the Bible. Her friends from high school became like family.

During high school years her parents were 'separated for a short time' and high school was 'my strength'.

In a different but equally powerful way, Catholic school became important for Holly. Raised a Baptist, her exposure to Catholicism in elementary school was pivotal:

> We would have Mass every morning except for Wednesdays and then we would have religion class everyday. I loved religion class. I got the Religion Award every year. And the person who got the Religion Award was supposed to be the person who crowned Mary in the May Procession. But it had never been somebody who wasn't Catholic before and they wouldn't let me crown Mary.

Missing out on First Communion hurt a great deal: 'I cared even more than a lot of those kids did and I just couldn't partake in it because I wasn't baptised Catholic yet'. At 18, Holly's parents gave her permission to become a Catholic. She attended initiation classes and was baptised during her senior year in high school. All in all, Holly says, 'there have been very few supports for me as far as being Catholic. . . . Mass for me is very individual. Like, it's me and God . . . I don't rely on somebody [else] . . . I depend on myself to go.'

On moral and political beliefs, a marked individualism is obvious among the young adult core Catholics. While many hold clear, and somewhat conservative, stances on moral issues, few extend their personal preferences to judging others. Most do not believe that premarital sex is a good idea but 'sex happens', as Pam notes. A third of the interviewees volunteer that they do not drink. Most female cores and married male cores do not believe that abortion is morally right; most single males are less certain or say it's a 'woman's issue'. There is less unanimity (or even clarity of personal positions) on the death penalty, and even less on euthanasia or homosexuality. However, the Church's position on birth control is considered 'out of date'.

Like Victoria, a third of the core Catholics describe themselves as somewhat 'democratic', 'more liberal than conservative' or 'liberal Republican'. Most, however, are ambivalent or cynical: as Sam says, 'I'm republican but it doesn't matter anyway'. Over two thirds are tolerant of other religions. A few attribute this to the fact that Catholicism is not a majority faith in the United States and particularly in the South. Most have close friends who are not Catholic. The majority of married interviewees' spouses have converted to Catholicism from some other Protestant faith; many young cores express appreciation for the fact that their Catholic schools were racially and economically diverse:

> I like to consider myself as very open-minded. My best friend was Hindi and I've been open-minded enough to go to a Baptist University. I think

more than anything by being friends with people of different religions, it enhances your own religion (Katie).

My Catholic friends see Catholicism as the best religion in the world: not being the 'right' religion but the one that is right for them. It may have some outdated principles but they still find that religion very applicable to their lives and can deal with the things that don't fit (Pam).

Like Victoria, most young married cores appreciate the Vatican II reforms. While very active in their local parishes and comfortable with their Catholic identities, they still are interested in change and in a more liberal direction for the Church. They explicitly wish the 'Catholic Church had more going on' (Jane, Paul and April) or were 'more like Protestant churches' in terms of educational programming, mission action and evangelism. Interest in the hierarchy and the sacraments – particularly Confession – is quite low compared to enthusiasm for retreats, a meaningful Mass, engaging homilies, and approachable parish priests.

Three life histories provide especially interesting contrasts on the Church among young adult core Catholics. Paul has always been active in the Church; his single mother 'dragged [him] to *Cursillo*' (a Catholic commitment and community-style programme) when he was young. A series of compassionate priests have been 'like fathers' to him. At the University of Alabama he was very involved in the campus Catholic centre. He even considered the priesthood for a couple of years. Now both he and his wife lead youth ministry programs in separate parishes. Paul says:

I think we're dying for priests because they can't get married – and if priests could be married, yours truly here would be signing up to wear a collar: I mean, that's all there would be to it. Our views on women need to change. . . . They need to become more active and the Church needs to give them more power. A lot of our Catholic churches, especially in the South, are led by nuns – led by women, which shows that they are just as capable, if not more capable of running churches.

Carol represents a more conservative perspective. It is also a decidedly minority one among our interviewees. Single and a senior at a large, prestigious Catholic high school, she describes her home environment as 'protective, loving and sheltered'. She has been educated exclusively in Catholic schools, and is planning to attend a small Catholic college in Ohio. All her friends are Roman Catholic with 'good morals' and 'approve of things that come from the Roman Catholic Church.' Carol went to Denver to 'sing for the Pope' and says she 'got chills from the experience; there were so many Catholics'. She is concerned that her Catholic high school is too liberal. Teachers should 'teach the whole truth about the Catholic faith not just certain parts, even if they disagree'. Carol is proud that she has been on 'Mother Angelica's television show'. She and a close friend recently attended a retreat in Rhode Island for girls 'discovering a vocation'. But Carol remains undecided.

Joel, a 22-year-old college student attending a state university sees himself as neither 'conservative' nor 'liberal' but somewhere in 'the grey area'. He attended a public high school and became involved in a parish youth group: 'I started going and fell in love with it and that's really when I developed an understanding of Catholicism and really developed feelings about it'. He says, 'Vatican II . . . was the best thing that the Church has seen. . . . My biggest fear now is that a lot of people are going back to pre-Vatican II days.' He concludes that it is hard to know what a Catholic is because 'there's so many different Catholics out there'.

When asked about their life goals, young adult core Catholics talk about the importance of family, being a 'morally good' person and/or being what 'God wants me to be', and about specific values like 'honesty', a strong 'work ethic', and 'respect for others'. Jane says, 'I don't think you have to be in any particular religion to be close to God but I think I have to be a Catholic to be close to God because I grew up that way.' For John, 'being Catholic means being part of the church that God set up to achieve the ultimate goal'. For Holly, 'it's very individual . . . I think it's the Mass, the Eucharist'. Paul agrees: 'to be able to go to Mass and to love God and to have a relationship with God, but then to actually physically have him as being part of you, to me that's what it means being Catholic.'

INTERMEDIATE CATHOLICS: FAITH
YOU CAN ALWAYS GO BACK TO

Cecilia grew up in 'a nice little Italian family' in Cleveland, Ohio. She explains her family was 'working-class Italian combined with middle-class suburban. I had a good solid start in life. A lot of people have this cultural vacuum. My grandmother was half Italian and half Polish and she decreed Italian-ness on [us].' Her father is an accountant and her mother a housewife. The neighbourhood she grew up in was 'multi-racial', and her neighbours and closest friends were Korean. Her family went to 'church every Sunday and every day of Holy Obligation'. Cecilia's earliest religious memory was Christmas: 'Dad hid Jesus at Christmas because you couldn't put Jesus in the nativity until Christmas Day. So the big challenge every Christmas was "Find Jesus"'. But, she concludes, religion 'didn't make much of an impression until you got older'. For example, before Church 'you take classes and practise with Ritz crackers. So it's Jesus, yeah [*sarcastically*]. And you get up there in your white dress. Now, it's like a miracle. It was bread; now it's the body of Christ. I was as deeply spiritual as a six year old can get.'

Cecilia's parents stressed respect for the Church but, above all, respect for intelligence and education. Cecilia attended public school through the third grade. During her elementary school years, the family moved to Birmingham, Alabama and she enrolled in a Catholic school in a 'gifted program'. Cecilia remembers the school as 'too easy' and the people as 'snotty'. She adds, 'there are very few people from the time that I still talk to'. The religious aspects of the school, however, were 'a very good thing'. Students went to 'Mass every Wednesday, choir practice and did the Stations of the Cross on Friday during Lent'. Most importantly, Cecilia recalls, 'they would teach about other religions'.

Cecilia had a chance to test her knowledge and interest in other religions when she attended a public high school for gifted students. The student body included 'Sikhs, Hindus, Muslims, Jews and even pagans and no one attacked you. It was like, "we believe this, what do you believe?"' Cecilia says the school environment promoted the development of your 'own moral and philosophical themes. . . . Three of my friends were bisexual and lesbian. [There were] lots of people with different sexual ideas than mine.' Though, she adds, it 'didn't change my perspectives' many of which were 'the cultural values that were passed down to me'. For example, 'Sex was not seen as sinful. It was explained [by my mother] as a natural thing – a wonderful gift'. Her school was academically rigorous. It was 'an ego-driven high school. There was competition but it was not vicious'. History, biology and German were her favourites. Cecilia was also heavily involved in extra-curricular activities.

College has changed little of Cecilia's intellectual drive and direction. She attends a small private university and is a double major in History and German. She tutors in German, proof-reads and edits texts for teaching German and Arabic, works with Amnesty International, and is active on the campus in 'Women's Forum' as well as the German Club. She wants to start 'a young Democrats society because the campus is solidly Republican – it needs another voice'. She also maintains a variety of friends, with three girlfriends who are particularly close. One is longstanding friend from high school: 'she's my bitch partner on e-mail'. Another, she met in karate class. Her closest friend 'is frighteningly compatible'. With two of them in college and the third in graduate school, they all work at least part-time. Their lifestyle is basically 'caffeine-driven: work, do this paper, study for this test'. At weekends they sleep, date sometimes, watch football, go to clubs. On Sunday 'some go to church and some don't'. What dominates their life? Cecilia explains: 'feminism, graduation, personal goals and dedication'.

Cecilia and her closest friend are avowed socialists. Her circle of friends also includes 'democrats, traditional and liberal Catholics and some [others] with strong religious views'. What all her friends share, however, is 'tolerance, a dedication to causes, having a focus to your life and respecting human rights'. She strongly believes in the 'right to religious self-determination'. With most of her friends disagreeing with the Church's stance on issues such as abortion, Cecilia remains adamant on 'sanctity of life' issues, although not on religious grounds. On abortion, 'you should take responsibility for your actions; if you made a decision to have sex, you should accept the consequences'. On euthanasia, 'somebody else generally decides for you; it's kind of Hitlerian'. On the death penalty she struggles and decides it is 'consistent to reject it'.

On homosexuality, not surprisingly, she is equally clear: 'I have lots of friends who are homosexual. The actions themselves are none of my business. The Church stands against them, but I am not going to judge. They are human beings, to treat like anybody else.' On faiths she answers: 'other religions are fine. People are people. There are good people in other religions.' She is less tolerant in her views of more fundamentalist groups. On the Church as an institution, she explains, 'the Church takes a very hard line and they have to. You can't be flexible at the lower levels if it's not clear and strict.' What does she think of the Pope? 'The Pope rocks', Cecilia replies playfully. She usually goes to church on Sunday but does not really have much time for it.

*   *   *

Like Cecilia, a third of the intermediate Catholic sample is from outside the South. Also like Cecilia, most were raised in middle-class, suburban and intact Catholic families. A few interviewees like Gary, married and a salesman, grew up in working-class families. Unlike other intermediates, Gary's parents are divorced. Four interviewees have Catholic mothers and Protestant fathers: Joanne, a college student majoring in religion and working as a classroom aide; Cal, a medical school student; Beth, an office administrator and currently engaged; and Sherri, a full-time student from Michigan. Kevin, a pharmacist, was brought up by Baptist parents, attended a Catholic middle school and converted when he married. 'I'm a Batholic', he says.

Like Cecilia, about half of these intermediates went to church regularly during childhood but, unlike Cecilia, the majority talk about their early church experience as 'boring' and something they were 'forced to do'. Jack, married and a computer technician, spent a lot of time moving around as a child: 'as a kid I hated [church], really. It was just something you were forced to do every Sunday – like it or not – go to church and [doctrine] classes and whatnot, and First Communion and all that stuff. . . . I didn't really care much for it until probably in high school.' Coleen, a housewife who is pregnant with her first child, expresses herself with similar words. But Brad, a native New Yorker and college student, and Anne, a third-year college student, both explain that their parents never forced Catholicism on them.

Intermediates raised by parents of different religious backgrounds tend to emphasise strictness and fear as part of their early experience. Sherri says her relationship with her parents was 'poor' growing up; children were expected 'to be submissive and controlled'. Beth remembers her parents 'would scare us and, I don't know if we were loud or said something bad, then [they] would say that we were punished. Like, if you say something and then trip over something, [they] were like "God just punished you".' In addition, most say they did not attend church regularly as children. Early exposure to religion was largely limited to Mass attendance for intermediates. In addition to Cecilia, only Chris, an attorney in his father's firm in Birmingham, and Randy, a third-year university student and track athlete, talk with some warmth about Confirmation, prayers and other religious observances at home.

Nearly half of intermediate Catholics went to public schools only. Some note that Catholic schools were 'too expensive'. However, Jack says, 'my mother, she went to Catholic school all her life and swore she'd never make her kids do that'. Chris attended private, non-parochial schools exclusively. Like Cecilia, Randy, Kevin, and Brad attended both Catholic and public schools. For Kevin, a Catholic middle-school education was pivotal. He became disillusioned with his Baptist church as a teenager: 'it got too cliquish. It was what you wore, how well you looked and who you knew. It had nothing to do with God.' In seventh grade Kevin 'started going to midnight Mass in a Catholic church. My friends would invite me. Pretty much every year they made it a point to invite me to midnight Mass, and I haven't missed one since then.'

Three interviewees attended only Catholic schools. Coleen's schools 'were trying to teach the children to be Christian but the education was important, also'. She recalls, 'we had Mass once a week; we'd say prayers everyday; say the pledge of allegiance every day'. Her early teachers were 'pre-Vatican II nuns' so 'you knew what you were supposed to do'. She accepted everything until seventh grade but, 'then I began to challenge. . . . By the tenth or eleventh grade, it seemed like religion was being pushed on me at school.' Beth's experience was similar: 'in grade school, I believed everything they told me. Church was such a routine; it was a chore. . . . In high school we had religion class every day . . . lots of stuff the Catholic Church believes in [that] I don't. Kids held up signs outside school: "Stop Abortion". They got on my nerves. They were also against homosexuality – like it's a sin and I don't believe that at all.'

Like Cecilia, other intermediate interviewees have a diversity of friends. About a third say their friends are 'religious' and another third that they are 'not religious at all'. These friends are Protestant and Catholic. They either 'don't discuss politics' together or see politics as irrelevant or 'not important'. Most interviewees spend their weekends involved in leisure pursuits: watching football or basketball, camping, hunting or 'just hanging out' as a break from work or school. Church is a part of these activities for most – but not a consistent or especially prominent part.

Intermediates hold a dizzying array of political and moral views. Their views on premarital sex, abortion, the death penalty, euthanasia, and homosexuality are divided between conservative, liberal, and ambivalent positions. On homosexuality and premarital sex, no matter their personal inclination, they are most likely to conclude, like Mary – in college with a steady boyfriend who is a 'strict' Baptist – 'who am I to judge?' This perspective is especially evident in discussions about the validity of other religions: 'everybody has their right to religion', and 'I don't judge' are typical responses. What dominates the lives of these intermediates? Most say work, school, impulse, freedom and self-reliance. A few married intermediates like Colleen and Jack talk about family, health, and happiness.

Half the intermediates go to church 'usually weekly', as Coleen says. 'I believe [religion] is important. I don't know if it is on the top of my list, though.' Coleen and Brandi, both married to non-Catholics, go to church on their own 'for myself'. Mary, engaged to a Baptist, says, 'I go to the Catholic church with my mother on Saturday nights. I go to the Baptist church with Richard's parents on Sundays.' The remainder go less often. Beth, whose fiancé claims no religious affiliation, was minimally active in the Catholic Church prior to her engagement. She mentions that she visited a Unity church and liked it: 'anybody who wanted to could come'. Lately, however, her participation in the Catholic Church has increased as a part of marriage preparation. Beth admits, 'I am very interested in finding a church of a different faith. Brian and I are really anxious to go somewhere together'. Most intermediates that attend less than weekly talk about busy schedules and lower priorities for religion. As Gary says: 'I have little time for church [but] I could make more time'.

Like Cecilia, most intermediates are vaguely positive about the Catholic Church. Kevin and Mary echo the sentiment of Joanne: 'it's a good institution. It's stuck around for 2,000 years and they must be doing something right.' Brad sees the Church as 'very political; a money-maker'. The Pope is generally considered an 'important man' and nuns and priests are 'impressive' or 'dedicated' because they 'work for nothing'. Beth admits, 'I don't really know much about the Pope', and Randy wonders, 'I don't know if it's Catholic preaching or belief still to say that the Pope is infallible but I don't agree with that . . . I don't think anybody is completely unsinful. But I think the Pope is a key figure.' When asked her opinion of the Church as an institution, Sherri says, 'I think each person sees it differently. I see it as a place that allows me to come in contact with people of my own belief . . . and then, I guess if you have a problem with it, leave and find somewhere else.' Brad reflects a very similar stance. Being Catholic 'is a part of life. It doesn't become your life.' And if you don't agree with the Church, you can still be a Catholic or you can leave. Randy imagines what might happen if he married someone who was not Catholic:

> If my wife was not Catholic and she was really against Catholicism, I think we'd have a problem. But I wouldn't put it past myself – and I don't think it would be wrong or anything – to change my denomination. . . . I think it's all [about] being a Christian. . . . I like being a Catholic but I wouldn't say that's a major issue.

FORMER CATHOLICS: TO BE OR NOT TO BE?

The Distant

Mike and his older sister were born and raised in Mobile, Alabama. His father was in telecommunications, and his mother was a kindergarten teacher. Both parents were Catholics and graduates from Catholic high schools. Mike remembers that he was a 'handful' when he was young. 'I remember that I got caught shoplifting when I was in the second grade. I really got [in trouble] about that.' When he was eight, the family moved to Birmingham. For the first four years, he attended public schools and found it hard to make new friends. Sixth grade was particularly difficult: his grandfather died and he took it really hard. Mike then 'got caught skipping school for a total of about seven days in a month. . . . I can't really put my finger on any one thing that made me do that except for just the fun and adventure of it.'

When he was little he found church boring:

> I wanted to be somewhere else. . . . I would have to just be calmed down, and I remember having to be taken into the baby's cry room. I was one of the older ones in there at that time. For my father, when we were in church it was time to be serious, to listen, and take in. To me, it was more than I could handle to sit still for that long.

He attended a Catholic school from kindergarten through third grade and also a Catholic high school:

> I didn't really enjoy school that much until I got into the high school. I really started having a lot of fun and actually my grades were better the more fun I was having. When it seemed like I was under [somebody's]

thumb and being pushed and told 'you have to do that' I didn't enjoy it at all. Towards the end I began to appreciate it and take more pride in it.

He also had a variety of friends: 'I had friends on the football team, friends that stayed in trouble all the time, friends that were just straight "A" students. I pretty much got along with all'. Mike admits, 'I had probably quit attending Mass regularly when I was in the eleventh grade'. Adolescent rebellion was part of the reason. Another major change came with Mike's experimenting with sexuality:

> Catholics are supposed to be abstinent until marriage. . . . I don't believe in abstinence; I do believe in sex before marriage. . . . There are quite a few priests on my dad's side. . . . At one point . . . family members thought I might go into the religion. . . . I felt that maybe that would be possible, but a priest cannot be married.

Mike attended a major state university for about a year, but:

> I don't feel that I was able to accept the responsibility of everything I was given. I immediately walked into an apartment and a room-mate that wanted to party as much as I did. I came back in 1990, went to some classes [at a commuter college] off-and-on, and never really did get serious. . . . [I quit College and now] I have a business that does car sales and car repairs that I own myself . . . I enjoy myself. The business is young so I'm on a tight budget to keep up my responsibilities as far as my bills and maintaining my credit . . . I go on vacations; I still live at home. It helps me out not having to pay utilities and rent for a separate apartment.

Several of Mike's closest friends work in computers. Most of their time together is spent in leisure pursuits including watching football, going fishing, and camping. Neither Mike nor his friends are 'religious'. But he says:

> About 60 per cent of [those] I hang out with the most – they all have a spiritual side to them. They will actually recoil if anyone starts putting down their religion or God . . . I'm among them too. I have my beliefs. I'm not necessarily what you would consider a Catholic . . . I have very few friends that still practise . . . unless they do it on their own terms. Not in a group.

Mike thinks of God as 'an energy. . . . I kind of feel . . . I have my own relationship with God . . . I don't feel like I have to be at Mass to do that. I . . . go to Mass but it's usually for the big events.' On the Church he adds:

> I think it's 'old school' and has been very slow . . . on changing to modern times. . . . What used to get me the most when I was growing up, when I was first being taught about the different sins . . . they said suicide was one. . . . You would automatically go to Hell if you committed suicide. Is it not accepted in society that someone is usually unstable when they do something like this, they need counselling, they have problems? Why would someone be damned to hell for doing that?

All in all, Mike considers himself 'very tolerant. . . . If I meet someone who is Jewish, I don't want them to try to explain to me how Jesus didn't exist . . . As long as someone is not going to . . . tell me what I believe in is wrong, then I can get along.' He holds a similar view of homosexuality: 'I disagree with it. I don't really like to be around people that I know are like that. At the same time, I guess I respect whatever they want to do.' He's personally against abortion and euthanasia although he admits that in some circumstances they are necessary choices. On the death penalty, Mike reasons, 'if you're going to put yourself in that almighty, powerful position you had better be able to suffer the consequences'.

What dominates Mike's life is 'trying to succeed'. He wants to be 'happy, somewhat successful, not super-rich. . . . I like to have my cake and eat it, too'. Politics and other social or moral issues are clearly 'something personal and an individual thing'. This is true for his religion and especially Catholicism: 'it's not a subject open for question . . . [my parents] go to Mass regularly and I don't go at all. . . . It's not something I want to talk about. . . . I don't tell people how to carry on and I expect the same respect.'

*   *   *

Mike is a former or 'distant' Catholic. Though he considers himself Catholic, he rarely practises: he is 'not religious'. Half of the former Catholics we interviewed are 'distant' by this definition. They include Nick an insurance representative, Doug a production assistant, Margaret a customer service agent, Stella a dietitian, Ryan an account adviser, and Suzie, Ryan's wife, an assistant manager. Compared with other life-history groups, 'distants' are older, out of school, and working full-time.

Mike, Nick and Stella were raised in metropolitan suburbs of Alabama. Doug was born in Boston, Ryan in California. Margaret's father was an army colonel – consequently, she spent most of her childhood moving from city to city. Suzie is from a metropolitan suburb in South Florida. All the fathers of these interviewees had white-collar jobs, half of their mothers worked in lower-level administrative positions, and the rest were at home. Like Mike, Margaret, Stella and Ryan are from intact Catholic families. But only Mike's father practises. Neither of Margaret's parents is involved much with the church: 'we went on Easter and Christmas to Mass. It was not something that was happening in our daily lives.' While Nick and Suzie have Catholic parents, these are divorced; although both mothers remain active, their fathers are not: 'because both [my parents] had been married previously, their marriage wasn't recognised by the Catholic Church. . . . So they could never take Communion. . . . I guess my Father just decided if the Church doesn't want me I don't want them. So he never went' (Suzie).

Like Mike, most 'distants' were taken to church regularly as children and most found it boring. Ryan recalls, 'I never really got anything out of going to the Catholic Church. It's like clockwork. The same thing every week.' Similarly, Stella says, 'Mass is kind of the same ole, same ole, over and over'. Although Margaret's family was not active, she does remember Christmas, Confirmation classes and learning the 'Hail Mary'. But, she concludes, 'I didn't have any feelings for it'. Suzie remembers, 'I learned my prayers, probably, from doctrine classes and from my mom'. Still, religious practices and church rituals, Suzie says, 'were just something we did'.

Suzie, Ryan, Margaret and Nick attended public schools. Suzie remembers, 'the closest we got to religion [in public school] was a moment of silence when somebody passed away or something like that'. Ryan and Nick said they never enjoyed school. Ryan was more involved in sports, and Suzie remarks that she didn't work very hard but still made good grades. Many talk about being somewhat 'rebellious' as adolescents. Like Mike, Doug and Stella attended Catholic schools. Stella says she 'loved it' and felt she received a 'good education'. Doug only attended Catholic high school after moving from Chicago to Birmingham:

> We wore uniforms. We paid more money . . . there were folks that were wealthier. I didn't like that. Dad and Mom kept us with people they felt comfortable [with] but, at the same time, we were constantly taught that if a friend has more than you do or less than you do, it doesn't matter. . . . Being a Catholic school, I had to pass the theology class. I learned a lot from it but I always [begrudged] the fact that I had to pass that to pass high school. Once per month, we had to attend a Mass. This did not thrill me.

The closest friends of 'distant' interviewees are from high school or college. As with religion, some of them are 'opinionated' about politics. Margaret has friends who are Republican, and Suzie says she is 'registered Independent but leans towards the Democratic point of view'. Others, like Ryan, Stella and Nick 'just don't care' or say politics 'is a turn-off'. Doug summarises: 'most [of my friends] are opinionated but everyone has their own opinion. They are trying to live *in* society peacefully and in harmony.'

When asked about opinions on premarital sex, abortion, euthanasia, the death penalty and homosexuality, most agree with Margaret that 'everybody just chooses for themselves'. Nearly all of these interviewees had premarital sex or cohabited at some time. Ryan's attitude is common: 'we lived together before we were married so I never saw anything wrong with it'. But most find commitment, safe sex, and responsibility important.

On religion, there is unanimity about an individual's right to believe as they please. Margaret says, 'I think, yeah, that's their thing', Doug echoes, 'if you want to be religious, that's great. . . . if I don't want to be religious, that's great, too. Don't push it on me. Live and let live.' Ryan agrees, 'I really don't look at them differently. If that's their belief . . . I don't judge them at all.' Suzie reasons, 'I think if I was raised in a Muslim environment, I'd be Muslim. I think people are just what their parents are.' Still, they don't necessarily do what their parents do. Suzie admits that her parents are 'more conservative' Catholics than she is and that Ryan's relationship to the Catholic Church is 'a one hundred and eighty degree turn' from his mother's. Like Mike, these former Catholics do not attend Mass any more, and only Suzie expresses specific opinions about the Church:

> I think praying to God is having a conversation with Him, not some recited prayer . . . [and] Penance (Confession): I haven't gone much as an adult so I don't know if it differs much. But I remember as a child I'd list my sins and [the priest would] say, 'Okay, say three Hail Mary's'. And that's supposed to make it all better – saying three Hail Mary's? I just don't agree with that. . . . I think women should be priests. I think priests should be allowed to marry. I have no problem with the Pope, with the hierarchy and the whole structure. . . . I just think the Catholic Church is very ritual-oriented.

Neither Doug nor Margaret is sure what God has to do with their lives now or in the future. Ryan says, 'nothing I do is based on religion' but Suzie, his wife, argues 'everybody needs something to believe in . . . I believe in a supreme being guiding us through life . . . he lets us make our own choices. I believe that there's something after death.' Ryan is less sure about God's form or function: 'I believe that there's something out there that watches what everybody does but doesn't do anything . . . there's something after death [but] I don't know what it is.' Much like Mike's, these life histories indicate work, success, and family as the driving forces in their lives. Suzie and Ryan 'just want to have a family'. Suzie, in particular, wants 'to contribute to society in some meaningful way'. Doug says with a smile, but quite seriously, 'I want a wife, a dog, two kids, two cars, a [circular] driveway, green grass, and a white picket fence.'

The Dissociated

Julie was raised in a small town in south Alabama. Her father was a lawyer and her mother a schoolteacher. Since both parents worked, Julie was raised by an 'older black woman who would come and stay with me throughout the day'. There were not many children in the neighbourhood 'so the significant relationships in my life were with older grandmother-type figures that were neighbours'.

Julie remembers, when she was young, going to Sunday school and church every week. There was a young Sunday school teacher named Lois: 'I enjoyed being close to her. There was a warmth to her personality.' But Julie's positive memories of Church end there:

Then I got into Catechism classes with First Holy Communion, and there
was a coldness there, and I didn't like being there. . . .

The whole family was Catholic, but it's not like we had any daily
devotional times. When I would go to bed my parents would teach me how
to say prayers . . . it was always [the same] every single night. It was like it
could not change a lot. I felt like that was a very formulated way to talk to
God. I did it. I was faithful in doing it every night but it was very
formulated.

Julie's parents quit going to church when she was in middle school: 'my
dad really wanted to play golf on Sunday, and my mom just didn't have
the desire to, so she would drop us off'. Julie initiated the Confirmation
process herself but saw it as an extension of parental pressure to 'excel':
'I was excelling in academics . . . I wanted to excel in spiritual things,
too'. She attended a private elementary school and then public school.
Her parents expected good grades and good behaviour, and Julie
complied, at least through middle school. High school years, however,
were quite different. She was 'rebellious' and became 'more interested in
the partying scene and drinking'. At 15, Julie started dating 'an older guy
that I very much wanted to be accepted by. . . . I didn't actually have sex
until I was probably a junior'. However, 'I started to experiment with
drugs. . . . I lost any interest, really, in going to church'. In her senior year,
Julie's parents were divorced.

She 'ran away' to New York City and attended college there for a year.
She returned home after a year of 'partying' and started attending a Church
of Christ congregation with a friend:

> I heard messages on salvation and that's when I became a Christian. I guess
> I understood the reality of hell, and living a life devoted to Christ is more
> than going to church on Sundays. . . . [Still] there was a real struggle when
> I came back . . . I wanted to get back into my church – the Catholic
> Church. . . . So I had a really hard time letting go of the Catholic faith. . . .
> The main last straw was when I went to a Catholic priest . . . and con-
> fessed . . . I told him that I was questioning the Catholic faith and whether
> it's the right way to meet God. He said, 'That's not a sin . . . you are doing
> right in exploring that'. And so, for me to walk away from a Catholic
> priest that just affirmed my explorations . . . was kind of a sign . . . a release
> from the faith.

Soon after her conversion, Julie went back to school and completed her
undergraduate and graduate degrees. She became friendly with an older
woman through the para-church college group Intervarsity. This woman
became a spiritual mentor, and because of her, Julie has started attending
an Episcopal church. She says this is 'almost weird' because the Episcopal
Church is 'very similar to a Catholic Church'. Julie thinks she can
appreciate the Episcopal Church because she's worked through her anger

toward the Catholic Church. 'Why', she wonders, 'did you let me go through all this time and not introduce me to Jesus Christ as a person?' Her subsequent conversion and other evangelical experience are a kind of antidote: 'because of my experience in charismatic churches and interdenominational settings, there's a much greater sense of freedom in my spirituality'.

Looking back, Julie concludes, '[my parents] didn't have a real focus on the Lord, a real personal relationship'. She attributes her spirituality to the black woman who cared for her as a child:

> She was a Christian woman . . . had a very strong and personal faith . . . her prayers and her influence on me certainly created – even at such a young age – a hunger and a desire to know God. She was rocking me in this chair and she said, 'I knew that you didn't have really a Christianity around you and I just prayed that the Holy Spirit would come and take you and that you would be God's forever'. There was this pull, this desire to be close to God . . . it just felt like the hunger never got satisfied in the Catholic Church and I had to go outside.

*   *   *

Julie is a 'dissociated' former Catholic. She was raised Catholic but no longer considers herself a Catholic. Like the rest of the dissociated Catholics in our sample, she drifted away from Catholic practice in her teens and was 'saved' in a conservative Protestant context as a young adult. Some of our life histories, one intermediate and two formers, refer to siblings that were raised Catholic and are now 'atheists'. Our contacts, however, did not yield young dissociated Catholics who claim no religion. In American culture, and especially in the South, considerable social stigma is still attached to disaffiliation if not inactivity.

Like Julie, most dissociated interviewees have experienced divorce in their immediate families. Krystal, a customer service representative, was born and raised in rural Maine by a nominal Catholic father and a reluctantly converted Catholic mother, his second wife. Amy, a dorm manager and student, says her mother died when she was three, her father remarried, and later divorced. She now lives with her stepmother. Katy, also a college student, grew up in a large, blended family. Both of her parents were previously married. Only Peter, a married businessman, was raised in an intact – and Italian – Catholic family. Unlike Julie, most interviewees experienced considerable disruption during childhood. Alexandra, married and a day-care worker, was born and raised in the Dominican Republic. Her mother was divorced, remarried and spent several years as a political prisoner. Consequently, Alexandra's Catholic grandmother raised her and her sisters. Maria, a graduate student, and Rebecca, a housewife, both tell similar stories of family upset.

Most of their parents, usually the mothers, went to church early on and then stopped going altogether. Katy's parents were Catholic but they would attend for a few weeks and stop again. Going to church 'was something that . . . I was supposed to do, so I did'. Amy recalls that her family 'went to Mass every week' when she was a child: 'I always dreaded going. It was boring'. She 'never understood' Catholic rituals. Her confusion deepened during adolescence:

> In seventh grade I was completely boy crazy . . . we all knew it was forbidden to have sex and probably didn't really even know why. I mean that's a lot of the problem I had with the Catholic faith, at least for me personally. There were a lot of things that I was always taught, 'this is what you believe', and maybe I agreed with them and maybe I didn't. But I just wanted to know why that rule was there and I didn't understand it.

Amy, Maria and Katy attended public and Catholic schools. Katy's experience is typical: 'it wasn't required that nuns were our teachers but religion was openly talked about. It wasn't pushed.' Like Julie, Krystal and Rebecca attended public schools. Their parents stressed academic achievement and, Krystal recalls, 'a very strong work ethic'. Paul and Alexandra both attended Catholic schools – although neither remarks on the particularly religious aspect of their education. Paul, in fact, observes that his Catholic high school included 'a lot of non-Catholics' who experienced more freedom than he did: 'I think that's really when I started getting into some battles with my parents, because suddenly I wanted to start having more freedom.'

Amy, Katy, and Rebecca, like Julie, had stopped going to church by the time they went to college. Like Julie, their relationships with their parents were also strained. All three of these young Catholics were 'converted' by evangelical friends they met in college. Amy explains:

> I had the idea of a Christian – and my entire family still thinks this – being a Christian means you are a good person. You try to do the right things and you are accepting of other people . . . you kind of let people have their own religious beliefs. [But] my religious life has changed dramatically, and I'm so glad for that. I mean I have a daily relationship with Christ. I learn and grow every day.

Krystal and Maria hold similar views. Both have converted to Conservative Protestant denominations. However, Maria fell largely under the influence of her Baptist father, and Krystal of her evangelical brother. Alexandra and Peter, ethnic Catholics with family ties to the Church, are both active in evangelical churches. Peter admits that he was not very involved in Church after college. Even his Episcopalian wife, who converted to Catholicism at the request of his mother, was more active. Since the death of a close 'Christian' friend and co-worker, Peter has decided to 'really start putting God first'. He has joined a men's Bible study and is attending a non-denominational church. His major objections to the Catholic Church include the routine, the poor preaching, and Confession. He is appreciative of his Catholic upbringing but it is not enough.

Julie, Rebecca, Amy, Katy, Maria and Krystal are all young evangelical converts. As such, they share the political and moral views of the conservative Protestant subculture. As Amy says, 'we all stick with the biblical views of things'. They are pro-life, pro-abstinence, opposed to homosexuality, and wary of other religious views and groups outside evangelicalism. Peter and Alexandra are older and more sanguine. Like our core Catholics, they are slightly more liberal on political issues and conservative on moral issues, including abortion. What dominates their lives? Like most new converts, the exploration of a fresh religious identity and practice are a primary preoccupation.

CONCLUSION: THE DISSIPATION OF CULTURAL CATHOLICISM

Our interviews of young American Catholics are not at odds with historical or empirical research. A comparison of the life histories of core, intermediate, and former young Catholics illustrates the effects of two – sometimes complementary and sometimes contradictory – forces: the erosion of the American Catholic subculture and the explosion of secular individualism. Generationally, there is strong evidence of a linear decline of Catholic belief and practice. Whatever disrupts socialisation in the Catholic subculture appears to weaken first religious practice, and second religious identity. Increases in divorce, exogamous marriages, educational, occupational and geographic mobility and declines in parochial education all work to loosen ethnic and religious ties.

At the same time, strong individualist themes pepper the thought and action of young American Catholics, who do not leave the Church and stay in spite of the growing gulf between the Vatican, American Catholicism and, most importantly, the local parish. At the same time, and for a number of young Catholics, a growing sense of religious and spiritual autonomy also promotes, not a social drift away from the Church, but an intentional movement towards something else. Whether for practical reasons they do not need the Church or religion for personal fulfilment, or for spiritual reasons they need something more for personal meaning, an intentional decision is made to stop going to the Catholic Church or to go elsewhere.

Cultural Catholicism appears to be dissipating, eroding erratically as a response to both external *and* internal forces. In a sense, young adults are seeding the American Catholic subculture with increasingly individualist concerns. They carry a virulent individualism that is less American and more global, less conventional and traditional and more innovative and secular. Yet the effects are hardly uniform because of the variegated sub-cultures in which they are raised and the divergent political and intellectual currents to which they are exposed. And, as many of our interviews show, the content of much of their early growth appears fragile and unformed.

7

YOUNG ADULT CATHOLICS IN ENGLAND

John Fulton

THE SAMPLE AND ITS ENGLISH CONTEXT

The majority cultures of the United Kingdom of Great Britain and Northern Ireland have their own impact on the sample for England. This nation-state entity paradoxically has a multi-national content, based first on the historic development of the dominance of the English over the Celtic fringes of Ireland, Scotland and Wales. Most of Ireland left the Union in 1922, but was forced to leave two thirds of the Irish province of Ulster behind as 'Northern Ireland'. Even so, the continuing influx of the Irish into the other three countries of the Union over the whole of the nineteenth and twentieth centuries has had a major impact on British and Catholic culture. After the Second World War, their influence was also partnered by inflows first from the Caribbean, and later from South and South-East Asia. There were also transfers of smaller populations from European countries from the turn of the century, and from former white colonies since the Second World War.

Most Roman Catholics in England are descended from migrants. As noted in chapter 1, this predominantly white church retained its 'ethnic Catholicism' roughly until the coming of the Second Vatican Council. This ethnic Catholicism has all but disappeared in today's young adult English Catholic generation, though it lives on in Scotland and Ireland at varying levels of strength. There may be as many as four and a half million Catholics by name in England, but the actual number registered with parishes is nearer three, and only 1.2 million appear in church on any given Sunday (*Catholic Directory of England and Wales* 1998). As with most other countries featured in the book, young people are noticeable by their absence from church on Sundays. The increased marginalisation of the lower classes from society is one probable cause for this, and the collapse of ethnic Catholicism from the early 1960s is another. One can also mention the likely absence from church of young Catholics living with partners (Fulton 1999).

The English sample of young adults affected by Roman Catholicism consists of 52 life histories. As can be seen in figure 7.1, there are 19 core, 17 intermediate and 16 former Catholic life histories. As with the American sample, *super core* Catholics soon appeared as a category within a category, and it was decided to give them special attention. It was also obvious the 'distant' would have to be distinguished from the 'dissociated' within the 'former' group. However, the English dissociated group is very different from that of the US, as will be seen. Note that the majority of 'partnered' Catholics are female. It is also interesting that we found their partners not to be Catholic. This suggests that partnering for Catholics may be more prevalent where the other partner is of another church, faith or non-religious persuasion, easing the pressure to marry that two Catholic partners would experience.

Figure 7.1. Young Catholic life histories for England

(Total: 52)	Core (19)	Intermediate (17)	Former (16)
Single Male (16)	Alan, Eddie, Ian, Luke *super core:* Walter	Doug, Frank, Harry, Neil, Peter	*distant:* Colin, Kevin, Malcolm *dissociated:* John, George Barry (sect)
Single Female (18)	Crystal, Debra, Gill *super core:* Frances, Linda, Paula Teresa, Sara	Anne, Breda, Cathy, Eileen, Helen	*distant:* Freda, Wendy, Yvonne *dissociated:* Beth, Evelyn
Couples or individuals with partners or spouses (18)	Nicola Rachel (f) Oliver, Vince (m) *super core:* Zack (m) Dee (f)	Gina, Jane, Karen, Olivia, Ursula (f) Rob (m) Terry (m)	*distant:* Vera, Sally (f) *dissociated:* Irene, Maureen (f) Sam (m)

It may be that the way young people in England were contacted brought super core Catholics to light to a greater extent than in other national samples. The Roman Catholic population in contemporary England is mainly urban, and clusters around the great cities and former manufacturing towns. This urban concentration and the small size of the Roman Catholic population, at seven per cent, combined with financial constraints, all directed the writer to construct a sample of young adult Catholics and former Catholics through contacts in the densely populated areas of south-eastern England. Two kinds of networks were used: outside the periphery of Greater London, priests and practising Catholics of the parent generation were contacted in six parishes; within the periphery, the staff and students of a state-funded Catholic university college were approached. Clearly, with these kinds of contacts a number of super core were bound to show in more significant numbers than less church-focused means.

It proved difficult to develop contacts with parishes and parishioners in suitable working-class and other minority areas. Consequently, there are few minorities other than Irish in the sample and only seven members of it are skilled or semi-skilled. Four of these have great difficulty staying in employment and have experienced periods without work. Their marginal social status also affects their church attendance, as they are more likely than middle-class respondents to work long hours, six days a week, and sometimes Sundays. This is a reminder of the life conditions of lower-class people, who still make up half the English Catholic population, and who may be more likely to discontinue practice as a consequence. The skewing of the sample towards middle-class Catholics at least places attention on those who are now the mainstay of parish organisation and activity. Roughly a third of the sample is composed of teachers or teacher trainees. A further third also has a university background. So while only one third of the young adult population of Britain has a university experience, over two thirds of the English sample for this research have been through or attends university.

CORE CATHOLICS

Gill and the Core

In what follows, the numbers at the end of quotations refer to the line numbers in the life-history transcripts. We begin with Gill's life history. While being unique, it shares in common with the rest of the sample a number of social bonds. These include ethnic as well as denominational ones. Gill's father, one of nine children, is second generation Irish and married to an English woman. His wife converted to Catholicism at the time of the marriage. Gill's family is middle class and lives in the counties to the north-east of Greater London. She has two brothers and is the youngest in the family. They visit family in Ireland as well as numerous extended family that live in and around their own area: 'we always played together. I've got lots of cousins who live nearby, and they were always coming in and out . . . both sets of grandparents were always around too' (14–17). Her father's job allowed him to work from home, though sometimes business would take him away for weeks. Even so, her mother was never absent. This happy childhood was followed by a relatively smooth adolescence: days out regularly with the family into East Anglia and the coast, and at home rarely separated from the cheerful company of brothers, cousins or child friends. She attended a pleasant primary Catholic school with caring staff. There is a complete state-funded Catholic elementary and secondary school system in the UK and Gill's was one of such schools. There are even Catholic state-funded university colleges. Gill's parents were very loving and stricter with the boys than with her. In fact at home she was rather spoilt, while in primary school her brothers protected her from unruly children. Religion was a part of family life, which in turn was integrated into the parish:

> We were all taken to Mass every Sunday. We all had to go together until we were all quite old really. . . . It was a proper family Mass, full of children and singing. My brothers were altar servers. . . . Grandad would come over to our house afterwards. He would bring sweets, and if you'd been really bad you weren't allowed them (307–8).

Gill remembers her first Communion but, like virtually all others interviewed, does not remember the sacrament but only the dressing up, the party and the gifts. The most important thing for her was its role as an initiation ritual: she would no longer be left alone while other family members went off to receive the sacrament; she would no longer 'miss out – it was all about being part of the gang' (320).

Most religion was fairly routine:

> A lot of it you did because you always did. It was fairly well drummed into me at home that you were a Catholic and you were to believe. . . . Mum was always telling us little Bible stories. . . . my dad had grown up the same as I had . . . he didn't speak about Catholicism. . . . But my mum was always the one we did homework for . . . [mum dealt with] any question on Religious Education. . . . That is what I always used to think of my mum: because she made a choice [to become a Catholic] that made her feel stronger (502–12).

Gill's mother never used the term 'wrong' to identify bad behaviour:

> My mum was always one for 'that's not nice, look at the other side'. In a row she'd always say 'put yourself on the other side of the fence', she was very much for that. . . . I never felt guilty. . . . and I was never frightened. My nan (grandmother) and grandad had a picture up in their house of the Sacred Heart. . . . I was frightened of that, I really was. . . . The whole religion business was not something that was spoken about, but was always there (513–31).

Her secondary education was at a convent school, for which she had to pass an entrance exam, and have a reference from the parish priest confirming she was a practising Catholic. Most of her girlfriends went there, so that was all right: and the nuns who made up a third of the teaching staff also turned out to be all right: 'the headmistress, Sister Frances, was lovely . . . she was really nice. And Sister Brid I had for religion, and Sister Pat for Maths' (359).

The teenage years brought some friction, arguments about going out with her girlfriends, and spending hours telephoning them. Even so, she was 'a good girl' and no deviant: 'I can't keep a secret anyway so I did tell mum most things. I was never interested in smoking . . . I did try once or twice . . . I did start drinking earlier than my mum and Dad thought . . . probably 15 or 16, so not terribly young really' (388–402).

She was introduced early to public houses, bars and night clubs, mainly because she went with her elder brothers, who kept a friendly eye on her and took her home afterwards (404–38). But then, when she was 16, the boyfriend entered the scene:

> My mum used to make me laugh. She used to say, 'He's computer picked. He could not have a problem, he comes from a lovely family, he is a Catholic boy, he has done all his A levels.' He was absolutely perfect. . . . But then I didn't want to go out with my brothers, and [mum and dad] would say: 'Be in by 11.00' or 11.30. And whatever they said, I would always push it a bit further. . . . Looking back now, I think, 'Oh, you were a real cow sometimes', but at the time you don't think. . . . And then of course it all backfired and they would say, 'If this is the influence he is having on you, you can forget seeing him.' . . . I just stopped seeing him anyway, so it all blew over. But I made it plain it was because *I* didn't want to see him (442–62).

Such episodes were rare. After all, she did have considerable freedom and found her parents very reasonable: 'they never said "no" out of spite' (475–5) and always gave a reason. Making up was more difficult with her father than with her mother, but her father always came round in the end (478–86). As she went through these teenage years, religion and morality became more sensitive issues:

> Basically, when I got to secondary school . . . we had long debates on abortion and contraception. . . . But I would always take in my view as well as the Church's. I was quite aware that you should know what they say and what you think – and I always used to come home and talk about it. I talked to my mum an awful lot and she was good . . . she would always listen. . . . To this day she still does the same. I remember coming home one day [aged 15]. We had had this huge topic on abortion. I came home to my mum and I was absolutely beside myself. I could not make up my mind what was right or wrong. We had been through all the case studies in class. And I said to Mum: 'a lady was raped' and so on, and could she have

an abortion, and I got very upset over it. . . . Other than that, I just formed
my opinion and listened to both sides basically. . . . I never just say, 'Yes it's
right because the Church says so'. I have my own opinions on things . . .
things like contraception . . . my own view is that it's just not practical, it's
just outdated (537–69).

The really sad things in life for Gill have been four family deaths,
including those of grandparents. Her father crying at his mother's funeral
made a big impact on her. But something else happened when she was 16
that has affected her religious outlook substantially. She agreed to go to
Lourdes with disabled children, at the request of one of her brothers:

> I thought, 'I'm in charge of a child for a week and I can barely look after
> myself!' And going to a strange country! But from the minute I got there, I
> absolutely loved the place, I really did. I would never go without the
> children, never. But the first time I went down to the grotto I was going to
> go during the day. But my brother said, 'Don't go now. Wait until later on.
> Wait until it's dark and empty and then we will go down together.' I did as
> he said, and it was absolutely amazing. I cried my eyes out. . . . It never
> really stops having an effect on me [she has been seven times]. I think it has
> changed a lot of my religion. . . . I was at the stage my brothers went
> through, when they were growing out of it. But just getting there [to Lourdes]
> and seeing so many people there together . . . so helpful and so kind and I
> just think: 'there is something bringing this whole thing together'. . . . One
> day of the week we have a big 'Trust' Mass (The Handicapped Children
> Pilgrims' Trust) which each of the groups attend. There are about 5000
> people in the Basilica. It's just amazing. It takes my breath away every
> time. . . . I think it just came to me at the right time. . . . I was just sixteen
> and going off to do my A levels [the two years for high school graduation].
> And everyone was a bit more of an individual: there were friends of mine
> who used to be obliged to go to Mass every week and didn't go any more.
> And you know I started not to go, too. . . . Lourdes definitely strengthened
> me (609–39).

Gill was one of eight in the sample who had experience of Lourdes. For
Gill, the experience led to efforts to say her prayers every night. But the
effect always wore off a few months later. Then she would go to Lourdes
again, and the effect would be greater religious application, always
wearing off with the passage of time. Then, as she finished school, she
went to work in retailing, but was so bored with the job that within a
year she applied to go university. While doing her degree, she worked
part-time, as most English students do nowadays, because of the abolition
of welfare state grants. She used her mother's car during the week and
took it back home for weekends. Her parents helped make up her fees
and board. When interviewed, she was preparing for her training year as
a primary school teacher. She remains a very sociable person with many
friends. Her day-to-day religious life has less sparkle. Receiving the
Eucharist has no particular significance: 'it's just something that happens

from going to Mass. I do feel a bit guilty if I don't go to Mass on a Sunday'. Her experience of Confession is shared by a majority of the sample, including other core members:

> I haven't been since I was really young. . . . I get so nervous, I don't know why. . . . I would rather say sorry to God as I went along in life than do that. When we were at primary school classes, Confession used to take place once a month, and all of us had to go. And I ended up inventing my sins, saying that I had had a row with my brother, when I hadn't. . . . I would rather say sorry during my prayers or whatever. . . . Saying sorry to a priest doesn't do much for me. . . . I suppose I gave up when I went to secondary school. I only ever went to Confession in primary school up to 11 years old. . . . When I was working in town, I used to pop into an empty church during the week, or sometimes go to Mass early morning. But I would rather do that than go to Confession to get something off my mind (954–95).

Her views on cohabitation mirror those of the majority of the sample, including other core Catholics. One of her brothers cohabited for a number of years before breaking up:

> I can see both sides of the argument, for and against cohabitation. I personally don't know if I would do it. But that is more to do with the fact that it upset my mum and dad so much. They never openly said that to my brother, but it was not what they would have chosen for him. . . . It is a practical arrangement for a steady couple. I see more reason to live together if they are getting married in a year or so. I think what upset me the most about my brother was that they were just girlfriend and boyfriend. They were not even engaged! But as I say, with a view to marriage, I can see more reason for it. In today's world, it can be more practical. I have got no strong feelings either way (1098–105).

She is equally liberal on the issue of promiscuity, perhaps more liberal than the majority of the core group:

> Different people want different things out of life. . . . I know people who are promiscuous. Some can handle it . . . I have no quarrel with them, but I do get quite upset for some girls because they can't really handle it. I think sometimes it really hits them what they have let themselves in for (1114–17).

Gill, like many students, does not vote in elections yet. But she knows she will follow in her parents' footsteps as a Labour voter, and does not like the state of the country:

> I definitely think the Health Service should have a lot more money piled into it. I think the education system should get money as well. I am very much against any form of private medicine and private school. I don't like the idea of that at all. Everyone should be offered the same chance in life (1186–90).

She also finds the divide between rich and poor in Britain, and especially the condition of the homeless, to be 'outrageous' (1215). On all these issues, the majority of young adults interviewed share her views.

Gill has a lot of respect for those who give up their life as celibates for work in the Church. She has a high regard for the Pope as a person. However, 'I find it hard to comprehend when I see him in Rome surrounded by the Vatican, and I sort of think, "put that in the context the third world" . . . I find it a bit hypocritical – though you don't expect him to live in a shack' (1232–9). She thinks the Church could make itself more attractive to young people, and that people of her own age or younger would do more for the Church and the community if they were given more encouragement. She recognises the shortage of clergy and wants changes, though of what kind she does not know. Unlike most core Catholics interviewed, she still wants a celibate priesthood, yet has no problem with women priests.

Her views on abortion reflect the overwhelming majority view in the entire sample:

> I don't agree with abortion at all. There are situations where someone has been raped . . . I can see why they want it. But, just in my mind, it is the murder of a baby. And I think, if you had a baby there, you would not murder it, so why abortion? And the idea of abortion months and months into pregnancy quite sickens me really. I think it is a very selfish action. I'm really against it. But it is hard for *me* to say. . . . I mean, luckily I've got a loving family that would help me. If it were me, things would be all right. But not everyone is so fortunate. I think people have got a right to choose, but I don't think it should be that easily offered (1295–305).

Gill is a person who wishes to do things for other people. Her present commitments are still the Lourdes pilgrimage with the disabled and the fund-raising that goes with it. She also has her part-time job and her boyfriend of one year. Her main hopes for the future are being involved with the disabled as a teacher and having a large family of her own. Life has treated her well so far. She remains very close to her mother, and feels highly valued by her father. She still goes to church every Sunday, though without her brothers. Even so, one of them still goes with Gill to Lourdes, so although he does not go to Sunday Mass, 'we both go together to Lourdes every Easter, with the handicapped children' (589).

*   *   *

The account of Gill's life is one of an English core Catholic, defined within that context as one whose frequent religious practices are part-nered by some other form of church-oriented activity. Gill is one of 11 such Catholics. The others are Crystal, Debra as the other two single females; Alan, Eddie, Ian and Luke as single males; and Nicola (married),

Vince (partnered), and Rachel and Oliver (married couple). They all have Catholic family backgrounds, except for Oliver, whose father was a non-religious person, and Debra, whose father is Church of England. Alan's father, an Irish Catholic, left home for another woman, but returned a number of years later. His parents now sleep separately but otherwise get on well. Eddie, Ian and Luke had intact Catholic families, along with Crystal, whose Catholic home is outstanding in commitment terms.

Vince was brought up in Scotland in a traditional Catholic family of the pre-Vatican kind. He is the only traditionalist in the core sample. Rachel's father stopped going to church when she was in her teens, as did Vince's father, but because of disillusionment with the modern church. All core members have had experience of Catholic schools. Like Gill, Alan has been affected strongly by the Lourdes experience, Ian by charismatic renewal, Debra by spending a year in a convent in India, and Eddie by his strong Catholic fiancée. Luke is the only non-graduate, a skilled crafts-man, who raises money for Third World projects through his charitable activities. They are all anti-abortion and pro-life, but refuse to judge others who have abortions and, with the exception of Vince, only want amendments to the freedom of abortion laws, not their total abolition. Politically, they are on the left and support Catholic social teaching on poverty, the Third World and the environment. They all feel secure in their faith, even if they often feel weak in carrying out its moral precepts.

The Super Core

The remaining eight core Catholics in the sample devote a significant part of their life to church-oriented activities. They are all graduates or final year undergraduates. Their greater life involvement is such that their life seems bound up with the fate of the Church, and they have 'put their eggs in one basket', almost leaving no other career open to them, except perhaps teaching religious education. These are what we have termed super core Catholics. I came across only two males in this category, while I had little difficulty in finding super core females.

Only one, Zach, has a business life, but such is his religious commit-ment that the career seems almost a second string to his bow: he is simply incredibly resourceful, and devotes as much attention to his unpaid Catholic youth work and work for the handicapped as to the secular business partnership he runs with two Christian, but less active, friends. In addition, the youth work he undertakes is also done by his equally energetic wife: they married at 21, an unusually young age for today, made more understandable as the marriage came at the end of the last decade, with Zach only just qualifying by age for the sample in 1998.

The other seven super core members have more normal levels of energy. Frances, Teresa and Paula are full time in varying forms of mission – Frances at a retreat centre, Teresa doing parish work in both church and school, and Paula a political activist on life issues as well as a member of a Catholic community. Walter and Dee are learning to be religious education teachers, having spent four years in full-time work for major religious charities and retreat centres. All of them have had a strong Catholic upbringing in family, church and school terms.

The two remaining ones differ in this respect. Linda holds a full-time job in social services while working a significant amount of time, including weekends, in diocesan and parish liturgy work. But she came to Catholicism via Protestant evangelism. Before that she came from an anti-religious family, in which being an evangelical had to be accomplished by stealth. Sara came from an inter-church family background in which she rarely experienced affection. Her Catholic primary school was also an unpleasant experience. Relationships at home were very disciplined. On one occasion at 15, when she did not want to go to a Sunday evening Mass, there was confrontation that ended in tears. She finally went to Mass because she would otherwise have been banned from going to Anglican youth group meetings, which was her major source of friendship, spirituality and enjoyment. In fact the youth group was her way into religion and was the centre of her life. She could not get enough of their summer camp activities:

> Everyone would go to a couple of talks in the morning, then have the afternoon off and go to the big event in the evening. I went to every single talk, going from eight in the morning until about eleven at night. I was very anxious to know more and more about the faith. I went for quite a few years running, and still I wanted more (290–6).

Linda and Sara had a common experience of finding evangelicalism too exclusive and condemning of those on the outside. While Linda found her answer in the first Catholic church she walked into, Sara found it first within Methodism but in the context of charismatic renewal, which she then found crossed over the denominations. Then, when she started her university course, she came across Catholics with a similar outlook to herself, and left the exclusivist aspects of the evangelical movement behind. She has since worked in a Roman Catholic retreat centre and would love to take part in the work of Christian Catholic evangelism on a full-time and whole-life basis.

As one might expect, religious experiences become more prevalent in the sample as one moves to the super core. Here there are more life commitment decisions to God or Christ, and to Christian apostolate. Some of these are related to places of pilgrimage, others to retreats, or simply periods of prayer. The making of an articulated, enthusiastic and fundamental choice in life for Christian commitment is common to all those in the super core group, and some of these choices and experiences are renewed with greater or less frequency. For Frances, the most important set of experiences has been 'reaching an acceptance that I am accepted and loved by God, a sort of affirmation', and the second is 'a wonder of creation' (1341–3). She also has 'a strong sense of the Spirit working within me' (1168–9). The experience of being accepted and loved by God is also linked closely to her religious life. For she frequently experiences the sense of not having done enough, of always achieving below her best, and needs to know and feel that acceptance (677–723). For Teresa, music is one of the vehicles of her religious experience; the other is her membership of a small prayer and relaxation group of like-minded and like-tasked lay apostles. Linda has both music and evangelical commitment as her religious experiences, as well as other personal and private moments. She has such experiences when they are 'needed' in her life (1148–9).

For Paula, an activist rather than a contemplative, the single most important experience was sparked by her utter loneliness in an African convent as a lay helper:

> It was a time when the only thing I clung to was God. . . . I did not want to run away. I asked God 'What shall I do?' I really prayed. I experienced what I class my dark side. I sort of . . . lost my identity almost totally out there, because there were no channels through which I could be the 'me' I knew. . . . I discovered a lot within me that I did not know before and it scared me. This is when I would say I came close to God, but at that time it was not yet the heart experience. The turning point came later. Basically I had been finding Scripture and prayer very sustaining. But there came a decisive point. I was in the chapel one night and I was trying to decide whether to go home or not. I did not want to be running away, I wanted to persevere. And I said to God, 'You know, I can't be doing this on my own any more!' And that was the last thing I said. The next morning it was just sort of beyond my control. It broke the 'me' as I had experienced it: 'I can't do it on my own any more'. And as soon as I relinquished the self-will, or the self-reliance, God just came in. Then things happened that confirmed it for me, and indicated what I should do. Like there was space on a flight. Before, I had been told there would not be space for a month (1997–2270).

Sara appears to have the richest profile in terms of experiences in these terms, having both evangelical and charismatic religious experiences and, most importantly for her life course, the experience of the prayer and spiritual support of a group of lesbian Catholics in accepting and embracing her sexual identity.

The secular and moral politics of the super core group is generally oriented to welfare and egalitarian values. Super core Catholics and most core Catholics feel strongly about social justice: the need to fight poverty, unemployment and homelessness, to develop an egalitarian society by tackling racism in society, supporting equality between the sexes, and having an adequately funded and equal opportunity educational system. They all feel strongly about the plight of the Third World, and support moves such as the abolition of debt and 'sustainable development' policies. Interestingly, the more one moves away from the super core towards the disaffected, the less agreement there is on such matters within the sample, although there are still more people on the left than the right in all of the remaining quotas. However, only a minority are political in the sense of committing themselves to a political party. None of them is interested in a career in politics, despite the past candidacy of one super core member for the Life Party and a core member's past work for SPUC (Society for the Protection of the Unborn Child) – to the right of the spectrum of Catholic life politics in Britain and Ireland.

The super core are also strongly pro life, being against the death penalty, euthanasia and abortion: though in the case of abortion they all support the right of the mother to choose; and on the issue of euthanasia, they support the view that it is sometimes more necessary to relieve pain than to sustain life. Contraception is seen as positively moral, a position adopted by all other core Catholics with the exception of Vince, a member of SPUC. Living together before marriage is seen partly as a practical issue, an approach that has been adopted by Dee. The rest commit themselves to marriage first. Only Frances seems likely to consider celibacy as a religious option. The strongest criticism of the institutional church comes from its super core members, as do the most radical proposals for reform: married clergy, women clergy, the decentralisation of the Roman Catholic Church and the reduction of the Roman Curia.

INTERMEDIATE CATHOLICS

Because we have spent significant time on the super core group, the intermediate group is only examined briefly. Let us recall that Gill is a core Catholic according to the definition for England that she regularly practises her faith, and is also involved in religious pilgrimages with disabled children: she has some apostolic activity. We can remember too that, for the English sample, the middle group, the 'intermediate' Catholics, is those who have from fairly regular to less frequent church contacts, but who are not involved very much in other church activities, or in any specifically Christian apostolate. On this point, we decided not to include Catholic teachers in Catholic schools as such an apostolate, as it is possible to find nominal Catholic teachers in such schools in England. There are five relatively strong figures among the intermediate group, all of whom practise weekly. Anne, a girlfriend of a core Catholic from

Malta; Breda, a graduate preparing as a teacher and committed to the pilgrimage for the disabled; Cathy, who has experienced a violent father, has very strong ties to her long-suffering mother, and has found solace for her pains in her relationship with God; Harry, an Oxbridge undergraduate who plays a key role in his parish services, but is the only Catholic in the five who has been educated entirely outside the Catholic sector, though attended a Catholic-leaning Church of England high school; and Doug, a College undergraduate corralled into chaplaincy liturgy by his girlfriend and glad to have survived his teenage romp with drink and soft drugs.

Then there are six respondents that sit roughly in the middle of the intermediate group. Karen, a graduate and trained counsellor, likes the Bible and goes to church about once a month, but is finding life difficult because she not only has problems with a father that still tries to rule her life even though she is nearly thirty, but also has to cope with the recent separation from her partner of one year. Her secondary education was in the secular private sector of education. All the remaining interviewees had a mainly Catholic primary and secondary education. Neil has a two-subject Honours degree in philosophy and theology. He works in the media business, shares a flat with four other upwardly mobile young adults, feels his faith is very frail and only goes to Mass when he is at home with his parents. Jane left school at 16, and spent two years living in semi-destitute circumstances with a man who spent all their money on drink and soft drugs. She has recently returned to her religious practice, and has found steady work as a mechanic. Jane, Karen and Neil are all in their late twenties. Like Jane, Peter, a semi-skilled 19-year-old mechanic, left school early and works a six-day week for very low wages. He goes to church when he is not sleeping all day Sunday, has no money for entertainment and lives with his unemployed parents. Terry, also an early school leaver, has at last found steady employment at 25, having 'skilled up', repairing computers for a stock-market firm. He has come back to religious practice having found a girlfriend that teaches religion classes in a Catholic high school. Gina still goes often to church, and feels she has had a strong Catholic education, is marrying a non-religious person, but does not want to spoil things by living with him until they are married.

Finally there are five respondents who attend church only a handful of times a year or less, but still have ties to the religious community. Frank, just about to finish his degree, still practises when he goes home, clearly believes in God and still experiences strong religious though non-authority pressures. But though he is relatively knowledgeable about the faith, has a mother who teaches religious education and is close to him, he has always found it difficult if not impossible to pray. In fact he is quite uninterested in religious issues, and has little concern for the Catholic perspective on the problems of the world. He generally supports a fully liberal stance on abortion and euthanasia while conservative on the death penalty and homosexuality: he 'cannot stand' being near homosexuals. Rob, late twenties, is an assistant bank manager, lives with his non-religious fiancée, goes to church occasionally, but feels it is very important for him to bring up his future children as Roman Catholics. Ursula, late twenties and married to a non-religious sailor, does not go to church at the moment mainly because of ill-health, has relatively little knowledge of the faith, despite her Catholic schooling, but has a deep commitment to Catholic life values and the Catholic education of her children. The youngest of five children and with Irish parents, she describes herself as 'naturally good' as a child. 'I used to pray a lot. . . . When I went to Ireland [for holidays] we would say prayers before meals and when going to sleep. But in our family we didn't do that. I just used to say my prayers off my own bat' (315–22).

Helen has broken most religious links except when at home, some-thing she still goes along with, as she relies entirely on her Irish parents for her income. Like Helen, Eileen is on the edge of the intermediate group. One of two children and also of Irish parentage, she was never taught at home to say any prayers. Her mother stopped going to church when Eileen was 11 or 12, and her father who drinks never really went at all. Eileen herself only went to Sunday Mass until she was 18. She was forced to go while her friends did not: 'I found it really hard. I never stopped believing but I didn't like to go, and I didn't like being forced' (382–6). Even so, last year, she often dropped into church to pray, 'because I did find it helpful' (393–4). She found Confession helpful as well, one of the few in the whole sample who have done so, and admits also to feeling much guilt in her present uneasy situation of whether to give up her practice completely.

FORMER CATHOLICS

We now come to the life histories of 'former' Catholics. These fall more or less easily into two groupings: those who have 'dissociated' themselves from the church, and those who are 'distant' from it or whose links with it are made tenuous by absence from religious worship and loose ties with the religious community. The distant still call themselves Catholics, and probably are, in so far as they either believe in God, or consider them-selves associated with church membership, or believe that they have been affected by Catholic moral teaching and wish to be recognised as accepting it. But this is to put words into their mouths. Let us look at the relevant aspects of the life histories for the two groupings.

The Distant

There are eight life histories of distant Catholics. The most distant is Colin, a young man about to join the army in the footsteps of his father and grandfather before him. His father has died, and there is only his sister and mother left; this small family has weak contacts with extended kin. His father was Anglican and his mother a Catholic from Ulster. There was some contact in the past with the church. But was there ever any sense of being in a Catholic or religious home?

> COLIN: 'I wouldn't say overtly, no. I have always been brought up with Christian values. But there was never – I mean, we would go to church once in a while . . . apart from that, not particularly. There was a time – on my father's side, my uncle was an Anglican priest and when we used to come into contact with him we went. Otherwise we used to go to church once or twice a year.'
>
> J.F.: 'Did you ever have any Christian initiation or education?'
>
> COLIN: 'I remember once or twice . . . over in Germany there used to be Sunday school . . . it was within the army, so I do not think it was a separate Catholic thing. I could be wrong' (351–75).

Colin has no memory of making his first Communion, and is not sure if he is baptised. He has only one or two close friends, though since his father died about five years ago from an illness, friends of his father from the army have looked after him more: there is a certain sense of solidarity within the British Army of looking after your own if an army parent dies. His friends are grown-up army children, and they are very active in the open-air life, sport and keep-fit. They have 'integrity' and Colin thinks that 'at the end of the day, they wouldn't sell me down the river. I think that's quite important, that you can trust a friend' (770–4). But in the army you are also expected to look after yourself and to show you have a strong and independent character. Colin recognises this influence, and shows it in his independent life style. He has 'high expectations of himself' in terms of military career and 'fear of failure' (631–4). The things he is concerned most about in society are homelessness, the need for more education, and a better health service. He also thinks that people generally in Britain do not love their country as much as people in most European countries do, and that Britain is fractious and not united enough. But this does not run counter to Europeanism in his case: he is European in his politics and thinks the European Union a good thing. Because he is not sure what he is, it seemed wise to rank him inside the distant category. We are dealing here with self-definition rather than church definition. But does he have a position on God?

Six or seven months ago, I started thinking. . . . Well, there has got to be a point to your life. It's not some sort of, you know, manic game, where people are buzzing around and doing nothing. There's got to be something there. And I think to myself, well, how and why are we here? Yes, I do think there is something – I don't know what – and I have not really looked into it (1086–94).

After Colin, there remain nine other distant Catholics. We can look at them in terms of their likelihood or otherwise of increasing or returning to their practice of Roman Catholicism. Firstly, we look at those who appear less likely to return. These are Kevin, Malcolm, Sally and Wendy. This does not mean they have no strong feelings for issues often related to the contemporary Catholic consciousness. Two of the four have only one religious parent: Kevin's father practises and so does Wendy's mother, who is separated. Both Malcolm and Sally have two Catholic parents and both sets practise. Only two, however, Wendy – single and from a one-parent family, and Malcolm, single with most relatives back in Ireland – remember saying regular prayers at home.

Malcolm went to church until he was 20, and then suddenly stopped. He admits that the Church provided social and sporting opportunities for him as a youth, and that was really why he went (327–52). The fact that he continued to practise for so long could be down to his Irish parents' insistence and to the fact that he has always lived at home but for six months, even though he is now 29. At the moment, while he is still playing sport, he is somewhat aimless, dissatisfied with work and with the fact he has not settled down. He still believes 'there is a God, but not as strongly as I used to . . . I'm more irreligious than religious now . . . God has helped me sometimes and I do pray' (879–90). Sally is equally vague: 'I don't know if there's a god. There must be, there probably is something, but I don't know what' (1349–52) and she agrees that religion is now relatively unimportant to her.

Malcolm and Wendy have both known priests personally, and Wendy finds the priest in her mother's present parish a good man. Wendy, like Beth, also helped run the children's liturgy. And her mother is a dedicated while open-minded Catholic. Kevin went to church because it was required, but as he entered his teens he began to feel religion more irksome. Again, at his Catholic secondary school – he had been to a state primary – religion became 'annoying'. Sometimes he would gain an insight at a religious assembly and was affected by Princess Diana's death, but with most other religious issues, 'normally you would just blank it. . . . But to hear – I know this may sound a bit nasty – Jesus on the cross, crucified, [well] I had heard it all before and it did not impact' (638–88). Kevin sums it up: 'I still regard church and religion as old-fashioned. Young people who are heavily into religion tend to be boring. I would say it holds more value [for me now], but I still don't get into it' (897–901).

Wendy is interesting from the point of view of lifestyle choice. At 15, she made her Confirmation and clearly accepted the sense of commitment to her Christian life. But one year later, she was already 'drifting off' (401), which upset her mother: 'I was a real nightmare . . . even now I get really bad pangs of guilt . . . I was so difficult, taking drugs and doing other things . . . my mum is very religious . . . and I could tell her what had happened, I could confide in her' (435). But it did not stop her blazing her own independent trail. Her lifestyle is conducted in what could be called a religion-free way.

The second group of distant Catholics are perhaps closer to the Church than the above, to the extent that they may return. These are Freda, Vera, and Yvonne, all women. What makes them different to the members of the other group? First of all, at least two of them had a sense of prayer in the home. Yvonne's father, a super core Catholic of his own generation, would always come into the bedroom to say some night prayers with the five children. Freda remarks that she had to go when she was small and often found it boring, but there were good moments too, with singing and taking part in processions (112–88). Vera articulates her sentiments differently: 'it was a combination of something you should do and something I wanted to do. It was good discipline . . . gave structure to the day, which is quite nice. And also sometimes especially at Easter time and Christmas time it was special, and gives you a sense of purpose' (196–206). She made her Confirmation with commitment: 'this is my religion, this is my faith'. But soon problems developed: 'I started not to find answers to the bigger questions in life . . . and I started to become more cynical about it' (527–39).

Yvonne, who has moved house and parish five times, living in different parts of the country, never remembers being bored at Mass while a child, and has happy memories of the clergy in at least two of the churches. It did become more irksome when she was twelve, because the family would sit at the front of the church – 'terrible' and mortifying – and also she began to realise none of her friends went. But this was on the eve of her teenage rebellion. However, even in those years, when she avoided Sunday Mass as much as she could, she would be paid for showing up in jeans and spiky hair to play the organ for someone's wedding. An accompanying theme was that she felt her parents, deeply religious activists, were given a hard time by the Church's religious and educational institutions in which they had always worked very hard. Even so, she is no longer rebellious – and she has always held to strong moral principles, on sexual relationships for example. It seems that it is more resentment towards the Church's representatives than anything else that keeps her negative.

The Dissociated

Those who no longer consider themselves Roman Catholic are Barry, Beth, Evelyn, George, Irene, John, Maureen and Sam: eight in all. Barry is different from the rest, in so far as he switched from Roman Catholicism to a small and localised evangelical sect, the only one in the sample who has done so. In contrast with the US, 'switchers' from Catholicism to Protestantism in the UK are not easy to find among this generation. Part of the reason for this is that fundamentalism has little attraction for English Catholics and ex-Catholics. Barry is deeply committed to the Christian Gospel and leads his life accordingly. Though the membership of his sect tends to condemn those on the outside, he himself still maintains the tolerant views he brought with him from his former background. Sam differs from others in the group, in so far as he sees himself as having gone beyond organised religious forms, having found tranquillity in the contemplation and creation of the aesthetic. He is a professional artist, and works spiritually through a variety of art forms and crafts. However, Evelyn, George and John no longer believe in God. Beth and Irene have left the practice of Catholicism not through choice for clear and positive alternatives, but because they no longer find a place for it in their lives. Maureen has left because she could not bear the guilt she experienced, though remained guilt-ridden for some time after. Let us deal with Beth and Irene first.

Irene has very few roots in Catholicism. Her childhood was mostly difficult. First her mother was a single parent. Then she married Irene's father. Later her non-religious father left and then divorced her mother. Mum never went to church and Irene went because her grandparents took her. She herself found church boring, but still loved being there because she had her loving grandfather all to herself: 'Mum was kind of rejected from the Church. When I was a child, I went to Communion; and I did turn to the Church when I went to primary school, and I was very interested in it. But it changed, you know, as I went along. . . . I don't think I stopped going to church because of my mum. I just lost interest and I then lost my faith as well' (411–13). In fact when her grandfather died she stopped going to church at 13 years old. However, by then, her unhappy childhood had been replaced by a relatively happy family life, when her mother remarried shortly before her grandfather's death.

Beth stopped going to church at 17, and her younger sister and brother followed her soon after. She never enjoyed going and was never attracted to religion. She found the local parish priest and most of the nuns at the local primary convent school frightening. She enjoyed Mass only at the private school to which her brother went, and then mainly for the jolly sermons and the singing. By the time she was 16, her way out of sitting through boring Masses was to lead the children's separate 'liturgy' or activities. Additionally, her Irish mother was her only Catholic parent and her father rather made fun of Catholic beliefs and practices. Beth believes there is probably a God but sees no point in institutional religion.

Maureen, one of two children, went to church under duress as a child. Her father was a traditional Catholic, with very strong views on church attendance and moral conformity. Maureen says she turned against Catholicism because she experienced a great deal of authoritarianism and guilt as she grew up:

> As much as I have always fought it, I fought it not knowing what alternatives there were. I sort of retaliated and rebelled against this dictatorship: you know, no sex before marriage. . . . I never spoke to my mother about sex in my whole life. I did not dare broach the subject. If it was ever on TV, we were forced out of the room. It was just taboo, which I think was very sad – which in itself was really interesting: because it gets you on to the topic of Mary Magdalen and her position in society – you know, in terms of the Bible and how women were cast out. . . . It is something I have lived with, it is an image of yourself as a woman. You are evil, and you are not allowed to have any emotional feelings towards a man because you are giving in. So your interpretation of your relationships is very warped, because you have this underlying guilt to deal with all the time. And by that, you do not have self-respect. I would say, after talking to a lot of Catholic girls, that we have to learn self-respect, because otherwise, if you have any kind of relationships, you are doomed. You see where I am coming from?' (Maureen, 302–26).

Once she was at college and away from home, she left her religion in a burst of sexual liberation, but only rid herself of the guilt years later, when she met her present partner:

> He says to me, 'I have never done anything wrong in my life'. And I thought, 'What a funny thing to say'. He says, 'I have never tried to kill anybody, never tried to hurt anybody, never sinned'. This was an absolute revelation to me. It was like, 'Oh my God! Some one who believes they do not sin!' This was incredible. And I took this on board and my whole life changed (372–81).

Maureen remains focused on her own career and enjoys business. If she has any religious sentiment now, it is towards New Age and discovering one's links with the natural world through self-healing practices.

George has a non-believing father. He also went through a major crisis at the age of 12 to 13 over the existence of God, but then settled for a while in his belief, only to come to the conclusion at the age of 18 that there was no God, a position he still holds. He is an intellectual, and the only person in the entire sample to have such a focus on the philosophical aspects of faith. He also has a dedicated background to the physical sciences, which he partners with his love for music of all kinds. Evelyn, too, has a non-believing father, and is closer to him than to her believing mother. She has stopped believing in Catholicism or Christianity, but is still unable to tell her mother with whom she goes to Christmas Mass every year.

John's realisation of religious choice came at 14:

> [Many] ideas that Catholics stand for are fine, and I would go along with them. But the basic idea of what it is and why they say, 'I am a Catholic' or 'a Christian', I don't agree with. Basically I do not accept the idea of there being a God . . . and the idea that Jesus came down and died and then came back to life again. Possibly I would like to believe it but I can't, so that's that. There are values that I accept, like helping people, helping the poor, giving to charities, things like euthanasia – fine, I go along with it, also its views on abortion, but not entirely. . . . And I wouldn't say 'I'm not going to do that because Jesus wouldn't want me to', but I would say 'I'm not going to do that, because I don't think it's right to do that'(467–92).

At the moment, Beth is sexually liberal, and also longs for a communitarian existence, in which she will have plenty of children to care for, but with no male partner in the picture. George wants to have more good and trusty friends, is uncertain what path to follow in life, and is a little lonely. He has no partner and finds promiscuity distasteful. Despite his disbelief and more morally affirming than John, George treasures Catholic social teaching, actively promoting, via chairing a local group, the lot of Third World peoples. Evelyn too is angry about the environmental pollution and poverty that exist in present day UK, and the poverty of the third world. Beth, George and Maureen appear close to their mothers, with Beth fearing and Maureen antagonistic towards her father, while Evelyn is closer to her father. Beth, Evelyn, George, John and Maureen have few people on whom they can rely, and apart from their mothers, there is no substantial relationship with a religious believing and practising person. Could this be a significant aspect of religious detachment in the modern western world for former believers?

CONCLUSIONS AND FURTHER REFLECTIONS

As one might expect and almost by definition, the life histories bring one to the conclusion that the closer an individual becomes to the super core Catholic experience, the more religious experiences and events predominate: conversions, other religious experiences, retreats and pilgrimages, the presence of role models with significant religious commitment and enthusiasm, exposure to enthusiastic religious education, as much if not more on the moral issues of the day than on the Bible and the Gospels. Again the frequency of these appears to be conditioned by one or more of the following institutional frameworks: belonging to a family of which one or more members have enthusiastic religious commitment, attending at least one Catholic educational institution where a living and inclusive type of religion is encountered, and having the support of enthusiastic religious friends.

While all core Catholics experienced at least one of the above events and social environments, some core members had several of these. Linda and Sara were unusual in having really only one environment to nurture their religious consciousness, namely religious and evangelical friends, though both school and church youth club provided the crucial first environment in both cases. There are, however, cases of former Catholics that had elements of such environments, but which did not lead to the continuance of religious practice and the development of commitment. George had only his mother for religious support, lacking a wider familial religious culture, and was not impressed by his primary Catholic education, though had some 'quality time' in Sunday Mass. It is noticeable that Beth, Evelyn, George, John had counter role models to religion in their sceptical fathers. At the same time a majority of former Catholics have clearly been influenced by Catholic social teaching and deprecate an uncaring society, showing their dissatisfaction with the British one in which significant inequality exists. The 'intermediate' group also show the impact of such social awareness. We have already seen the generally left-wing views of the super core on secular politics and the radical character of their critique of Roman Catholic Church structure.

We suspect the sample is close to the pattern of experience and life orientations of most middle-class young adult Catholics in England. Core Catholics have probably become with this generation a largely 'progressive' force, and are likely to continue to be such at least for the first few decades of the twenty-first century, as they take over lay leadership of their church, provided that they are encouraged and given the freedom and support by their pastors to do so. Only one person among our core (Vince, a Scot who settled in England) is a traditionalist, follows the papal line on sexual morality and believes in 'clear' standards and dogmas. There are no other signs of traditional ethnic Catholic values, with the exception of Marian devotion which, however, is now recast in the twin progressive moulds of community celebration and altruism towards the disabled (for this aspect, see Fulton 2000). It would be difficult to govern such a church in a traditional way, because there would be a clear rejection of traditional subservience to papal and priestly authority. People must now be convinced, if they are to act in accordance with enunciated norms. They must follow their consciences, and cannot take directives on trust. In this sense, the members of our sample demonstrated autonomy, and most showed also responsible semi-autonomy in their approaches to moral and political questions.

The profile of intermediate Catholics suggests that the present levels of Roman Catholic Church activity and participation might be sustainable for the first decades of the new century, at least in terms of its middle-class constituency, provided that the organisational changes intimated above also take place. The diverse patterns of dissociation and distancing might well also prove to continue a national trend, and it will be whether 'returning' to religious practice outweighs permanent 'leaving' that will ultimately determine the issue of the sustainability of Catholicism in England. These issues, however, deal mainly with church viability, which is clearly difficult to predict even if there were a thorough statistical research programme to verify the trends which Hornsby-Smith has in the past indicated in his substantive research programme (1987, 1989, 1991). Clearly, it would appear that thin layers of religion do exist among some of the distant Catholics, though it would be to misrepresent them if one saw them as people without meaningful human values and commitments. If one looks at the dissociated, one can see that the assertions of George, John and Sam are of positive commitments and concerns, and Barry remains a deeply committed Christian. Irene and Maureen are hardly immune to life's difficulties and show thoughtful responses to their situations, with human ideals that they hope some day to fulfil. Beth is the only one who has not yet sorted herself out. But then she is 22, while Irene is 24 and Maureen 29. What the research of Bynner et al. (1997) and McNamara (1981) tend to show is a settling down process that appears to begin in the mid-twenties, where life choices and commitments are firmed up and experimentation is over for the majority.

Consequently, this author views that, in so far as our sample is concerned, there has not been an 'end to grand narratives', be they religious or humanistic as prefigured by the postmodern interpretation. Among our sample, sense, sensibility and concern seem very much alive, with little sign of indifference. Nor does religious unbelief appear as a hot wire to human indifference for former Catholics. As the majority non-church going population shows, the roof is not set to fall in on the moral bond at the core of meaningful human relationships, despite the lack of specifically religious overarching frameworks. Of course, Catholics and former Catholics represent only about seven per cent of the British population. Still, this is one subculture which takes on a critical stance towards world politics and economics, and which could form alliances with other similar critical groups within the context of future social movements. These young Catholics and former Catholics are critical, in the sense of recognising both good and bad: critical of their church and critical of British and international society. They are definitely not postmodern in the strict sense, and definitely have purpose. But they do see that their personal integrity comes first, and that they have to be true to their conscience. This is why authoritarianism has collapsed in the everyday life of English Catholic young adults, and not because moral standards have disappeared. Moral principles are largely clear, but it is not easy to know how to work them out in terms of personal relationships and the wider political and economic arena.

8

YOUNG ADULT CATHOLICS AT THE MILLENNIUM

John Fulton

INTRODUCTION

From the beginning of the book, we set out to explore the life experience of young adult Catholics aged 18–30 in six different countries with a single purpose in mind. This was to gain insights into how they live in a late modern or postmodern world, and to what extent they embrace or reject the cultures they inhabit and the religious and moral tradition into which they have been socialised to varying degrees. In order to undertake this task, we explored in chapter 1 the changes in culture and socio-economic structure of the West in general. We then covered the relevant particularities of each national experience in the separate chapters. We also provided similar information on Roman Catholicism in terms of both its late twentieth-century reform and the national circumstances of each country.

We formulated the key questions to which we would seek answers, for our own country and for the six countries as a whole. We also laid out the structure of our inquiry, the sampling method we used and how we applied it in each national case. It is now necessary to bring together common and particular findings, and to understand the likely reasons for these, particularly explanations in terms of country, western culture and church-promoted change. Then we shall address the issues of whether a general direction for religion and morality is indicated, and the extent to which this direction hinges on the will of human kind, the religious institution, or on more globalised or even uncontrollable forces of the social dynamic in which the contemporary world finds itself.

It is helpful at this stage to recall the questions we intended to ask of our data, once it was collected. These we listed in chapter one (page 21) and are worth recalling here. To what extent and in what way does late modernity affect the religious and moral consciousness of young adult

Catholics and former Catholics? Is the result a religious orientation that survives only on the surface of their lives, without any deeper impact? Have they become materialistic, deprived of a supernatural or other spiritual consciousness? Are we seeing the end of Catholicism in the West and if so, why? Has the Catholic Church as an organisation promoted its own downfall? If there are no easy answers to these questions, do we need to be more perceptive and careful in our interpretation? Are we able to apportion different effects to modern culture and to a failed or successful church reform?

Before we answer these questions it is necessary first to clarify some differences in emphases in the way we applied our method and gathered our data. The reader will have noticed variations in the amount of ground covered on several substantive topics: the three religious categories – core, intermediate and former Catholic; the various stages of the life course – childhood, adolescence and young adulthood; the social institutions of family – schooling, higher education, and marriage; the coverage of relationships and moral and political matters. There are two main reasons why we sought variety here rather than a weighted conformity. First, total standardisation would have made the reading monotonous. Second, and more importantly, there were specific aspects in some of the countries that merited further inquiry, at the expense of other items. In some cases, as with travel in Malta and core Catholics in UK, there were new research findings worth highlighting. This led Anthony M. Abela to show how travel has an impact on sexual behaviour in an island known for its strong cultural and religious traditions. It led me to make space for a lengthier treatment of religious experience and social and personal morality among its progressive core Catholics, equally present in the US data. Teresa Dowling chose to concentrate on religious education in Irish secondary schools, as it appears to have little impact there as a tool of religious socialisation. Penny Marler has given more attention to inter-mediate Catholics, as there is little research on this group in the US. Luigi Tomasi was particularly struck by the high levels of individualism in his sample from Northern Italy, and consequently has openly raised the postmodern question of the modern religious person as a consumer at the supermarket of post-material and spiritual goods.

DIFFERENCES AND SIMILARITIES

We can now move on to consider the differences and similarities between countries, in particular the following tendencies. First, young adult core Catholics are present in each country, though have different political-religious and social orientations and varying moral attitudes and judgments. Second, there are differences in the three different religious quotas that are related to particularities of national culture, especially in terms of its link with Catholicism. Third, there are similarities that appear owing to the influence of Catholicism itself as opposed to modernity and others that appear owing to the influence of late modernity, but which also have been reinforced by tendencies within contemporary Roman Catholicism itself. We shall take each of these findings in turn.

Core Catholic Young Adults

In an age often considered postmodern, it is a significant social fact that there still is a core of committed young adult Catholics in the population, and that they are relatively easy to find. They could be considered as part of the constituency of the 'musically religious' or the *virtuosi*. For Max Weber, these were the ever persistent minority in traditional societies that kept religion going, while the majority were taken up by the problems and issues of the mundane aspects of existence (Weber 1968: 452–556, especially 538–41). This is true for our core catholic young adults, though their religious function in and outside church culture lies somewhere between that of Weber's religious virtuoso and that of simple laity. Core Catholics certainly make a succession of religious decisions that continually determine their life horizons, whereas intermediate Catholics see their religion as central only in major life-shaking events.

Common characteristics of these core Catholics in the young adult age group throughout the six countries are participation in sodalities and prayer groups such as the following: Legion of Mary, St Vincent de Paul Society, Catholic Action, and the Society of Christian Doctrine also known as M.U.S.E.U.M. They may even belong to an even more structured 'community' such as the Community of Good Friends in Poland, or to a small community such as that of Paula in the UK, or one of the more conservative Roman Catholic movements such as the Neo-Catechumenate and Opus Dei. Another common characteristic is that the majority of them do not see joining a religious order or becoming a priest as their goal. They are, therefore, distinct from the traditional 'set apart' group of priests and religious orders. Even so, it is quite clear, at least in Poland and Ireland, that some core Catholics view themselves as different from the rest of the laity.

There are, however, differences within the core Catholic constituency in what we might term their political-religious orientation. Whereas in the UK and US traditional core Catholics are relatively difficult to find, the same is not the case in Ireland, Poland, Italy and Malta, where traditionalist tendencies among core members appear more easy to find than progressive ones. One can note that in England the traditional Legion of Mary has virtually disappeared and that the new but tendentially elitist Neo-Catechumenate is quite small. In the UK and US, progressive young adult core are the rule rather than the exception. While traditionalists still focus on the Papacy as the ultimate authority and a principal source of spiritual nourishment, progressives focus on the local church and the religious community in both narrow and broad terms. While traditionalists are more likely to support a strongly hierarchical church and traditional roles in both church and society, progressives are more likely to look to further reforms of church structure, such as married clergy and women priests, and to other processes of enculturation into the home nation state to further the Christian mission more successfully. These are very different perceptions of the Roman Catholic project.

Even so, when it comes to current moral debates, it is interesting to note that core Catholic women rather than men across the countries are more progressive on sexual matters, and more readily disagree with the official church line on contraception and sexual mores in general, including sexual orientation. Again, while mostly disagreeing with the practice of abortion they are much more likely than those in the four 'Catholic' countries to point out exceptions and to query the use of state law and criminalisation to affect its practice.

It is not necessary to agree with Weber's theory of the religiously musical to accept that the presence of young core Catholics of the kind described are a sign of religious vitality within our countries. Though we are unable to say just how many they number, no one found it difficult to trace them. Also, there may well be as significant a number of super core Catholics as were found in south-east England. There, at least two or three young super core appeared in each parish – and English parishes are very small by US and European continental standards: often fewer than 1,000 registered of all ages.

Core, Intermediate and Distant: Differences by Country

Secondly, there are differences in religious and moral orientations in the three different religious quotas that are related to particularities of national culture and nation-state structure. For example, in Ireland, core Catholics tend to be seen as 'holy Joes': too religious for one's own good and not quite normal. We saw the same in Poland, where intermediate Catholics did not want to 'exaggerate' the extent of their religiosity. This attitude does not seem to be the same in England and the US. At the same time, there is a clear association in Ireland and Poland between being Catholic and being Irish or Polish, even among some former Communists in the case of the latter.

But already in both countries there are signs of an unravelling of these identities, not simply in declines in mass attendance, but also in the space respondents put between their interpretations of personal and sexual morality and the official statements of church leaders. Of course, the church leaderships in Ireland, Italy, Malta and Poland on the one hand, and in UK and the US on the other, have very different foci for their actions. In the former, there is still a battle that can be fought to retain the presence of Catholic traditional values in some sectors of society. In the latter, both of them Anglo-Saxon countries and deeply affected by Protestant cultures, the task is seen more as seeking ways to provide forms of religious gathering which will promote both a deepening of faith and forms of Christian action, and to dialogue with, rather than face down, the personal opinions and values that young Catholics have formed in the light of their own experience. The semi-autonomy of young adults is accepted as a presupposition for religious communication in the US and UK, but not yet in Italy, Malta and Poland, with Ireland coming somewhere in between. In this way, the communication structure in relationships between young adults and priests is already quite different, even though in places like Italy and Ireland there is almost as much autonomy as in the US and UK, with greater independence from the family of origin in the latter pair being perhaps the most significant difference. Again, the presence of parental authority in religious matters is still at its strongest in Malta and in the rural areas of Italy and Poland – perhaps less in Ireland where a separate rural culture has almost disappeared. Ordering youth to go to church in the UK and US is almost unheard of, unless the parents are first generation immigrants and come from places such as Italy and Poland.

Finally, there are differences among former Catholics according to country that also tend to follow the divide between former monopoly Catholic countries and countries where Catholicism is a minority faith, though such differences are far less noticeable than those in core and intermediate Catholics. In Poland, Ireland, Italy and Malta, it is very difficult for former Catholics to break their link with the church, particularly when it comes to bringing up their own children. They have to negotiate the pressure of their own extended family networks and neighbours. Such pressure seems to succeed in making them have their children baptised, educated in a Catholic school – there is almost no other kind at primary level in all four countries – and submitting them to the further initiation rites of Confession and First Communion. But, if anything, such pressure only results in many of them being even more critical of the church, especially in Italy. Here the anti-clericalism of the Latin countries remains, though in a weaker form than in Spain, where the bitter civil war of the 1930s still has its legacy. While agnosticism and atheism grows among former Catholics in Britain and US, there is much less criticism of Catholicism, which is more often either remembered fondly or judged as irrelevant and its god outdated. While there is some criticism of being schooled by unsympathetic nuns and the overbearing Catholicism of other educators and parents, it is generally irrelevance and unbelief that lie at the heart of moving away from 'the faith'. This may be attributable to varying degrees of materialism. But one suspects that the young adult population as a whole is more closely allied to the materialism of the struggle for survival than to hedonism. For many in late modernity, as well as in post-Communist Poland, families and individuals seek better work or even any work to earn the money which is so necessary for putting a roof over one's head and for having minimal access to comfort, especially among the lower echelons of the social scale. The signs of out-and-out pleasure seeking were sporadic in our data, though such persons more than others might be expected to self-exclude from this type of life-history research.

Similarities Caused by Catholicism and Late Modernity: Late Modern Religion

If there are differences between the religious and moral culture of our national samples, there are also similarities. It may be possible to apportion the causality of some of these similarities to Catholicism and others to aspects of late modernity and its cultures. Let us first of all list some of these similarities. We have already noted the presence of core Catholics in all our countries and that it was not difficult to find them. This is clearly a product of developments within Roman Catholicism itself. Also, many of the religious activities of these core laity are nourished and encouraged by the clerical church, though within certain limits, for example permitting male married deacons, but not female ones. There is also an absolute ban from Rome on conferring priestly ordination on these married men.

Part of the ease with which we found and recruited core Catholics was the result of sampling from educational establishments or parish networks where such people were likely to be found, rather than random sampling wider populations. The US sample is taken mainly from students with a college or university education: but then US participation rates in higher education are 50 per cent, the highest in the world. These young core Catholics were therefore also educated people and members of the middle classes. However, it is in all likelihood true that, with the exception of the Latino growth in the US, our churches are becoming more rather than less dominated by the middle classes. It is certainly true that Catholicism, unlike some forms of Protestantism, never established itself in the industrial heartlands of Europe except as the religion of migrant populations of Irish, Poles, Italians and others – and in all these cases with success only for one or two generations. Traditional rural cultures continue to disappear. Those who still live 'in the countryside' easily adopt an urban pattern of employment and unemployment, similar to those in the lower social strata of urbanised societies. Rather than depopulation of the countryside, country people are becoming saturated through travel and media with contemporary urban cultures, as well as being replaced by urban commuters. Rural Catholicism is already under threat in Ireland and Italy, and is likely to decline in Poland at a later date within the same low social strata, with the image of the rural Catholic peasantry as 'salt of the earth' disappearing along with it.

We have said that religion is becoming more a middle-class phenomenon throughout our countries, as the middle classes expand in number while working classes become more fragmented and increasingly powerless. Does this mean that, as people become more prosperous, they become more materialistic? In turn do they become less religious or more superficial in their faith, which thus becomes a matter of consumer choice, one possibility in a range of religious and other spiritual options? Do young people in particular believe 'less' as a result of modernity and does this appear in our life histories? Perhaps we should reverse the order in which we deal with the answers to these two questions, and in both cases answer using as a vehicle our young adults, who, after all, form part of the most powerful group of consumers in contemporary markets. Do young Catholics believe 'less' than previous generations? There is an ambiguity in the meaning of belief. One the one hand it refers to specific creedal statements the most central of which in the Christian context, put simply, are: belief in the existence of a personal and loving God, belief in Jesus Christ as both God and human, and belief that he came into our human world to show God's love and to reconcile us to God. We rarely asked our interviewees to confirm whether they believed in this core tenet. Nor did we often ask them about beliefs surrounding it such as the afterlife, its heaven and hell options. What we concentrated on was rather that other definition, where recognition of having a relationship with God and the sacred both privately and publicly, through prayer, rite and attention to Scripture, is matched by seeking to lead a life within the context of that commitment and as a member of the Roman Catholic Church community.

We do not know the extent to which our sample would affirm items such as the existence of hell and heaven. But we do know the nature of their overall personal disposition and the tenor of their life, as testified by their life-history accounts. Thus we know whether they experience and have a commitment to, and *therefore* believe in, the personal God of the Christian faith – or not, as in the case of some of our former Catholics. Our young people probably do not have a lively belief in heaven and hell, though whether they do or not we cannot be certain. However, we must bear in mind that popular belief in heaven and hell in the Middle Ages was also bound up with an entire perception of the physical cosmos as in a continuum with these other two worlds, the one below and the one above, a physical world so close to the others that supernatural forces and devils were forever taking over people's bodies or erupting into society.

The emptying of the enchanted world was accomplished by science and by the population's acceptance of science through modern education and media systems. In a world where such a perception of the super-natural is severely cut back, we suggest, religious belief is more able to survive in late modernity if there is conviction first of a relationship with God, on the basis of which beliefs about the afterlife and others associated with the creeds and teaching of the church can have plausibility. A modern religious faith requires a self-motivating trust that can carry one through the modern distractions of life: financial and emotional insecurity over work and income, and negotiation of the strong pulls of consumer society and the cult of the self. It requires a sense of God's presence or of God's purpose to replace the sacralisation of this-worldly experiences.

What are the possibilities of recovering the experience of the sacred for Christians generally in the modern world, beyond, or even leading to, this perception and/or feeling of God's presence? From the life histories, we suggest the experience of the sacred in late modernity occurs on the one hand in the private and public cult experiences of which we have spoken, and, equally importantly, at the interface between moral perception and the contemporary world in its physical, cultural, historical and social realities. In the strictly religious sphere of institutionalised religion, silence, music, prose, poetry, handshakes and sacramental rituals weave the reality of sacred space and time. At the interface between moral perception and the world, humanity and its environment become icons of God, as people commit themselves to abolish poverty, support justice for Third World peoples, the oppressed, the wrongly imprisoned, the tortured. Charities, NGOs (non-governmental organisations), and even the UN become the vehicles of God's work. Each human person can become the 'tabernacle' or dwelling place of God, as each one is urged to self-respect. Both humanity and self become stewards of the fragile earth and the forms of life that live in and on it. These too become sacred, and have to be treated with the same respect and reverence. We thus experience growth in the quasi-religious forms of vegetarianism, pro-animal activities, environmental consciousness and anti-nuclear and disarmament politics.

We have seen that in the experience of core Catholics, there is strong adherence to their religious way of life. Some have had religious experiences, others deep commitments to their faith and to ways of living it out in their lives. There is a strong communal theme to the spirituality of many. In this sense, the question whether the Catholicism of young people is significantly weaker than that of previous generations is answered negatively. Modern faith is different to a devotional or sin-cycle form of faith. It may mean that young core Catholics are more content and less guilty than previous generations. But it does not mean they are less religious. Also, there is no sign among core Catholics that religion has simply become a matter of superficial consumer choice. There are, however, signs among some groups of intermediate Catholics of what we might term superficiality in matters religious. While there are signs of such across all our samples, the most apparent are those in monopoly Catholic countries where religious affiliation is much more related to the dominant or exclusive association between being Catholic and being a true member of the nation. We suggest that it is this ethnic role of performing religious ritual or affirming religious identity, which imposes religious obligations that are not necessarily felt deeply within the person, and which consequently render such people 'superficial' in the eyes of their fellow core believers. But such superficiality is not the fruit of postmodernity, but of monopoly Catholicism, which can only induce religion from without rather than from within. In a late modern society, we find religious and moral value responses coming more from within the subject rather than from without.

As well as the specifically religious convictions and experiences our young people had, there were precisely the kind of beliefs we might expect of a late modern consciousness for which the sacred lies in new places and new subjects. The majority of our young people had strong beliefs in the value of human life. The nearer one was to the core Catholic experience, the stronger the convictions about the value of the child in the womb, the killer on death row and the person suffering from painful illness. However, in the case of opposition to both euthanasia and abortion, these convictions were often tempered by sympathy and by the conviction to respect those who make such choices. It was also interesting to find some of those who no longer believed in Catholicism still supported it in terms of respect for human life.

In those countries where the theme was explored, there was also strong support for action to help Third World countries as well as the poor at home. There can be little doubt that some church hierarchies, particularly in US, UK and Ireland, have pushed these issues in the parishes, and that this sensitising of the Christian conscience has helped national campaigns by more secular charities and political parties of the left to increase pressure for action by national governments. Of course, we are here witnessing late modernity partnering religious consciousness on such issues. The moral imperative of both modernity and religion are here one and the same. Where young adult core and some intermediate Catholics are concerned, there is not much sign of a diminution of a religious social conscience, even if traditional Catholic ethnic and class identities have disappeared. This could be an indication that a modern religious consciousness aids citizenship values: but it would need testing by comparing them with a group of secular young adults of otherwise similar home and class background and education.

If the sacred is spread more widely across the canvas of human action than the secular-religious divide provides for, what of the traditional internal religious linking of the organisational church? Certain trends are undeniable, particularly the gap between the institutional church's position on personal morality and the views and practices of most young believers. This gap is most apparent in the contrast between our young people's sense of personal responsibility for moral judgements and the continuing Vatican drive to enforce its own external moral authority in areas such as sexuality and human life. The reality appears to be that individual conscience has displaced external authority in the matter of social and personal ethics and that personal experience itself is used to uncover norms of conduct. Individuals then refer to whatever they know of the official church's position to see if it is any help in clarifying their judgement. For young modern Catholics, morality has become internal first and external only second. There is no doubt that the present generation of young adult Catholics and former Catholics varies significantly from their forebears. They are significantly more 'protestant' in their outlook and much less distinct from their secular counterparts than previous generations and will do what they feel is right and proper rather than what has been announced by the Pope.

Our concern here is to understand the significance of religion for those who still believe and practise. As a folk, national or ethnic religion, Catholicism has declined numerically in our culturally plural countries and is likely to diminish further in our monopoly Catholic countries. But despite the difficulty of finding them in church on Sundays, there are still young adults who are committed and want to hand on their faith to their children when they come along. But whether their children will experience the same depth of conviction as their parents is debatable. There is no longer the massive support provided by external forces of ethnic identity, the sin cycle of yesteryear, the high sacrality of Latin liturgy or the novenas, rosaries and other devotions which saturated church activities for the first 65 years of the twentieth century. If and when religion is passed on seems to be an issue decided only partly in the family, sometimes reinforced in school, and sometimes only decided upon in early adulthood. From then on it is sustained by individual commitment, but with some 'community' extensions that reinforce belief and galvanise moral and social action. While these community experiences have to be chosen – they do not usually arise automatically in everyday life and require making time – we have seen that many young people are choosing them: Sunday church celebrations, group meetings, pilgrimages, sodalities both old and new and friendships. Also, it is true that only some of them go out of their way to espouse causes, movements and organisations against abortion in particular. But they are environmentally aware, have their own standards in sexual behaviour, and are strongly supportive in the main of life issues. The more progressive equally stand by the right to act according to personal conscience, placing caveats on authoritarian and other social pressures, as well as opposing, for example, the use of criminalisation against those who have the burden of choice in moral matters. It does seem that semi-autonomy and personal responsibility do figure together for these young religious and moral people, including the majority of former Catholics, though many of the latter do stress freedom more than responsibility. However, the person-based religion of the majority, linked in with various forms of religious community celebrations, has become a bearer for a new social type of religion that is very difficult to define beyond certain minimal aspects. For want of a better word, let us call it *late modern religion*, and see if we can describe it further.

One thing is clear: there is a fusing of messages which originate on the one hand from the surrounding secular social world of late modernity and on the other from the tradition and actuality of Roman Catholicism. Some origins are unclear. They might come from humanistic and humanitarian sources that end up triggering conscience and consciousness to the sphere of the generally religious, or Christian, or even specifically Catholic religious themes and sensibilities. Whereas, at one time, the authority of the clergy and pressure of local face-to-face community would have often provided a ready-made prescription for action, today it is more likely that such themes come from a range of sources and in much weaker form, and that, in the religious sphere at least, the subject must motivate the self and deliberately listen to their influence.

This need for self-motivation in the strictly religious sphere is not necessarily replicated in moral matters. One could argue, as in chapter 1, that the moral sphere is simply there for everyone, and no functioning society has ever been found where morality has not been articulated (see Colin Turnbull 1972, for a society collapsing in on itself also morally as a result of famine). But this argument does not necessarily have to be made here. For, contrary to popular belief and the much-heralded message that 'anything goes' in today's environment, there *are* moral principles throughout our prevailing popular cultures, whether enunciated through mass media or mediated by social interaction, that face people when their judgement and decision making are required. People talk of being respected and respecting others, of not interfering in other people's lives. They also know when people are going 'off the rails', who the dangerous people are and not just fear but recognise the evils of rape, murder, public disorder and mayhem, and the massive evil of genocide. In terms of the field of personal and interpersonal morality, moral consciousness is sensitised by the vast array of TV soaps positively laying bare the moral dilemmas of cheating, lying and doing damage to other people. Of course the script writers turn and twist the characters in an almost schizophrenic way to squeeze out all the moral angles and dilemmas of personal existence, and in this sense they caricature life. But young people, just like the old, do talk about the dramatis personae and their good and evil ways, and discuss their weaknesses and impossible situations.

For young adults, who have come through the years of puberty, but who also experience greater forms of dependency in all our countries than their parents' generation, 'settling down' now involves a larger slice of their life than previously. Half of our young adults have not entered the job market and most are still unmarried. It was therefore not surprising that the majority of the research team found it difficult to fill their quotas of married and partnered life histories. Social commentators on youth find an association between the uncertainties that lack of settlement produces and the tendency to risk-taking and breaking moral codes characteristic of the young. For example, research has pointed out that over half the crime committed in many of our western countries can be attributed to the 14–25 age group. Additionally, in Britain, while at the end of the 1970s the 14–17 age group had the highest crime rate, this wooden spoon award moved by the end of the 1980s to the 18–20 age group. This is precisely at the end of the period where this shift in insecurity up the age structure was taking place (Furlong and Cartmel 1997: 86–7).

We would expect such insecurities to pass on to the field of morality even for practising Catholics. And this is what we find in the data. But, then, in a society such as ours, negotiating a possible relationship with the opposite sex does not have marriage as a proximate end in view. For most people in their early twenties, this is simply not financially feasible, because of work insecurity. It is also true that many of those seeking a partner in the intermediate term simply cannot find a partner who would put up with the financial insecurities. Consequently in Britain, there are as many lonely single people as partnered people in this age group and, as we have previously pointed out, there is a growth of steady partnerships on entering the post-24 age stage. This is probably as true of practising Catholics as the rest of our population. To quote one priest, 'all of the couples getting married in the parish this summer have been cohabiting for some time. Today, cohabitation is so widely accepted' (Pastor Ignotus 1999). In terms of the moral quality of life therefore, the evidence points more towards the existence for the majority of a liminal, and either difficult or exciting phase of life – in some case all three – that young people are forced to go through, rather than a period of abandonment of body and emotions to the fleshpots of pleasure, though some young adults do precisely that. Uncertainty and experimentation do not amount in themselves to a practical philosophy of hedonism.

Clearly, some of the basic conditions of life for our young Catholics are imposed by the state of our late modern economies or, in the Polish case, by the state of an economy too quickly abandoned to the spirit of the market after over 40 years of a Communist command economy. Our societies have also been pluralised by ethnic migration and greater freedom of expression. The resultant cultures permit a wide range of beliefs and practices, but also aim at personal inviolability and respect for the rights of others. Of course, other cultural forces tend to 'dumb down' diversity and standardise taste: at least that is where the mass markets are (Ritzer 1993). This is one of the key contemporary environments within which religious persons have to work out their moral existence. What we are seeing in our countries is young adult Catholics doing precisely that. From whatever national background they come, they work on what the world gives them, unifying their decisions into a biographical trajectory that is ever sustained by the faith and trust they have developed over the period of their growth to young adulthood. Making up their basic trust and faith are their faith and trust in God, in the religious and moral principles they have been establishing, in their way of life, and in the people and society which surrounds them, even if they often fail through either bad faith or genuine error. This modern faith and trust is not syncretism, unless by that term one means what human beings have always had to do: make sense of the world in which they live or withdraw from it for either an hermitic or sectarian lifestyle. Religion does not become one's own unless one makes sense of it for one's personal and social life, in other words unless one interprets one's cultural surroundings in the light of religious faith and chooses the good from the bad and the sense from the nonsense. There are no other fully human alternatives. Being part of a religious community still means keeping in touch with fellow believers by regular face-to-face encounters, prayers and celebrations, rather than living within a sect-like structure separated out from the world. The modern life synthesis of culture and religion is still founded on the personal-community axis of experience, with all the joint reading of religious symbols and personal encounters this involves. But it is also underpinned by late-modern sources of faith and trust as well as the more narrowly religious sources: personal relationships of family and friendship on the one hand, scripture, sacrament, prayer and religious community on the other.

In sum, we have been able to answer a number of the questions we listed on the first page of the chapter. The first of these was: to what extent and in what way does late modernity affect the religious and moral consciousness and outlook of young adult Catholics and former Catholics? We have answered that it tends to remove authority and social pressure as resources for religious behaviour, and the taken-for-granted supposition of a sacred world to which we are externally and socially responsible. It replaces them instead with a focus on individual purpose and personal responsibility for one's own beliefs and values, and requires both a more personal relationship link with the sacred and also the experience of supportive networks to provide a sense of belonging to a religious-motivated community. We have seen that religion is alive in both the context of the private individual faith and moral experience as well as in the social-faith (church) and social-moral (humanistic and environmental) field of real and imagined (worldwide human) community. Moral consciousness has not disappeared but, in the field of personal relationships and sexuality, is far more based on individual judgement than ever before. In the social field it is ever more based on an increasing humanism promoted by modernity and turned by it into a sacred value, one which is consecrated by the subject's own perception of religious faith and reinforced by whatever Catholic social teaching has got through. Religion may exist on the surface of the lives of many intermediate Catholics, but for others and for all core Catholics it is profoundly rooted. This rooting does not depend on everyday life experience, though it has benefited in most individuals from being established within the basic ontological trust system they have acquired in primary socialisation. The deep roots are mostly the result of the extra efforts they have made to chart a religious trajectory through life. It is consequently far more likely to be resilient and not to disappear when people change their cultural milieu. In this sense, late modern religion travels well. But the extent in numbers of such a faith and morality is limited. Going, or already gone, are the days of an ethnic religion, unless by reason of ethnic conflict they continue.

So have even religious people become materialistic, shorn of the perception of the supernatural and the spiritual? The answer is that it varies. The core may be morally frail and do not always live up to the standards they desire to achieve. But they are religious stalwarts in their perception and choices. The intermediate vary. And one sometimes finds deeply spiritual and altruistic people among the former Catholics. Losing faith in God does not mean people necessarily lose their commitment to a better world or to the personal happiness of those they meet or seek to encounter on life's way. Then again, what do we mean by 'materialistic'? The term is commonly used to describe pleasure-seekers and the selfish. But it can mean being forced to pursue money because one has none and therefore cannot provide for loved ones. The phrase 'post-material age' refers to the contention by Maslow (1954, 1968) and later by Inglehart (1977, 1990) that in advanced industrial society an increasing number of people will be (Maslow) or have been (Inglehart) freed from the constant preoccupation with money for survival, and can turn their interests to the more spiritual things of culture and self-fulfilment. Unfortunately the real Western world, even the most advanced, still has between a third and a half of its people living in the thrall of financial uncertainty. Leaving behind self-indulgence or money-grabbing materialism for post-material goals is for others, and not for the poor and insecure. Our samples give indications of these realities, but most of our materialists are compelled to seek money for the sake of survival, and most of our post-materialists are religiously committed, with only some focused on cultural as opposed to religious values, as in the case of part of the Italian sample.

THE FUTURE OF CATHOLICISM
IN THE WESTERN WORLD

We now turn to the last major issue of this final chapter. With the changes in Catholicism that appear in the lives of young adults, are we seeing the end of Catholicism in the West? Or can it survive and even expand in the future? Has the Catholic Church as an organisation promoted its own downfall? Or has it or can it develop a plan for a successful future? Up to what point can changes in the structure of the institution strengthen or weaken the Catholicism of its people? Has the development of secularity already put paid to whatever methods it tries?

Predicting the future is a risky business. Hence, sociologists like to speak of trends, and social policy analysts indicate the likely outcomes of particular strategies or forms of social engineering. Predicting the future in the case of religion is doubly dangerous. Not only might the trends be misconceived, but also charismatic leaders and events might totally change the political or religious landscape. As Weber rightly noted, both politics and religion were, at least in the past, supercharged with potential for the radical change of their societies: 'Within the sphere of its claims, charismatic authority repudiates the past, and is in this sense a revolutionary force'. It can produce a life reorientation 'born out of suffering, conflicts, or enthusiasm. It may then result in a radical alteration of the central attitudes and direction of action with a completely new orientation of all attitudes toward the different problems of "the world"'(1978: 244–5).

So while we might be involved in late modern living, with its apparent orderly and rationalised economy and bureaucracies, we might still be threatened or destroyed by an international stock market collapse, a sudden ethnic war, a nuclear explosion or fallout engineered by terrorists, or the release of deadly bacteria or gas by a religious or political fanatic or sect – perhaps the most likely way for humankind to disappear off the face of the earth. And why may it not be possible for a sudden religious movement to appear that takes the world, or a huge section of it, by storm on the back of some major human disaster? Perhaps not in the West, one might say. If not, what are the possibilities of change if churches and their believers are left to their own devices of reviving charisma within their own midst? What likely directions might religion take in such circumstances?

We mentioned above that the present generation of young adult core Catholics and many intermediate ones are likely to persist in their faith throughout their lives. However, survival of Catholicism in the long term in the West does not depend on the fidelity to death of these believers, but on having others to replace them when they die. In the past century, the largest single cause of Catholicism's growth in the West has been migration, particularly in the English speaking countries. With the exception of Latino growth in the US, this source of Catholic population renewal has been switched off, and Catholic populations have been left to their own devices. The traditional additional 'method' of religious population renewal has been larger than average families and the religious socialisation of offspring: 'handing on the faith' as catechists say, or 'religious transmission' as sociologists have recently called it. Though we have few statistical indicators on this matter, the general impression of priests and core laity wherever one goes is that more of their children distance themselves from Catholicism than stay close. If this is the case for core Catholic parents, how worse might it be for others?

But parents might be consoled by the fact that even in the last century and earlier decades of this century, 'handing on the faith' only ever worked in conditions of ethnic-type separation of Catholics from the host community, or in situations of Catholic monopoly control of mainly rural populations. It was never successful among the urban-industrial populations of Catholic Europe. It might be argued that a 'genuine' Catholic school system could bring about a 'Catholic revival' simply by doing their job of education, catechesis and worship better than at present. This is a possibility, and believers might hope that a renewed church and school structure might be able to achieve such a goal. But it certainly has never worked in the past, and even those within the schools cannot see a return to a form of separatist evangelism. This strategy, along-side the renewal of the parish as a religious community, is the one in which the present church leadership in Europe puts its faith. If one talks to bishops about it, they clearly are not too hopeful in human terms, but hang on to it as the 'only hope' barring divine intervention.

There are, however, other problems, which go beyond those of schooling, but do affect parish renewal. One of these is Vatican teaching on contraception, which may in itself have been a major cause for the loss of Catholics in the late 1970s and throughout the 1980s. A second is church discipline on divorce, with remarried Catholics being marginalised and having little hope of 'religious renewal' for themselves within their church even if they want it. It also looks as if the divorce rate for Catholics is similar to that of the rest of the population. The Roman Catholic Church's rules themselves thus operate a social closure, one about which even many priests are worried. The same could be said of the loss of quality human resources through the resignation of priests who wish to marry, and the return of men and women religious to the ranks of the laity for the same reasons. It is not uncommon for all three groups of people, and numbers of homosexuals and lesbians, to suffer exclusion from mainline church activity. Clearly, together with the prohibition of female clergy, such practices militate against inclusivity and possibilities of expansion rather than retraction. It may well be that English-speaking countries are more likely to follow the pattern in mainland European countries with regard to Catholic practice, one of steady decline at least for the foreseeable future. The only relevant question in such a scenario is if such a decline could be slowed down or even stemmed with or without the end of such exclusions.

This reflection brings us to a major issue. Is there anything the Catholic Church can actively do to reverse its western decline, which the presence of core young adult Catholics only delays? The state of 'the world' has always been a sorry one for religious virtuosi and the present western one is only different because an aura of enchantment does not automatically cover its institutions or the physical world that surrounds it. The dilemma for the Catholic Church's leadership, as with any major denomination, is who to include and who to exclude, and not just in terms of laity but also of those who would be candidates for its ministries. Are decentralisation, enculturation, partial democratisation and the use of regular Councils – the main items of church reform for progressive Roman Catholics – appropriate measures for the development of a church appropriate to contemporary western societies?

There would be no certainty of success in taking a leap into such reformation-type decisions. The right wing of the Church would threaten schism, but would have to accept the decision, provided that they were allowed to hold on to their practices within the structures of a more pluralist church. The sociologists that support a thoroughgoing secular-isation model of contemporary religious institutions would predict that this new liberalism would eventually disassemble the Catholic Church, just as it did to mainstream Protestant churches. However, there would remain the possibility that another interpretation could be right: that by so doing the Roman Catholic Church might have just converted itself to a new type of organised religious movement, on the way to reinventing itself as a relevant source of religious power in the world of the twenty-first century.

Changes in the institutions of Catholicism are possible. But their out-comes, as with most major changes in the modern world, are unpredictable. The major sources of change in religion have been either through the growth of new religious movements, both internal and external, or through reformation. At the moment, the Vatican policy is to facilitate only those movements which do not threaten the present internal organisational structure: in other words only those that keep the male and celibate priesthood of the Latin Rite intact, and preserve the dominance of the Papacy, the Vatican dicasteries and the diplomatic corps structure. Religious liberation movements, particularly the base community move-ment inspired by liberation theologies and spiritualities, have been either squeezed out or come under the control of the Vatican or conservative local bishops, many of whom have been Vatican replacements for liberation-friendly bishops.

It is not that things have stayed the same since the 1960s. Roman Catholicism has seen considerable internal religious change in the West over the century. The development of Catholic political consciousness pushed elite lay members more and more into the arena of national and international politics. Their most powerful expressions were in the Kennedy phenomenon in the US and in the building of the European Union, founded on a Catholic dream and on the Catholic principle of subsidiarity. Also, in many countries, experiments with multiple ministries have taken place, as lay people, both men and women, have replaced priests in many parish-related duties. There has been a shift in Catholic consciousness partly away from the clerical caste mentality, and towards Luther's understanding of 'the calling', a vocational consciousness affecting all aspects of life, thus elevating the lay and married states, though even these have had limited success with the tendency to reassert clerical dominance via liturgical and organisational practices embodying clerical superiority. So far reform has been a semiconscious movement towards modernity by the Roman Catholic Church. The biggest move in this democratisation of ministries has been the ordination to the diaconate of married men particularly in the US and UK, but only because of 'priest shortage' and not for ideological reasons. Perhaps a radical decentralisation of the church, with the papacy only retaining extraordinary powers over local-national hierarchies, would be of assistance in permitting a more genuine enculturation of the church, and the development of local canonical traditions. Even that would involve a major experience of charisma if it were to take place. It is certainly something that Anglo-Saxon young adult Catholics want to happen. In fact some of them have to turn away from continuing full-time ministries of evangelisation in the Church and move into schoolteaching or other vocations, as the church structures do not provide them with a vocational path that would allow them a wage sufficient to raise a family.

Such a decentralisation would, however, be only half the story if Roman Catholicism were to have a chance of turning round its progressive western decline. For young Catholics, and many older ones, pay little attention already to papal statements and interventions, as we have seen in the present volume. The Catholic culture that has developed in the West over the last 40 years of the twentieth century implies semi-autonomous intellectual and moral autonomy as essential for survival in late modernity. The variety of lifestyles we have found is directly related to this core fact and value. To tell the truth, the real power of the hierarchical church has already been defused and decentred. The present holders of clerical positions will have to adjust to this new situation if they are to perform any real religious function for their lay believers, as indeed a number of priests and bishops are already doing, but by themselves and with stealth.

Some of the means for bridging the clerical-lay divide were, of course, already suggested by the Second Vatican Council: greater collegiality, dialogue and diffusion of authority. To these should be added the use of new technologies for decentring the management of the Catholic Church from a top-bottom Roman bureaucracy model towards a web-network society, and the further development of local team ministries, with priesthood itself becoming part of the sharing. But change on this scale appears a pious hope as we begin a new millennium. God only knows what lies in store for the Roman Catholic Church and for those inside it of all ages and conditions who wish to see it prosper in religious terms.

REFERENCES

Abela, A. M. (1991). *Transmitting Values in European Malta: A Study in the Contemporary Values of Modern Society.* Rome and Valletta: Editrice Pontificia Università Gregoriana.

Abela, A. M. (1992). *Changing Youth Culture in Malta.* Valletta: Social Values Studies.

Abela, A. M. (1994). *Shifting Family Values: A Western European Perspective.* Malta: Discern, Institute for Research on Signs of the Times.

Abela, A. M. (1995). 'Youth, Religion and Community Care in Malta'. *Social Compass.* 42: 59–67.

Abela, A. M. (1996). *Il-Harsien Socjali fis-Snin Disghin: l-Ewwel Rapport.* Msida: Institute of Social Welfare, University of Malta.

Abela, A. M. (1998). *Secularised Sexuality: Youth Values in a City-island.* Valletta: Social Values Studies.

Archer, A. (1986). *The Two Catholic Churches: A Study in Oppression.* London: SCM.

Ashford, S. and Timms, N. (1992). *What Europe Thinks: A Study of Western European Values.* Aldershot: Dartmouth Press.

Atkinson, R. (1998). *The Life Story Interview.* London: Sage.

Barker, E. (1997). 'But Who's Going to Win? National and Minority Religions in Post-Communist Society'. In I. Borowik and G. Babinski (eds): 25–63.

Bauman, Z. (1996). 'From Pilgrim to Tourist – or a Short History of Identity'. In Stuart Hall and Paul du Gay (eds). *Questions of Cultural Identity.* London: Sage: 18–36.

Beck, U. (1992). *Risk Society: Towards a New Modernity.* London: Sage. [1988. *Risikogesellschaft.* Frankfurt: Suhrkamp]

Beck, U. and Beck-Gernsheim, E. (1995). *The Normal Chaos of Love.* Cambridge: Polity.

Beck, U., Giddens, A. and Lash, S. (1994). *Reflexive Modernisation: Politics, Tradition and Aesthetics in the Modern Social Order.* Cambridge: Polity.

Bellah, R. N., Madsen, R., Sullivan, W. M., Swidler, A. and Tipton, S. M. (1985). *Habits of the Heart: Individualism and Commitment in American Life.* Berkeley: University of California Press.

Bertaux, D. and Thompson, P. (1997). *Pathways to Social Class: A Qualitative Approach to Social Mobility.* Oxford: Clarendon.

Bianchi, E. C. and Ruether, R.R. (1992). *A Democratic Catholic Church.* New York: Crossroads.

Blasi, A. J. (1995). 'On the Social Affinity Between Religion and Values: A Multidisciplinary Consideration'. In L. Tomasi (ed.): 29–65.

Boissevain, J. (1965). *Saints and Fireworks: Religion and Politics in Rural Malta.* London: Athlone Press.

Borowik, I. (1996). 'Religion and Sexual Values in Poland'. *Journal of Contemporary Religion.* 1: 89–94.

Borowik, I. (1997a). *Procesy instytucjonalizacji i prywatyzacji religii w powojennej Polsce.* (The processes of institutionalisation and privatisation of religion in post-war Poland). Kraków: Wydawnictwo UJ.

Borowik I. (1997b). 'Institutional and Private Religion in Poland 1990–1994'. In I. Borowik and G. Babinski (eds).: 235–57.

Borowik, I. and Babinski, G. (eds). (1997). *New Religious Phenomena in Central and Eastern Europe.* Kraków: NOMOS.

Breen, R., Hannan, D.F., Rottmann, D. and Whelan, C. (1990). *Understanding Contemporary Ireland.* Dublin: Gill & Macmillan.

Breslin, A. and Weafer, J. (1985). *Religious Beliefs, Practice and Moral Attitudes: a comparison of two Irish surveys 1974–1984.* Maynooth: CRD Report No. 21.

Brierley, P. (1994). *UK Christian Handbook.* London: Evangelical Alliance.

Bruce, S. (1995). *Religion in Modern Britain.* Oxford: Oxford University Press.

Brunetta, G. and Longo, A. (eds). (1991). *Italia cattolica: Fede e politica religiosa negli anni Novanta.* Firenze: Vallecchi.

Bynner, J., Ferri, E. and Shepherd, P. (eds). (1997). *Twenty-Something in the 1990s.* Ashgate Press.

Camilleri, R. (1999). 'Pentecost!' in *The Sunday Times.* Malta. 23 May: 14.

Campiche, R.J. (1993). 'Jeunes et religions ou le déclin des identités confessionelles'. *Informationes Theologiae Europeae.* 2: 181–96.

Campiche, R.J. (ed.). (1995). *Cultures jeunes et religion en Europe.* Paris: Cerf.

Campiche, R., Dubach, A., Bovay, C., Kruggeler, M. and Voll, P. (1992). *Croire en Suisse(s).* Lausanne: l'Age d'Homme.

Casanova, J. (1995). *Public Religions in the Modern World.* Chicago: University of Chicago Press.

Castelli, J. and Gremillion, J. (1987). *The Emerging Parish: The Notre Dame Study of Catholic Life Since Vatican II.* San Francisco: Harper & Row.

Catholic Directory for England and Wales. (1998). London: Burns & Oates.

Central Office of Statistics. (1998). *Abstract of Statistics 1996.* Malta: Central Office of Statistics.

Cesareo, V., Cipriani, R., Garelli, F., Lanzetti, C. and Rovati, G. (1995). *La religiosità degli italiani.* Milano: Mondadori.

Chirban, J.T. (1996). *Interviewing in Depth: The Interactive-Relational Approach.* London: Sage.

Cimino, R. P. (1997). *Against The Stream: The Adoption of Traditional Christian Faiths by Young Adults.* Lanham, MD: University Press of America and Religious Watch.

Coles, B. (1995). *Youth and Social Policy: Youth Citizenship and Young Careers.* London: UCL Press.

Constitution of Ireland. (1937). *Bunreacht na hÉireann.* Dublin: Government Publications.

Crook, S., Pakulski, J. and Walters, M. (1992). *Postmodernization: Change in Advanced Society.* London: Sage.

Curtice, J. and Gallagher, T. (1991). 'The Northern Irish Dimension'. In *British Social Attitudes: the 7th Report*: 183–216.

D'Antonio, W. D. (1994). 'Autonomy and Democracy in an Autocratic Organization; the case of the Roman Catholic Church'. *Sociology of Religion.* 55: 379–96.

D'Antonio, W.V., Davidson, J.D., Hoge, D.R. and Wallace, R. (1989). *American Catholic Laity in a Changing Church.* Kansas City, MO: Sheed & Ward.

D'Antonio, W. D., Davidson, J. D., Hoge, D. R. and Wallace, R. (1995). *Laity: American and Catholic: Transforming the Church.* Kansas City, MO: Sheed & Ward.

Davidson, J.D. et. al. (1997). *The Search for Common Ground: What Unites and Divides American Catholics.* Huntington Indiana: Our Sunday Visitor Press.

Davie, G. (1994). *Religion in Britain Since 1945.* Oxford: Blackwell.

Davis, J.A. and Smith, T. (1996). *General Social Survey Cumulative Codebook: 1973–96.* Storrs: Roper Center.

DEMOS. (1995). 'The Time Squeeze'. Special issue of *Demos Quarterly.* 5.

Diaz-Stevens, A. M. and Stevens-Arroyo, A. M. (1998). *Recognizing the Latino Resurgence in U.S. Religion: The Emmaus Paradigm.* Oxford: Westview Press.

Dobbelaere, K. and Voyé, L. (1992). 'D'une Religion composée à une religion recomposée'. In L. Voyé et al. (eds). *Belges heureux et satisfaits.* Brussels: De Boeck.

Dolan J. P. (1985). *The American Catholic Experience: A History From Colonial Times To The Present.* New York: Doubleday.

Donati, P. and Colozzi, I. (1997). (eds). *Giovani e generazioni. Quando si cresce in una società eticamente neutra.* Bologna: Mulino.

Drudy, S. and Lynch, K. (1993). *Schools and Society in Ireland.* Dublin: Gill & Macmillan.

Dudley, R.L. and Muthersbaugh, H.P. (1996). 'Social Attachment to Religious Institutions among Young Adults'. *Review of Religious Research.* 38: 38–50.

Dwyer, J.A. (ed.). (1994). *The New Dictionary of Catholic Social Thought.* Collegeville, MN: The Liturgical Press.

Elzo, J., Andrés Orizo, F., Gonzalez Blasco, P. and del Valle, A.I. (1994). *Jóvenes Españoles 94.* Madrid: Ediciones SM.

Ester, P., de Moor, R. and Halman, L. (eds). (1993). *The Individualising Society: Value Change in Europe and North America.* Tilburg: Tilburg University Press.

Faraday, A. and Plummer, K. (1979). 'Doing Life Histories'. *Sociological Review.* 27: 773–98.

Fulton, J. (1997). 'Modernity and Religious Change in Western Roman Catholicism: Two Contrasting Paradigms'. *Social Compass.* 44: 115–29.

Fulton, J. (1999). 'Young Adult Core Catholics'. In M. P. Hornsby-Smith (ed.). *Catholics in England and Wales 1950–2000: Historical and Sociological Perspectives.* London: Cassell: 161–81.

Fulton, J. (2000). 'Contemporary Young Adult Catholics in England: Faith and Education'. In M. Eaton, J. Longmore and A. Naylor (eds), *Commitment to Diversity: Catholics and Education in a Changing World.* London: Cassell: 385–401.

Fulton, J. and Dowling, T. (1998). 'Society and Belief Today: Roman Catholic Young Adults in Britain and Ireland'. *Informationes Theologiae Europeae:* 253–69.

Furlong, A. and Cartmel, F. (1997). *Young People and Social Change: Individualisation and Risk in Late Modernity.* Milton Keynes: Open University Press.

Gallup, G. Jr and Castelli, J. (1987). *The American Catholic People*. Garden City, NY: Doubleday

Ganado, H. (1974). *Rajt Malta Tinbidel (1900–1969)*. 4 Vols. Malta.

Garelli, F. (1996). *Forza della religione e debolezza della fede*. Bologna: Il Mulino.

Gee, P. and Fulton, J. (eds). (1991). *Religion and Power: Decline and Growth*. London: BSA Sociology of Religion Study Group.

Geertz, C. (1973). 'Religion as a Cultural System'. In *The Interpretation of Cultures*. New York: Basic Books.

Giddens, A. (1990). *The Consequences of Modernity*. Cambridge: Polity.

Giddens, A. (1991). *Modernity and Self-Identity*. Cambridge: Polity.

Giddens, A. (1992). *The Transformation of Intimacy: Love, Sexuality and Eroticism in Modern Societies*. Cambridge: Polity.

Grabowska, M. (1992). 'L'Eglise de Pologne a un tournant'. In P. Michel (ed.). *Les Religions à l'Est*. Paris: Cerf: 109–29.

Greeley, A.M. (1977). *The American Catholic*. New York: Basic Books.

Greeley, A.M. (1990). *The Catholic Myth: The Behaviour and Beliefs of American Catholics*. New York: Charles Scribners.

Greeley, A.M. and Hout, M. (1997). 'The People Cry Reform'. *The Tablet*. 1997: 388–90.

Grundmann, H. (1995). *Religious Movements in the Middle Ages*. London: Notre Dame Press.

Grzymala-Moszczynska, H. (1991). 'Worldview Orientations Among Polish Youth'. In Gee and Fulton (eds): 67–77.

Heelas, P. (1996). *The New Age Movement*. Oxford: Blackwell.

Herberg, W. (1960). *Protestant – Catholic – Jew*. Garden City, NY: Doubleday.

Hervieu-Léger, D. (1993a). *La Religion pour Mémoire*. Paris: Cerf.

Hervieu-Léger, D. (1993b). 'Present-Day Emotional Renewals: the End of Secularisation or the End of Religion?' In William H. Swatos Jr (ed.). *A Future for Religion? New Paradigms for Social Analysis*. London: Sage: 129–48.

Hoge, D. (1981). *Converts, Dropouts, Returnees: A Study of Religious Change Among Catholics*. New York: Pilgrim Press.

Hoge, D. (1986). 'Interpreting Change in American Catholicism: the River and the Floodgates'. *Review of Religious Research*. 27:4

Hornsby-Smith, M. P. (1987). *Roman Catholics in England: Studies in Social Structure Since the Second World War*. Cambridge: Cambridge University Press.

Hornsby-Smith, M. P. (1989). *The Changing Parish: A Study of Parishes, Priests and Parishioners after Vatican II*. London: Routledge.

Hornsby-Smith, M. P. (1991). *Roman Catholic Beliefs in England: Customary Catholicism and Transformations of Religious Authority*. Cambridge: Cambridge University Press.

Hornsby-Smith, M. P. and Whelan, C. T. (1994). 'Religion and Moral Values'. In C. Whelan (ed): 7–44.

Hornsby-Smith, M. P., Fulton, J. and Norris, M. (1995). *The Politics of Spirituality: A Study of a Renewal Process in an English Diocese*. Oxford: Clarendon.

Hutton, W. (1995). *The State We're In*. London: Cape.

Inglehart, R. (1977). *The Silent Revolution: Changing Values and Political Styles Among Western Publics*. Princeton, N.J.: Princeton University Press.

Inglehart, R. (1988). *Culture Shift in Advanced Industrial Society*. Princeton, N.J.: Princeton University Press.

Inglis, T. (1988). *Moral Monopoly: The Catholic Church in Modern Irish Society*. Dublin: Gill & Macmillan.

Johnston, H. (1992). 'Religious Nationalism: Six Propositions from Eastern Europe and the Former Soviet Union'. In B. Misztal and A. Shupe (eds). *Religion and Politics in Comparative Perspective*. Westport, CT: Praeger: 67–79.

Jones, G. and Wallace, C. (1992). *Youth, Family and Citizenship*. Buckingham: Open University Press.

Josselson, R. and Lieblich, A. (eds). (1995). *Interpreting Experience: The Narrative Study of Lives*. Vol. 3. London: Sage.

Kennedy, E. (1990). *Tomorrow's Catholics, Yesterday's Church*. New York: Harper & Row.

Kenny, M. (1997). *Goodbye to Catholic Ireland*. London: Sinclair Stevenson.

Koseła K. (1995). 'Religia przy tablicy- postawy wobec religii w szkołach'. (Religion next to the blackboard – attitudes towards religion in school). In K. Kiciński, K. Koseła and W. Pawlik (eds). *Szkoła czy parafia? Nauka religii w szkole w świetle badań socjologicznych*. (School or parish? Teaching religion in the light of sociological research). Kraków: NOMOS: 89–123.

Kungress tal-Lajci. (1987). *Lajci '86: Is-Sejha tal-Knisja fil-Knisja u fid-Dinja (10–16 ta' Novembru, 1986)*. rapport minn J. Aloisio. Malta: KDAL/KDZ.

Lambert, Y. and Michelat, G. (eds). (1992). *Crépuscules des religions sur les jeunes? Jeunes et Religion en France*. Paris: L'Harmattan.

Littwin, Susan 1986. *The Postponed Generation: Why America's Grown Up Kids Are Growing Up Later*. New York: Wm. Morrow.

Luckmann, T. (1967). *The Invisible Religion*. New York: Macmillan.

Luckmann, T. (1995). 'Morals in Communicative Process'. In Luigi Tomasi (ed.): 19–28.

Lyotard, J-F. (1984). *The Postmodern Condition*. Manchester: Manchester University Press.

MacGréil, M. (1991). *Religious Belief and Practice in Ireland: A Sociological Survey*. Maynooth: Dept of Sociology.

Mach, Z. (1997). 'The Roman Catholic Church and the Transformation of Social Identity in Eastern and Central Europe'. In I. Borowik and G. Babinski (eds): 63–81.

Maffesoli, M. (1995). *The Time of The Tribes: The Decline of Individualism in Mass Societies*. London: Sage. [*Le temps des tribus* (1988) Paris: Le Livre de Poche].

Malta Human Development Report 1996. (1997). Malta: UNDP, Media Centre Print.

Mariański, J. (1991). *Kondycja religijna i moralna młodych Polaków* (Religious and moral values of young Poles). Kraków: NOMOS.

Mariański, J. (1995). *Młodzież między tradycją i ponowoczesnością* (Youth between tradition and postmodernity). Lublin: Wydawnictwo KUL.

Market Research Bureau of Ireland (MRBI). (1998). 'Prime Time Survey (RTÉ)'. *The Irish Times*. 2 February 1998.

Martin, D. (1978). *A General Theory of Secularization*. London: Harper & Row.

Maslow, A.H. (1954). *Motivation and Personality*. New York: Harper.

Maslow, A.H. (1964). *Religion, Values and Peak-Experiences*. Columbus, OH: Ohio State University Press.

McNamara, P.H. (1992). *Conscience First, Tradition Second: A Study of Young American Catholics*. Albany: State University of New York Press.

Michel, P. (1994). 'Religion, Communism, and Democracy in Central Europe: The Polish Case'. In W.H. Swatos, Jr (ed.). *Politics and Religion in Central and Eastern Europe. Traditions and Transitions*. London: Praeger: 119–33.

Michelat, G., Potel, J., Sutter, J. and Maître, J. (1991). *Les Français sont-ils encore catholiques?* Paris: Cerf.

Mills, C.W. (1940). 'Situated Actions and Vocabularies of Motive'. *American Science Review*. 5: 905–13.

Mizzi O'Reilly, S. (1982). 'Women in Senglea: The Changing Role of Urban, Working Class Women in Malta'. Ann Arbor MI: University Micro Films. PhD dissertation, State University of N.Y. at Stony Brook.

Morawska, E. (1987). 'Civil Religion vs State Power in Poland'. In T. Robbins and R. Robertson (eds). *Church-State Relations: Tensions and Transitions*. New Brunswick, N.J.: Transaction Press: 221–32.

Nic Ghiolla Phádraig, M. (1976). 'Religion in Ireland'. *Social Studies*. 5: 116–29. Maynooth.

Nic Ghiolla Phádraig, M. (1986). 'Religious Practice and Secularisation'. In P. Clancy et al. (eds). *Ireland: A Sociological Profile*. Dublin: Institute of Public Administration:

Nowicka, E. (1997). 'Roman Catholicism and the Content of "Polishness"'. In: I. Borowik and G. Babinski (eds): 81–93.

Pace, E. (1998). 'I giovani del Veneto: dalla religione di nascita alla ricerca di nuove spiritualità'. In L. Tomasi (ed.): 57–74.

Pakulski, J. (1997). Cultural Citizenship'. *Citizenship Studies*. 1: 73–86.

Parks, S. (1986). *The Critical Years: The Young Adult in Search for a Faith to Live By*. Harper & Row.

Parliamentary Secretary for Women's Rights. (1998). 'White Paper: Proposals for amendments to Maltese legislation for the better protection of victims of domestic violence'. Malta: Office of the Prime Minister.

Pasek, Z. (1998). 'Wykaz zarejestrowanych w Polsce związków religijnych ułożony według tradycji religijnych. Stan na 1.1.1998r'. in *Kwartalnik Religioznawczy*. 22/23: 107–117.

Pastor Ignotus. (1999). 'Pastor Ignotus'. *The Tablet*. 3 July: 1924.

Pawlik, W. (1995). 'The Church and Its Critics: The Spell of the Polish Ombudsman'. *Polish Sociological Review*. 1.

Piwowarski, W. (1996). *Socjologia religii*. (Sociology of Religion). Lublin: Wydawnictwo KUL.

Plummer, K. (1983). *Documents of Life: An Introduction to the Problems and Literature of a Humanistic Method*. London: Allen & Unwin.

Richter, P. and Francis, L. J. (1998). *Gone But Not Forgotten: Church Leaving and Returning*. London: Darton, Longman & Todd.

Ritzer, G. (1993). *The McDonaldization of Society*. London: Pine Forge Press.

Roberts, K. (1995). *Youth and Employment in Modern Britain*. Oxford: Oxford University Press.

Schoenherr, R.A. and Young, L.A. (1990). *The Catholic Priest in the US: Demographic Investigations*. Madison, WI: Comparative Organizations Studies Publications.

Schwab, Ulrich (1995). *Familienreligiösität*. Stuttgart: W. Kohlhammer.

Stringer, P. and Robinson G. (eds). (1992). *Social Attitudes in Northern Ireland: The Second Report*. Belfast: Blackstaff.

Szajkowski, B. (1983). *Next to God: Politics and Religion in Contemporary Poland*. New York.

Tomasi, L. (1981). *La contestazione religiosa giovanile in Italia (1968–1978)*. Milan: Franco Angeli.

Tomasi, L. (ed.). (1995a). *Values and Post-Soviet Youth*. Milan: Franco Angeli.

Tomasi, L. (1995b). 'The New Europe and the Value Orientations of Young People: East-West comparisons'. In W.H. Swatos (ed.). *Politics and Religion in Central and Eastern Europe*. London: Praeger: 47–64.

Tomasi, L. (ed.). (1998). *La cultura dei giovani europei. Religione, valori, politica e consumi*. Milan: Franco Angeli.

Tomasi. L. (ed.). (1999). *Alternative Religions Among European Youth*. Aldershot (UK): Ashgate Press.

Tonna, B. (1998). *Attendance at Sunday Mass: The Best Opportunity for Evangelisation 2000: Report on the Third Census*. Malta: Discern, Institute for Research on the Signs of the Times.

Tonna, B. (1999). *A Surge in Quality: Report on the Signs of the Times 1999*. Malta: Discern, Institute for Research on the Signs of the Times.

Turnbull, C. (1972). *The Mountain People*. New York: Simon & Schuster.

Turner, V. (1967). *Forest of Symbols: Aspects of Ndembu Ritual*. Ithaca, N.Y.: Cornell University Press.

US Bureau of the Census. (1996). *Statistical Abstract of the United States: 1996*. Washington D.C.: US Government Printing Office.

Urban, J. (1998). 'Prawo wyznaniowe w Polsce po 1989 roku'. (Confessional law in Poland after 1989). *Kwartalnik Religioznawczy*. 22/23, 87–107.

Vassallo M. (1979). *From Lordship to Stewardship: Religion and Social Change in Malta*. The Hague: Mouton.

Weber, M. (1978). *Economy and Society: An Outline of Interpretive Sociology*. 2 vols. Berkeley: University of California Press.

Whelan, C. (ed.). (1994). *Values and Social Change in Ireland*. Dublin: Gill & Macmillan.

Whyte, J.H. (1980). *Church and State in Modern Ireland 1923–1979*. 2nd ed. Dublin: Gill & Macmillan.

Wilkinson, H. and Mulgan, G. (1996). *Freedom's Children: Work, Relationships and Politics for 18–34 Year Olds Today*. London: Demos.

Williams, A.S. and Davidson, J.D. (1996). 'Catholic Conceptions of Faith: A Generational Analysis'. *Sociology of Religion*. 57: 273–89.

Wood, R.L. (1994). 'Faith in Action: religious resources for political success in three congregations'. *Sociology of Religion*. 55: 397–417.

Wuthnow, R. (1995). *Learning To Care: Elementary Kindness in an Age of Indifference*. Oxford: Oxford University Press.

INDEX